THE GRACE GLEASON FILES

UNHOLY
MIND GAMES

THE GRACE GLEASON FILES

UNHOLY
MIND GAMES

A Novel Inspired by True Events

DONALD REICHARDT

JOYCE OSCAR

GLEASON FILES LLC

ISBN-13:978-1726232555

ISBN-10:1726232557

Printed by CreateSpace, an Amazon.com company.

Available from Amazon.com and other retail outlets, online outlets and book stores.

Other novels in The Grace Gleason Files series:

Justice On Hold
The Blue Wall

For more information, visit: www.GraceGleasonFiles.com

Dedicated to the children.

And their protectors.

ACKNOWLEDGMENTS

The authors wish to thank our advance readers for their invaluable input: Pamela Sammons, Sammy Beck, Nicole Valek, John Staton and Katelyn Dorrell

We're grateful to Monica for her tenacious proofreading.

Thanks also to William David for his book layout and brilliant cover design.
www.WilliamDavidCreative.com

PROLOGUE

"I don't like the feel of this," Thomas Putnam told his partner as he cranked up the heat and turned on the defroster of his county patrol car. Putnam and Jeremiah Smith squinted through the frosty film on the car windows as a bitter chill swirled outside. Their windshield wipers seemed to be working overtime against a light mist quickly turning to an icy mix.

"Me neither," Smith agreed. "I moved down here from Michigan to get away from this stuff. The last week in March? Man, it was seventy degrees yesterday. Now look."

"Nasty weather and ten damned o'clock at night is no time to be serving a warrant in this part of town," Putnam said. He furrowed his brow, making his hulky brown forehead fold oddly forward under his cap. The twelve-year veteran of Fulton County's sheriff's office ran a meaty hand over his daylong stubble of beard. "Especially to a real bad dude."

"I hear that," his partner answered. Jeremiah was twenty-eight, eight years younger than Thomas and in his second year as a deputy. He was clean-shaven and slender, the son of a Jamaican immigrant. He rifled through some papers. "Aahil Moghaddam. Previously known as Slay T. Jefferson, a proponent of violence in the California Lives Matter or CLM movement. Now a Muslim Imam. Just who are we dealing with, Tom?"

The older deputy shook his head. "String of offenses from car theft to impersonating an officer. But I guess he's a religious leader. Sheriff says the FBI thinks he might be recruiting young kids in his mosque for jihad. That's got nothing to do with this warrant, but I'm just saying…"

"Man, let's stay alert," Smith warned. "This guy has a huge history. Says here he might be armed."

"Yep," Putnam replied.

The deputy pulled the cruiser off Westview Drive. He turned down Lawton for several blocks and headed west on Walnut Street toward the small grocery store where they intended to serve the warrant on its owner.

Only a few of the streetlights in the area were working, adding an eerie peril to the deputies' task. Putnam slowed the car to a crawl as they reached the block where the store was located.

"That's the place right up ahead there," Smith announced.

"Kinda dark," Putnam nodded. "Looks closed. Supposed to be open till midnight."

"There's a guy," Jeremiah Smith spat out. "Right over there, standing next to the Mercedes. "See him?"

"Yep," answered the veteran officer. "That's him."

Dressed in a black trench coat, their quarry stood erect, staring directly at them as they approached and pulled to a stop. He looked much older than the photos from his CLM days, only a few years back when he earned a reputation for mayhem against law enforcement. His chin sported a scraggly beard. He wore a black stocking cap. His hands were concealed inside the coat.

The two officers stepped out of the car cautiously. "Sheriff's deputies! Show your hands!" called Putnam, wincing from the blowing sleet.

The figure did not move.

"Show us your hands!" Smith echoed his partner. "Now!" The two unholstered their .38 caliber pistols and simultaneously raised them toward the shadowy figure.

"Okay, here they are," the man responded. Instantly, he pulled two guns from under the coat—first an assault rifle, and then a 9mm revolver. A rapid-fire "thump thump thump thump" of bullets sprayed the hood of the cruiser. The deafening sound of exploding windshield glass ripped through the cold night air.

Jeremiah fired a shot and then jerked sideways to see Putnam crumple to the ground, the older deputy's body recoiling from several shots fired. Then, as Smith turned back toward the shooter, the impact of bullets cut his legs from under him. Jeremiah went down as two more slugs ripped into his body vest.

Struggling to crawl under the cruiser, Smith fumbled for his radio, his hands shaking. "Two officers down. Send help!" he screamed over the din.

The scene of cacophony and chaos went quiet, but only for a moment. Rapid footsteps broke the silence. A car door slammed. An engine fired up and roared against the violent squealing of tires.

Again, all went silent.

CHAPTER ONE: Savannah

Change. Grace Gleason had learned it was one thing you can always count on. She regarded life's churning movement to be a constant reminder that the polar opposites of joy and pain are always in transformation. First one, then the other, each extreme approaching or fading away like the day itself. And sometimes, in between the two, a calm settles in, as remarkable as the early morning hour between the night birds and day birds when shadows conceal secrets.

Here, in beautiful Savannah, Grace finally reached that harmony.

Grace was sitting on a weathered wooden bench along Savannah's River Street. She realized she was stalling for time, not wanting to disturb this deeply needed relief from the reporting wars she left behind. A massive container ship glided by, silhouetted against the glow of a brilliant rising sun. Even the blare of its colossal air horns failed to fully rouse her from this daydream state.

Directly across the bay, she saw in her memory, from just two days before, tiny Tybee Island. She had wandered the beaches, completely immersed in the charm that idyllic paradise oozed, stopping for a delightful, unhurried lunch at the colorful little Tybee Inn. Then, returning to Savannah, she commenced the walks along the tree-lined streets she had enjoyed the past few weeks.

It had been a perfect time—the live oaks covered in Spanish moss greeted her along the cobblestoned streets filled with quaint shops, historic sights and haunted cemeteries. How remarkable all of this picturesque inspiration was, a mere stone's throw from a seemingly endless river. The humidity mingling with the sweet smell of honeysuckle comforted her aching mind and body like a well-worn blanket. Even the critics and naysayers who decry the invading crime in all cities, including tourist-haven Savannah, failed to dampen her affection for this place.

Her hiatus from the newsroom provided a badly needed breather. But Grace Gleason had a well-developed instinct. She knew in her gut the sand would be shifting once again. After her weeks-long absence from work, she sensed the rumblings of a changing, moving, unsteady ground at Big Six News. She would never be able to explain these impulses, but they were rarely wrong.

She had come by her refreshed state of mind gradually. Many times during those delightful weeks she sat on this very bench, watching the barges come in from faraway places—Asia, South America, Europe—wondering what hidden treasures might be inside the containers with foreign signage on them. The scene unfolded like the steady beat of life itself, always shifting, rolling on this peaceful river, bringing closure, healing, peace.

When her job stress made this sabbatical a necessity, she first hoped her daughter could join her. But with Megan immersed in courses at Georgia Tech, that wasn't practical. As it turned out, the solitude proved to be good for Grace.

But this would be her last day in this paradise. Soon, nirvana would give way to reality. Her uncluttered mind would yield to thoughts of work and exhaustion and the challenge of life.

Emerging from her dream world, Grace thought back through the past year at Big Six News. As the station's go-to crime reporter, she poured everything she had into the police connections she so carefully nurtured. She recalled the pain and disappointment she felt after losing a friend, a police officer who succumbed to his own dark character flaws and paid the ultimate price, death. Many events had shaken Grace as she chased down a story of big-city greed and exploitation. But it was officer Eduardo Cruz's passing that jolted her the most.

Grace's efforts to expose drug dealers and bad cops had not gone unrewarded. The accolades heaped on her police corruption series were exactly what she dreamed she could do if given the chance to shine.

Just before she left for this much-needed break, the station manager told her ratings had never been better. "Your series has won every time slot," Harvey Silver said. "Not insignificantly," he went on with a wry smile, "station ad revenues have hit new heights."

She remembered nodding and blushing slightly, unaccustomed to such praise from her management. But she also recalled feeling uncomfortable, even sad, accepting the subsequent awards her reporting garnered. Most notably, she recalled the huge event at the Hilton ballroom when she was given a Southeast Regional Emmy for best investigative series. The smile she forced as she walked to the podium hid her profound desolation over what it took to get to this place. She wondered, looking out over the audience of colleagues and friends warmly applauding at the reading of her name, if they really knew how wounded she felt deep inside.

That evening, returning to the station's table, she felt incredibly small as Silver arose from his chair and greeted her with a hug. "I know you need time off," he whispered. "But Grace, Big Six News wants you back as soon as you can hit the ground running."

She left the next morning for the much needed vacation. Now, as the blossoming day warmed her in Savannah, she realized how much her management understood that the complicated, sometimes violent twists of her award-winning crime stories left her exhausted and fragile.

Grace had always been driven by the good she could do, exposing corruption and informing her audience about the community and the world. It would feel good to get back to what she did best, digging, searching for answers. Yet why did she feel so conflicted, so unsteady, so not ready to dive back in and shake things up?

There would be plenty of time to sort that out during the two hundred fifty-mile drive home, headed west on I-16 toward Macon and then I-75 North all the way to Atlanta.

Grace pulled her tablet from her bag. She had shut off her

texts, news alerts and news broadcasts while visiting Savannah. She was astonished she had been able to do that. It was time to flip the switch and see what was going on in the rest of the world. Completing the internet connection, she pulled up the Big Six newscast.

Christina Cruz was delivering the morning news. Her dark eyes burned into the camera, reflecting her usual fervor. "Two Fulton County deputies were shot last night as they attempted to serve a warrant in Southwest Atlanta. Dead is thirty-six-year-old Thomas Putnam, a twelve-year veteran of the sheriff's office."

Hearing the officer's name jolted Grace. She remembered talking with Putnam several times when covering stories.

Christina continued, "His partner, Jeremiah Smith, twenty-eight, is in serious condition at Southbend Hospital with multiple gunshot wounds. Scott Matthews is on the scene at Southbend. Scott?"

Grace sat up straight, staring at the screen. Scott Matthews was in a sense her project. When he was new at the station, a recent University of Georgia journalism graduate, she began to bring him in to assist with her investigative stories. And when she left abruptly on the sabbatical, she entrusted him with delivering her final monologue to close out a series on one of the most sensational police corruption incidents in Atlanta's history.

And now here he was, doing a story that should be Grace's.

"Thanks, Christina," Scott stood in front of Southbend Memorial Hospital, his delivery deadly serious. "So far the media have been denied access to the wounded deputy. He is in serious condition here, but a county spokeswoman told me his chances of survival are good. Meantime, he reportedly has identified the shooter as the man he and deceased deputy Thomas Putnam were attempting to serve a warrant on. That suspect is Aahil Moghaddam, the Imam of a small mosque in a Decatur neighborhood. Moghaddam is probably better known as the former Slay T. Jefferson. His born name was Monroe Jefferson. He was most notably a leader of California Lives Matter, or

CLM, in San Francisco who espoused violent disobedience to protest several police shootings of men of color in that state. After serving time for bombing a police station and converting to Islam in prison, he came to Atlanta several years ago and organized the mosque."

Scott continued while the station ran footage of Federal agents assembling and climbing into vehicles to commence a search for the killer. "A nationwide manhunt has been launched, headed up by the FBI. Here in Atlanta, followers of Moghaddam are reportedly organizing a street protest. Leading that effort is Khalila Noorani, a community organizer reported to be a close friend and adviser to the Imam."

Back on camera, Matthews said, "I attempted to interview Ms. Noorani, who is a lawyer, earlier this morning. She declined comment. I will continue to follow this story and the search for the fugitive. Scott Matthews reporting for Big Six News."

"My God," Grace said aloud. She wanted to hear more, but there was no time to waste. Her instincts as a reporter were kicking in, pushing aside the doubts and fatigue that brought her to Savannah. She had to get back to her hotel, collect her bags and car and get on the road. She would get further details then.

Within thirty minutes Grace was speeding up I-16 on the normally boring route back home. Today there would be no time for boredom. This was a major story, and she would be needed. Her mind spun, working on the questions she wanted to have answered. She connected the speed dial on her car phone and called the news director.

"Good morning, Big Six News television," the receptionist answered.

"Hi, Mrs. Nicholson, it's Grace Gleason. Please put me through to Vivian Ellis?"

The receptionist paused a moment. "Ms. Gleason, wait one second, please." Her voice sounded halting and she put Grace on hold.

"Grace, it's Harvey Silver. Where are you?"

"Driving back from Savannah," she told the general manager. "I just heard about the cop shooting."

"Nasty business. The perp is on the run. That surviving deputy has identified him, and there's a massive manhunt going on."

"Mr. Silver, why am I talking to you? I asked for Vivian Ellis."

"Vivian is no longer with the station." The words shook Grace. Several years earlier, one of Vivian's first actions as Big Six's newly hired news director was to travel to Texas and pitch a job to Grace. It was to be groundbreaking work, exposing the underbelly of Atlanta's worst elements. Grace made the move, and the two got along famously. Now, Silver's words confused and disheartened Grace.

"What happened? Where did she go?"

"CBX Network News hired her away. It's a great career move for her. I've already hired a replacement."

"I can't believe she didn't contact me. I thought we were close."

"It happened pretty fast, Grace. They swept her up and whisked her away to New York in less than a week. You'll probably hear from her."

"Right now I have to get back and cover this Imam shooting story."

"Scott Matthews has it. He'll be knee-deep into it by the time you get back. Go home. Rest up from your trip. Come in tomorrow morning and we'll talk."

Grace was always the stoic one, the rock. She rarely got rattled. She had endured much worse developments than this. Still, she felt tears welling up uncontrollably—not only because of the dreaded sense of losing a friend and mentor, but also because she knew she had been right. *Today is the beginning of the first day back, and everything is about to change. Again.*

CHAPTER TWO: Back to the Grind

Sitting on her back porch drinking coffee, Grace shivered at the startling cold wave invading north Georgia. Having grown accustomed to the softer, sultrier days in coastal Savannah, she didn't like this rude return to her Atlanta base. She hunched into her sweater and folded her hands around the warm cup, gazing out into the first backyard she had owned since she and her husband had gotten a divorce.

She liked her new neighborhood, Morningside, with its thick greenery and ample spaces to walk. It was more settled in than the Buckhead area from which she had moved and the postage-stamp lot of her townhouse there. The serenity here and the slower pace met her growing need for sanity amid the chaos of the news business. In just her first few weeks, she met more neighbors than she had known the entire two years she was in her Buckhead townhouse.

Her source for information about the neighborhood first came from across the street. An older woman who lived there arrived one evening with a carafe of pinot grigio shortly after Grace moved in.

"I'm Evelyn Bradshaw," the diminutive gray-haired woman said. "I saw your car pull in, and since I hadn't met you yet I thought, 'Hell, Evelyn, she's probably a wine drinker.'" Her eyes opened wide. "If you're not, I'll drink it all and you can do the talking."

Grace giggled and beckoned her in. "Evelyn, you were sent from Heaven. I'm Grace. I have a nodding acquaintance with some of the neighbors, but really haven't had time to socialize."

"Well, I can tell you and I are in the same boat—single ladies in a neighborhood of mostly old fogey couples who roll up the sidewalks at nine-thirty. Don't worry, I'll introduce you to everyone before you know it. Have you met your next-door neighbor?"

"The man on the north side? The one who has all his buddies over, huddled around the fire pit drinking beer and telling stories? No,

I haven't. But I've heard them go on into late night on several occasions."

The older woman's laugh was a cackle. "That's Horace Gunter. He's been here several years. Horace is a retired policeman from somewhere in Virginia, so we all feel safe living on this street. We never talk, though. He's a widower, and shortly after he moved here we had a neighborhood party at my house to welcome him. Well, Horace got a bit into his cups and thought maybe he'd..." her tone turned confidential, "...you know—stay for breakfast. He seemed sorely disappointed when I sent him home empty-handed. We haven't spoken since."

They both laughed hilariously. Grace liked this firecracker of a woman.

"A retired cop? Fantastic," Grace exclaimed. "I'm familiar with so many of the police here, I wonder if he's gotten to know any of them. I'll have to look him up when I get back."

"Why? Are you going somewhere?"

Grace nodded. "Savannah. As soon as I can finish up a few odds and ends, I need to get away. Maybe you and Horace can keep an eye on things while I'm gone?"

They hooted again.

Grace smiled at the memory and then let it slip away as she took one last sip of coffee. But it served to remind her she wanted to meet Horace. She looked at her watch. *Time to get moving. Can't drag in late my first morning back at Big Six News*, she thought.

Driving toward the station, she thought back to the first day of her tenure at Big Six. Fresh from Dallas' number one news station, she was apprehensive about the move to Atlanta. But with the promise of her own news segment, more freedom to explore the underbelly of a city, and Megan's acceptance at Georgia Tech's school of architecture, she made the leap. It reaped rewards and bestowed awards. But the foray into crime and corruption was also punctuated by danger, fear and stress. Her exhaustion was so debilitating she desperately needed the sabbatical she just emerged from.

She felt whole again. Her batteries were charged now, after whiling away several weeks in South Georgia, rummaging through shops, enjoying Savannah cuisine, sitting for hours on park benches and the veranda of her hotel watching the world come and go.

She was ready to do battle.

Parking in the back lot, Grace entered the newsroom through the side door. She had an eerie sensation of not having been gone at all. Everything looked and felt the same—the walkway, the plantings, the entryway where every day she wondered what excitement, what challenge, what danger, lay ahead.

It was still early. The place was quieter than it would be later. Yet there was still a familiar low hum of computer keys clicking, the murmur of voices on the phone, the low-volume drone of monitors overhead displaying network newscasts. She was grateful to be there before everyone arrived and the low drumbeat of sound became tympanic commotion. She liked her colleagues but wanted no hoopla over her return. And she knew going in the front way would have drawn a dramatic greeting from Mrs. Nicholson. Just what she didn't want.

Pausing at the news director's office, she noted Vivian Ellis' name had already been removed from the door. The sinking feeling returned.

Grace was sure Harvey Silver would already be there. He was nearly always the first person to arrive.

"Hello, Mr. Silver."

He looked up from reading reports at his desk, seemingly surprised at first, then offering a huge, welcoming smile. "There's our top reporter. How are you, Grace?"

"I'm good," she answered, accepting his motion for her to sit. "Ready to get started. I stopped at the news director's office, but no one was in there."

He leaned back and nodded. "I really hated to lose Vivian. And I know much you valued her as a colleague. Someone at the network had to be watching her progress. They came to me out of the blue."

"And her replacement is…" Grace inquired.

"Buck Lohmeyer. Coming to us from Columbia, South Carolina. The number one station there, WXIS. The guy is top-notch, you'll like him. Buck had some personal business to attend to, but we expect him in later today or in the morning at the latest."

"Good," she said. "I want to get moving on this Imam shooting. The morning reports said they think he might have fled to Tennessee and they're on his trail. Mr. Silver, I'd like to get over there."

He paused and drummed his fingers on the desk. "No, I don't think so, Grace. It's still a nationwide hunt, and we could exhaust a lot of resources chasing every lead. We'll wait until they find the guy. And Grace, Scott Matthews will be on the story if they catch him. He'll do fine. I know you have a lot of confidence in Scott, his having helped you on the last big story, the strip club murder and that gang of crooked cops."

"Of course, Scott's a good young reporter. But Mr. Silver, crime is my beat. I'm ready to plunge back into it."

Silver stood and walked around the desk, perched on the edge of it and looked down warmly at his star reporter. "We're making some changes, Grace. I might as well tell you. Buck is bringing a reporter with him from Columbia—a top-notch crime guy. It was kind of a package deal. And Scott can be a big help to him the way he was with you." He hesitated. "We want you to try something new, Grace, and I think you'll be great at it."

Her silence begged the question.

"We've been taking a pretty bad beating from the Atlanta leadership—political, business and religious people. Most importantly, our advertisers. They think we've started sinking into the ambulance-chasing syndrome of the other stations, and that it will drag our ratings down. I'm hearing more and more criticism that we're ignoring all the inspirational stories that bubble up here every day. Grace, we're putting you on the religion beat so you can capture the essence of that positive side of our great city."

14

"Religion beat!" she exploded. "That's ludicrous, Mr. Silver."

"I don't think so," he recoiled slightly at her outburst. "No, it makes good business sense and good news sense. We need a tighter partnership with the positive things in our community, and you're just the woman who can do it." He returned to his chair and picked up his reports. "That's it. Talk to Buck when he gets in and you can sketch it out with him."

"Mr. Silver..." Grace interjected, not knowing whether to be bewildered or angry.

"That's it, Grace," he said with finality. "Talk to Buck."

Grace retreated to her cubicle, smoldering. *Religion beat? I won't do it. I signed up here for crime and corruption, not choirs and catechism!* She was hurt, disappointed, dismayed, baffled. Grace sat staring at her computer for a long time, options running through her mind. Move back to Dallas. Flip to another Atlanta station. Talk to the cable networks. She had options.

She booted up her computer. Pulling up the station's streaming news report, her senses immediately charged up. Live video showed a gathering crowd on Prior Street in downtown Atlanta near the county courthouse. As news cameras closed in, the protesters grew more raucous, waving hand-written signs saying, "Imam is Being Framed," "Aahil Moghaddam is Innocent," and "Stop Police Brutality." The burgeoning mob chanted noisily, "Free Moghaddam! He is innocent!" repeatedly.

"The protesters started with about a dozen followers of the Imam," Scott peered into the camera. "But as they march and chant, the group is picking up steam and growing in numbers. I continue to ask for an interview with their apparent organizer, Khalila Noorani, but she has only committed to a press conference at a later date."

Suddenly a surge of the crowd moved in behind Scott, screaming and waving signs in the direction of the camera. Several jostled the young reporter as he struggled to hold his on-camera position.

"As you can see, things are getting dicey with this crowd,"

Scott shouted over the uproar, his voice getting unsteady.

A large man wearing traditional African clothing leaped in front of Matthews and glared into the camera. "The Imam is being framed! Aahil Moghaddam didn't kill nobody!" The camera shot became violently shaky, as if the photographer was also being manhandled.

Scott sidestepped the protestor and yelled, "This is Scott Matthews signing off. We'll have more on this story as it develops." The final words were nearly inaudible because of the clamor, and the picture cut off immediately.

Grace gazed into the screen, aghast. *I should be there,* she thought. *Scott is good, but he has never experienced this kind of line-of-fire reporting.*

She grabbed her smart phone and texted him: *Are you OK?* There was no immediate response. Grace was sure the police would have arrived by now and would ensure that Scott and his photographer were safe. She felt a knot in the pit of her stomach, knowing she wasn't involved in this big story. She sat back, miserable, thinking. *Of course. Silver said they want me on the religion beat. Moghaddam is a religious leader. I might not be allowed to report on it as a crime story. So I'll report on it from the Islam angle.*

Grace grew excited. She would talk to Scott as soon as he returned, and they could sort out their relative angles for coverage. Grace had mentored him when he first came out of the University of Georgia. She had tapped him not only to help her cover the dangerous corrupt police story, but also to deliver her final script to close out the series as she hightailed it out of town toward Savannah.

She was certain she could pull this off, given the opportunity. The only hurdle, a huge unknown to her, might be Big Six's newly anointed news director. Buck Lohmeyer was the wild card.

CHAPTER THREE: The Masjid

Scott was back by early afternoon and stopped at her work-station. "Good to have you back," he told her.

"Scott, are you all right? You didn't answer my text."

He chuckled. "Sorry. I must have had three dozen, and I just couldn't get them answered. We got a little busy for a while. By the time we fought our way through that angry gang to our truck, the cops finally got there. Everything turned nasty as they tried to restore some order, and they commanded all the media out of the area. Said it was for our own safety. Everyone's instinct was to stay, but truthfully after getting pushed around like that, we were happy to give our report and get the hell out."

"I'm sure the cops didn't want a news camera there if they started busting heads," she nodded. "I really need to talk to you about our coverage of Moghaddam."

"Sure. Have you had lunch?" Matthews asked her. "I missed breakfast, and after all that excitement, I'm famished. Can we discuss the story at the Varsity? I need a chili dog."

Grace grinned. "Sure thing," she answered. "I could use some of those onion rings myself."

They found a corner of the iconic old restaurant in Midtown and set their trays down. "I haven't been here in years," Grace told the young reporter.

He laughed. "Even though I went to school at the University of Georgia over in Athens, I know quite a few people who went to Georgia Tech just up the street. They subsisted on these dogs and burgers when they were in school. Now they get me over here once in a while. Hey, isn't your daughter Megan going to Tech?"

Grace nodded. "Architecture. But she's so busy with it, I hardly ever see her any more. Besides, she has a steady boyfriend now, so I'm playing third fiddle."

"Boyfriend, huh?" he eyed her slyly. "I missed out."

"You did," she winked. "You sleep, you weep. Okay, down to business. The new guy Lohmeyer hasn't come in yet. Have you met him?" Matthews shook his head no. "Well, he's bringing a crime reporter with him, and I'm being pushed off on some crusade to report goody-goody stories about churches and such."

"Man, that sucks," Scott responded.

"Maybe not. If I'm going to have the religion beat, then okay, I'm going to report about religion. And that includes a man of Islam accused of killing cops."

Scott's eyes widened. "If they let you."

"I have another reason for wanting to stay involved," she said, and her voice cracked a little. Matthews leaned back, intrigued, at seeing her eyes water up a bit. "I knew Thomas Putnam."

"The deputy who died?"

"I interviewed him a couple times for a story we did on the conditions of the county lockup. He was a good guy, very concerned about making court-ordered improvements in the jail. It looked to me as if he was fighting against the tide of the bureaucracy over there, trying to do things the right way."

"How long ago was that?"

She cast her eyes toward the ceiling, trying to recall. "About two or three years ago, I think. When I went over there for the second interview, his wife and two little kids were there waiting for him to get off work. Cutest little boys you've ever seen. And his wife struck me as beautiful and smart. When I heard it was Putnam who was killed, it felt as if someone had stuck a knife in me. It's personal, Scott."

"I get it," he said quietly.

Grace drew in a breath, wiped her eyes, and smiled at him. "I want a pact with you Mr. Matthews. You cover the day-to-day crime stuff—the manhunt, what prosecutors are saying if they find him, the courtroom process, interviews with the witness..."

He interrupted, the pace of the conversation accelerating, "... And you'll dig under the bark of the tree. Was he motivated by his faith? Was it an act of terror, supported by some organization like ISIS? Is he being framed, as they claim, because of backlash against Muslims? Or if he did it, was it simply a hangover from his early days of hatred for law enforcement? Yeah, Grace, I think we can make that work. Who do we have to convince?"

"I say let's just go for it. Get slapped on the wrist for sins of commission, not omission."

"Wow," he guffawed, "You're already getting this religion thing down pat."

She munched on an onion ring and watched him for a moment. "Want to get started right now?"

Scott grinned and leaned forward. "I have a head start on you."

She reached out and grasped his arm. "Have you been out there? Where the shooting happened?"

"Not yet."

"And the mosque he's the leader of?"

"No."

She grabbed her purse. "Finish those last bites. Let's go."

"What, you mean now?"

"When else? I'll drive you to the lion's den. Scene of the crime."

"You know exactly where it is?"

She looked at him askance, a silent rebuke.

"Of course you do," he continued. "I forgot for a minute who I was talking to."

Grace and Scott dashed for her car in the Varsity parking lot and within minutes, they were heading down Marietta Avenue. As they turned onto Ralph Abernathy Parkway, Grace asked, "You've read the deputy's report, right?" He nodded yes. "I'm going to take us the exact same route they took. That little store he owned is very close to the mosque. We need to get a feel of the neighborhood, of the sights and sounds those deputies might have experienced."

The area was distinctly working class with older, tiny homes lining streets that obviously needed more maintenance than the city was willing to provide. But what impressed Grace was that home-owners obviously made an effort to keep things neat and trim. Few yards were neglected. Some homes had apparently been recently painted. This was one of the city's poorer neighborhoods, but it wasn't a ghetto.

School was still in session, but toddlers played happily, nois-ily in front yards and on front steps. Some residents sat and chatted or smoked on front porches. She could see laundry hanging behind several of the homes they passed. This must have been, she thought, what life was like in small-town mid-America in the Fifties. Except for the demographics.

Grace wondered what people who saw them drive past thought about them—a white couple driving through their neighbor-hood, staring at the surroundings. Was it normal occurrence here? Or would they view these two interlopers with suspicion?

She turned the corner off of Lawton onto Oak, and about a block ahead they could see several unmarked police cars parked randomly. Several detectives were combing an area inside a large perimeter of yellow crime scene tape. A tow truck was winching a bullet-ridden Fulton County patrol car onto its bed. Grace stopped the car. "That's it," she said. "We're coming toward the shooting scene exactly the way the deputies did. See, there's the store Moghaddam owns. If he did it, if he shot those cops the way Jeremiah Smith said, he must have been standing right over there next to his getaway car."

She parked as close as possible and they jumped out. Grace

squinted skyward. The sun had broken through, beginning to push back against the unseasonal cold snap. As they walked to the scene, she could see small groups of residents milling around. They watched warily from a distance as the police picked up objects from the ground and bagged them, conferring quietly with each other as they worked.

"Hey detective," Grace called out to Mack Showalter. She knew him from a previous case.

The detective said a few quiet words to another member of the team and walked to the two reporters. "Grace, we don't have anything to tell the press right now," he offered pointedly. "When we do, we'll call a conference and get to you all at once."

"I know," she responded cheerily. "I just wanted to see what things looked like over here. Never been to this particular neighborhood before." She nodded to the curious onlookers. "Have you questioned any of these people?"

Detective Showalter laughed. "You think anyone is talking? Even if they know anything?"

"No, I guess not. Have you guys interviewed the woman leading the protests?"

"Khalila Noorani? Sure, we talked to her. She's been going around saying Moghaddam doesn't match the description Deputy Smith gave us of the killer. Even though he ID'd the guy's photo. We won't get anything useful from her. That's it, Gleason. Can't say anything more right now. Gotta go."

Grace and Scott returned to the car and drove for several blocks. Turning onto West End Place, Grace stopped in front of a tiny structure, more a cottage than a house. A sign over the door read, *Masjid Al-Emaan of Atlanta.*

"This is it?" Scott asked, astonished. "This is Moghaddam's mosque?"

"Yup. His mosque. Or masjid in Arabic. Who said a mosque has to be one of those grand structures you see pictures of," she answered, "or like that showy one over by the Georgia Tech campus? Technically, a mosque is anyplace where Muslims pray facing Mecca. It can just be a room somewhere.

"Some of the buildings would fool you," she went on as he listened intently. "There's a mosque in Brooklyn that was once a factory—the so-called blind sheik convicted in the 1993 World Trade Center bombing was once a leader there. There's a mosque in Cedar Rapids, Iowa, called the Mother Mosque of America, and if you discounted the dramatic green entryway and dome on top, you'd think it was some concrete block lawyer's office or small city hall. The women's mosque in Berkeley is a pretty modest place. The Masjid Al-Farooq in Brooklyn is a storefront."

"Man, you've done some research."

"A little. Of course, the major share of the mosques are grand in scope. I looked them up on the internet and was in awe at how—I don't know—ostentatious some of them are. Scott, if we're going to do this story right, we're going to have to understand a million things we don't know about Islam."

"That sounds more like your job than mine. I'll stick to the crime and courtroom stuff. Meanwhile, Grace, I'm getting kind of nervous being here. Can we go? We don't know who lives around here, what they think of two snoops driving around and what they might do if they decide we're up to no good."

"Don't be silly," she smiled as she pulled the car away and headed back toward the highway. "This is Atlanta, Scott. This is America."

Yet as cool and collected as her self-assured demeanor made her seem, Grace harbored serious concerns inside.

The truth is, she thought, *it's a part of America I don't know much about. How am I going to get involved in bringing a killer to justice if I don't understand who and what I'm dealing with? My ignorance scares the stuffing out of me.*

CHAPTER FOUR: Corporal Punishment

Six was pretty early for breakfast. But she hadn't seen Megan since returning, and her daughter had a seven-thirty class. Besides, Grace had a nine o-clock staff meeting. So there she was, walking into the Magic Plate Diner near the Georgia Tech campus.

The place was buzzing with early risers, but she didn't see Megan. Finding one open booth, she grabbed it.

"Coffee?" the middle-aged waitress asked with a friendly smile.

Grace responded, "Might as well leave the pot."

Within minutes, her daughter Megan breezed in with long blonde hair flying. She rushed up and flopped into the booth opposite her mother, laying her book bag on the table. "Hi, Mom." It was Megan's standard greeting for her mom, yet Grace knew she could never hear those cheery words tossed out often enough.

"Honey, you look tired. Are you still pulling forty-eight hour shifts?"

Megan nodded and heaved a heavy sigh. "Have a major-major project due in a week, and it's pretty complicated. I'm really burning the nighttime oil."

"Well, let's get some breakfast down you. I want to hear everything."

Nearly an hour later, they had each consumed an omelet and exhausted Grace's recounting of Savannah and every aspect of Megan's schoolwork. Megan asked about the stories Grace would be working on, and Grace related her concerns about not getting to cover the stories she preferred, instead faced with church feature stories that would probably air in off-hours and weekends.

"Mom, why don't you take Mr. Silver's advice? You deserve

to have some time away from those stupid, dangerous crime stories you cover. In Dallas it was a murderer who almost got you killed. After we moved here, it was drug dealers and crooked cops. You always get involved in incidents that put you in danger. I worry about you."

"Megan, it's what I was born to do. Next to being your mom, I believe my calling was to use my background and skills to help inform the community. And I have to do it my way. I'll be careful, I promise."

There was an awkward pause. Grace hesitated, but she couldn't resist bringing up one final subject.

"What about that guy? Are you still seeing him?"

Megan's mouth became a frowning pucker. She let out a noisy sigh. "'That guy' has a name, Mom. It's Joe Perez." Her tone was ripe with annoyance. "I've told you all about him, don't you re-member? His Australian mom? His Columbian dad?" Her gaze fixed more steely on her mother as she continued. "We're in architecture together? And yes, we're still a couple."

Grace sat back in amazement at how emotional Megan became. Her daughter's eyes seemed to plead for understanding. "Mom, Joe and I've become really close."

"I worry that a relationship while you're trying to finish your degree will be a distraction," Grace furrowed her brow. "Can't you put things on hold for now? There's plenty of time to explore your future with a man after you graduate."

"Is that what your mother said? You married Dad while you were both finishing college."

Grace's voice turned a notch harsher. "My mother was dead when I married your father."

Megan stared. "I know, I'm sorry. I didn't mean it that way. I was speaking figuratively about anyone who might have advised you and Daddy to back off and wait. Like you're doing to me now."

"Maybe we should have waited. Who knows if we would have gotten married or not?"

Megan sat up straighter. Her eyes burned into Grace, and her voice grew strident. "Right, then you wouldn't have had me, and we wouldn't be having this argument. Right?" She picked up her books and began to slide across the bench. "I have to go to class."

"No, no, Megan. I didn't mean for us to get cross-wise like this," Grace pleaded. "I just worry about you. Let's forget I brought it up."

Megan stood, angry, ready to bolt. "I would, Mom, but you never forget. You'll keep on and on about it. Well, I'm not going to stop seeing him. Talk to you later." She turned and headed for the door. Grace sat deflated, regretful. Their relationship had always been respectful and loving. Now it seemed she was losing her.

She sat for several minutes and pulled her phone from her purse. She looked up ShoutNet, an internet source she used often to get community updates because of its breaking news feature. Sometimes the site was as fast and reliable as texts from her management.

The top story jarred her. "Minister Jailed in Child-Beating Controversy." Grace sat reading the first sentences of the story, her eyebrows raised in disbelief: "Dontell Freeman, a black minister at the Church of Faith, is in jail with five of his congregation for spanking children in church. Some children were taken from their families and turned over to Child Protective Services."

Grace glanced at her watch. Nearly eight. She needed to get to the station well ahead of the morning meeting to prepare. She hastily left money on the table with the check and hurried out to her car.

Immediately after Grace reached her cubicle in the newsroom, Lateisha Robinson found her. The assignment editor appeared out of breath. "I've been looking all over for you," Lateisha gasped frantically. "I got a call about this minister who was arrested for..."

"Latiesha, I already know about it," Grace cut her off.

The young editor heaved a sigh. "I'm not sure how to assign it. They told me you're supposed to be the new religion reporter, but it's a criminal matter, too."

"Who called it in?"

"It was the mother of one of the kids who was beaten. She said something about filing a lawsuit." She handed Grace a piece of paper with the woman's name and number.

"We have a staff meeting in less than an hour. I'll say I took it off your hands. It's my story."

The young assignment editor beamed a smile of relief. "Great. With the new news director here now…"

Again, Grace interrupted her. "Buck Lohmeyer is here?"

"He came in an hour ago," Lateisha responded. "He's been in with Mr. Silver, so none of us have had a chance to meet him yet. I'm glad you're taking the story. Thanks, Grace."

Grace nodded, and Lateisha disappeared. Grace jumped for the phone. She needed to get as much information as possible about this breaking story before the meeting.

Just a few minutes before nine, Grace rushed down the hall. She was one of three stragglers barely getting to the conference room on time. She found an empty seat and deposited her tablet on the table, tapping it to pull up notes she had taken. She glanced around and nodded at the assortment of reporters, producers, editors and daytime anchors assembled there.

"Hey Grace, glad to have you back," a producer, MaryAnne McWherter, waved across the table.

"Yeah, Grace, welcome back to the salt mines," Scott Matthews winked.

Other colleagues joined in with welcoming comments. Before she could respond, Harvey Silver walked in with two men in tow.

"Folks, I'd like you to meet Buck Lohmeyer," the general manager said. "I think you all know why he's here."

Lohmeyer nodded to the muted laughter. He was portly, ruddy-faced, serious. "Glad to be here, everyone," he started in a deep, unctuous voice. "I'll be having one-on-ones with everybody here soon, just to get us all on the same page. Meanwhile, meet Bannister Walker. I stole him away from WXIS, because he's a good, hard-nosed reporter who will fit right in with all of you pros."

Bannister waved and found a chair. He was tall, slender with close-cropped hair and ebony skin. Grace was surprised at how young he looked, given his reputation as a veteran reporter. She joined everyone in smiling and waving back.

Buck Lohmeyer turned to the general manager. "Harvey, don't feel like you have to stay. I know you've got to go make us some money."

Everyone laughed, including Silver. "It's okay, Buck. I'll hang around just this once. I need to catch up on what's on tap for this group."

Buck nodded agreement but frowned slightly with annoyance. "Okay. So, before Lateisha here runs down what's been covered on the early casts, let me address the five hundred pound elephant—the Imam shooting. Scott, you did an exemplary job of covering the early activity…"

He paused as Matthews acknowledged scattered applause around the room.

"…Now we get into the long grind of the story," Buck continued. "I'm putting Bannister on the story as lead reporter, and Scott, you work with him as needed. When—not if—they catch this guy, all hell is going to break loose. I want Big Six in lead position on every breaking story. Got it?"

"What about Grace?" Matthews asked. "I think since the suspect is a religious leader, she should have a part in the coverage." Grace cringed, wishing Scott had left her to fight her own assignment battles.

Buck grimaced again. "Bannister and Scott will cover the story. Let's move on. Lateisha?"

"Before I go over the other ongoing stories we have," Lateisha said, "we got a tip this morning about the arrest of a minister who beats children in his church."

"Allegedly beats them," corrected one of the anchors, Jackson Davis. Grace had worked with Jackson for a while now, and she knew him as a pompous, aging broadcaster who liked to score points in these morning meetings.

Lateisha smiled patiently and acknowledged, "Allegedly beats them," she agreed. "Grace Gleason is already working on the story since she has been assigned the religion beat."

Buck interceded. "Seems to me since he's been jailed, we should cover it as a potential crime and court case. Let's reassign it."

Grace was smoldering underneath, but she attempted to respond with a calm demeanor. "Mr. Lohmeyer, I've already put out several calls to parishioners, both pro and con, and have a lot of quotes. I talked to the arresting officers and the D.A. And I plan to interview one of the mothers of a child who was beaten. She's going to sue the pastor and probably the church as well."

"Sounds like Grace has this one under her thumb already," Harvey Silver chimed in. The general manager walked toward the door, then turned back toward Buck and Lateisha. "Might as well let Gleason follow up and see what happens." He left, with Buck Lohmeyer's dour stare boring a hole in his back.

Grace inwardly sighed in relief. She would get to cover a firestorm her first day back.

**

Later in the morning, Buck Lohmeyer appeared at Harvey Silver's office door. "A word, Harvey?"

"Sure Buck," Harvey smiled. "Let me guess—Grace Gleason and the minister beating story?"

Buck sank into the chair opposite his boss. "You undermined me on my first day, in front of the entire crew. I know you're in charge, but that room is my bailiwick."

"I get it, Buck. Didn't mean to stick my nose in your business, really. But look at it from my perspective. Grace Gleason has been a real asset to this station. She's covered some huge stories for us and has been instrumental in building up our audience ratings. Grace almost got herself killed uncovering a big cop corruption case for us. Buck, we just spayed her with this assignment on religion to accommodate the guy you brought with you. Help me out here and throw her a juicy bone occasionally so we don't lose her."

Lohmeyer hesitated, then nodded. "I just don't want us to give everyone the appearance I'm a weak manager. By God, I'm not."

Silver smiled. "If I thought you were, I wouldn't have hired you. Just let Gleason have this story and if it becomes too big, your guy can handle the courtroom piece."

The news director sat back and surveyed his supervisor with a dour expression that appeared he wanted to hold his nose. But then he sighed and nodded agreement.

**

Grace was already back at her desk, talking to single mother Shaniqua Forrester. "Ms. Forrester, I was told you intend to sue the minister they arrested, Dontell Freeman. Is that true?"

"Damned right it's true," Shaniqua responded in a large, alto voice. "This man took over pastorship of my church four years ago, and ever since then he has been whupping children in front of the congregation for their transgressions. Half the congregation is against it, including me, but the other half support him. Ain't no way you can justify taking someone else's child and doing what he do. I'm going to sue his black ass."

"Do you have an attorney lined up?"

"I do. Lawyer name of Bruce Newton say he'll do it pro bono. Says any man of the cloth who has his parishioners hold a kid down while he tans they hide, should be held accountable. Mr. Newton is a religious man. He definitely took issue with the practice."

"Ms. Forrester, I'd like to come interview you. Would you do it?"

"Hellfire yes," Shaniqua answered. "Long as my attorney says it's okay."

"Bring him with you," Grace advised. "I'll interview you both."

After hanging up, Grace felt her pulse pounding. This was the old sensation coming back, her penchant for digging out a huge story on steroids. She could hardly wait.

CHAPTER FIVE: Hooked on Crime

Grace realized she was walking a tightrope. On one side, she was supposed to report on the positive religious stories that would satisfy her management. But on the opposite side, certain events were unfolding that cast some religious leaders in a different, dangerous light. How effectively she could keep the two ideas in play would determine whether she would stay upright or fall to Earth.

Riding with her favorite photographer, Steve Jankowski, gave her comfort. They worked together covering crimes several times in the past. He was a veteran, one of the good guys, and she trusted his judgment.

"What do you think?" she asked. "Look okay to you?"

"Good interview," he answered. "But you know…" He gave her a sidelong glance as he drove, half-smiling.

"I know, I know. It's not what I came to Atlanta for. But right now I don't have much choice."

He nodded and a full grin covered his days-old beard. "Missionary stories are a far cry from drug busts and murders," he said. "You'll figure it out, Grace. You're a pro's pro."

As Steve drove, Grace smiled, opened her laptop and pulled up the interview she just completed. The background was the massive Second Methodist Church in Midtown Atlanta. The subject interview was the church's missionary minister, a tall, thirty-something, enthusiastic man of the cloth.

"I'm speaking with Rev. Frank Richmond," Grace looked into the camera. *"Reverend Richmond, you and some of your con-*

gregation just returned from an annual missionary trip to Costa Rica. Tell us what you accomplished there."

"Grace, you should have been there," he bubbled. His collar bobbed as he talked, and it might have been comical were it not for the sincerity with which he spoke. *"Forty-five dedicated members of our congregation descended on that tiny Costa Rican town ready to do battle on behalf of the Lord. They transformed a dilapidated old church building into something beautiful in less than a month. New roof. New floor. Bright paint throughout. A kitchen. Modern bathroom fixtures. And the large bronze cross we had manufactured specifically for the project was the crowning touch. Those wonderful Costa Ricans who invited us to help them were astounded at what our people were able to accomplish in a short amount of time."*

"Where did the funds come from for the work?" Grace asked.

"Our missionary funding comes from donations of our church members," he responded. *"But many of the volunteers who went down there personally purchased materials and saw they were delivered at exactly the right time. And of course, each volunteer paid his or her own way. I'm happy to say, some took their teenage children to be part of the group. What better way to teach a young person how to minister to others?"*

Grace closed the laptop and looked over at Jankowski. "I can't watch the rest. I know it's a good story, a meaningful one. And it made me realize how little I've done outside the newsroom to make a difference in the world. But Steve, I don't want to do feel-good stories the rest of my career."

He cut loose a deep laugh. "I'll tell you what's wrong with you, Gleason. You have an addiction."

"Addiction?"

"You're hooked on crime," Jankowski said.

Grace joined his laughter. "Maybe so."

"Well," he continued, "This next interview ought to be a quick fix. From what you've told me about this church minister walloping kids in his services, you have a chance to expose another side of the religious paradigm."

"I know, but I wish it weren't the case."

He nodded and wheeled the Big Six News truck into a parking lot at the law offices of Bruce Newton and his partners.

Inside, the offices sported wood-paneled walls and marble flooring. The museum-like quiet presented a stark contrast to the busy street noise outside. A secretary escorted them to a large conference room, and Jankowski quickly, deftly, set up his camera and lights. Just as he finished, attorney Bruce Newton entered with Shaniqua Forrester. Newton was a small man, balding—about fifty, with a ruddy complexion. Unlike some of the blustery lawyers Grace had covered, Newton seemed reserved, given to small gestures and carefully contemplated comments. Shaniqua, on the other hand, filled the room, both with her physical presence and an aggressive, high-volume speech style. She wore a bright green dress with a multi-colored scarf. Her heavy makeup had been perfectly applied, punctuated by some of the longest eyelashes Grace had ever seen.

"Mr. Newton," Grace began, "if you agree I'd like to interview Ms. Forrester first. Then, if there's more to ask, I'll turn to you for additional responses."

The lawyer nodded agreement. "Okay. There are a few things we can't talk about. I've advised Shaniqua what not to get into, but if things wander off base, I'll let you know."

33

Steve turned the lights on, and Grace went to work.

"Ms. Forrester, the preacher at Church of Faith, Dontell Freeman, has been arrested, accused of spanking children during Sunday service. Meanwhile, you have filed a civil lawsuit against him. Why take this step if he's in jail?"

"Ain't no way to know how the charges against this man will work out in criminal court," she answered. "But my little girl Rosalee got a whupping two Sundays ago. Man pull her dress up and whacked her five times with a stick while others held her. I rushed up and got her before he could do more, but she wasn't the only one he whupped that morning. We're..." she hesitated and glanced at the attorney, who nodded to proceed. "...alleging... the man damaged more than skin on her backside, know what I mean? That's a harm she might not ever forget, might not ever get over. I won't go back until that man gets removed from our pulpit."

"Have any other parents expressed interest in joining your lawsuit?"

"Some, privately," she said. "But the man got a lot of powerful friends in that sanctuary. Many of the parents opposed to what's going on are afraid of what might happen. So they go along. Well, I ain't afraid. Not right, beating children, making sexual innuendos in sermons, taking these underage girls over to Alabama to get them married."

Grace nearly shouted. "What? What are you talking about?"

"You didn't know 'bout that?" Shaniqua Forrester asked. "Man takes them over where they will marry girls fourteen, fifteen years old. Marries some of them off to guys on parole from jail. Says it creates a stable life for both of 'em. I say if it's not a crime, it should be." She looked quickly again at Bruce Newton. "Lawyer agrees."

"Do you have proof this is happening?"

Again, the woman appeared hesitant and peered at Newton for approval. He seemed reluctant, but finally slowly gestured to go ahead.

"We have proof," she responded.

About to ask another question, Grace instinctively held back. She could see her interviewee's face contorting slightly and then growing puffy as Shaniqua teared up.

"Children got a right to go to church and learn about the grace of Jesus Christ, not the wrath of their pastor," the woman lamented, sobbing softly. The flow of tears accelerated, streaking mascara down her brown cheeks. "I can't stay quiet, can't say 'he's my minister so he must be right.' Can't just do nothing, Miss Gleason."

Grace started to speak, but Newton stepped in. "Ms. Gleason, I'm sorry, but that's as much as we can say right now."

Grace nodded to Jankowski and he turned the lights and camera off. She moved forward and embraced the large woman. "You did fine, Shaniqua," she whispered. Then, turning to the attorney, "Mr. Newton, is it a proven fact? He forces teenage girls to get married?"

The lawyer thought for a moment. "I warned Shaniqua not to get into that. You can see how passionate she is about it. We don't know if it will be part of our lawsuit, Grace. I know you've got it recorded, but I wish you wouldn't use it until we find out more. Can we speak off the record?"

Grace nodded. "For now, at least."

Newton motioned for everyone to sit at the conference table. Shaniqua Forrester sank into a chair, still crying softly, fanning herself with a piece of notepaper. Grace sat beside Newton.

"We haven't been able to thoroughly investigate this yet," the lawyer told her. "What we've learned so far is the guy identifies girls who have an unstable home life, whom he believes would benefit from a life of marriage and constancy. Ostensibly, that's his rationale. The other part of the equation is that many of the men he's marrying them off to are inmates from the Federal prison here who have just been paroled. So he supposedly tells them they will both be better off in a solid, married environment."

"You're certain of the girls' ages?" Grace asked. "I think the age of consent in Alabama is sixteen."

Shaniqua was getting her second wind. "Teens, some young as fourteen," she spewed angrily. "State of Alabama is lax about ages when it comes to marrying. There's lots of places over there where they can go do it."

"Are the girls being forced? What about their parents?"

"Therein lies the rub," the lawyer smiled at his own Shake-speare reference. "Look, you're right about the age of consent. Used to be fourteen in Alabama but there was a big stink about it, and the legislature raised the age. But it's still fourteen if the parents agree. All preacher Freeman has to do is get the parents to approve. Some are happy to grant it—gets the girl out of the house. There are other instances when we're not sure whether or not the consent is legitimate. Or if a few justices of the peace somewhere over there might be complicit."

He shook his head and glanced at Shaniqua. "At any rate, we haven't found a girl yet who objected to the idea. They seem to follow their pastor meekly, almost obediently, it seems to me. We haven't been able to establish—not yet, anyway—that any of the girls has been married against her will."

36

"It's hard to get my mind around why the girls wouldn't put up some kind of fight," Grace said. "Why would they stay so devoted to someone who forces his will on them that way?"

The lawyer shrugged his shoulders. "Not sure. There's always the Stockholm Syndrome. Not sure if this is some kind of related behavior, but it's a possibility."

"I've heard of it," Grace nodded. "But I really don't know much about it."

"The classic definition is that hostages develop a psychological commitment to their captors to survive," he said. Then, smiling, "I just told you all I know about it. Could be something like that is working in that church."

"I need to look into it, I guess," Grace acknowledged.

"There's a guy over at Emory University, a psychology professor, who is supposedly an expert on it," Bruce Newton told her. "I crossed paths with him when he appeared as a witness in a case I was trying. I can give you his information."

Grace nodded. "Thanks. But Stockholm Syndrome or not, it's hard to fathom those children and their parents following so blindly."

"As far as I know," replied the attorney, "none of those nine hundred followers of Jim Jones who drank poisoned juice complained, either, at least not publicly. As for parents, most of these girls have very little guidance at home. In fact, some are basically homeless. Or live in a household grateful to get them out from under their roof. I can see how easily the Reverend Freeman could pull it off."

"Jim Jones encouraged his cult followers to turn in anyone who was a dissenter or wanted out," Grace recalled. "He had armed guards to control the people at Jonestown."

Grace paused, waiting for comment, but Newton merely smiled, so she continued, "He became more powerful and the situation grew more dangerous for anyone wanting to leave or expose what was going on. Do you think that's the situation with this minister? Do you think he's dangerous?"

The lawyer didn't answer, his shoulders going up in a "who can say" gesture.

Grace turned to Shaniqua Forrester, who stared back with legitimate fright in her eyes. "I'll tell you my opinion. Yes, crossing this man could be risky. I'm watching over my shoulders. Miss Gleason, you getting deep into this subject now. Watch your back."

CHAPTER SIX: Feud and Fear

The long, slow days of her Savannah sabbatical had floated by like cottonwood seeds on a warm summer day. In contrast, the time since her return was churning wildly, like the tornadoes of August, as if the news gods decided once again to test her resolve.

Grace conducted the interview with Shaniqua on a Friday. Jackson Davis aired it on his Friday six o'clock newscast.

"Grace Gleason returns to Big Six this week," Davis drawled in his usual air of pomposity. "And what she uncovered about the so-called spanking pastor of the Church of Faith in Dekalb County is sure to have authorities take a second look at the man behind bars. Here's Grace."

The interview ran, but she edited out the reference to marrying off teenage girls. Grace believed Shaniqua Forrester, but she wanted corroboration from more sources before it aired. It would make a good follow-up story, especially if she could get over to Alabama and interview some of the people running those marriage mills.

"Good interview with the mom," Scott Matthews stopped by her cubicle early Friday evening.

"Thanks," Grace smiled up at him. "I was a little worried about a negative reaction from Buck Lohmeyer, but it never came. What're you doing here so late?"

"Some of us are going down to Piedmont Tap for a little TGIF cocktail. Why not join us?"

"No, I have some more work to do here. Then I'm going home. I'm beat."

"Old lady!" Scott taunted.

"Young whippersnapper!" Grace teased back as he disappeared out the door.

The truth was she was preparing for what could be a huge interview. An hour earlier, after multiple attempts, she had managed to get Khalila Noorani, the community organizer for Imam Moghaddam, on the phone. Grace was pleasantly shocked to hear the woman agree to an interview on Sunday. There was a lot of homework to do before then.

She worked all day Saturday, watching video of the woman, reading about her background and learning how she had connected with Aahil. Not wanting to ignore the minister-beating story, she also conducted an extensive internet search of locations in Alabama where young girls could marry. Grace was astonished when she finally looked at the clock and it said five p.m. Not only had she worked all day, but she had missed lunch.

Time to go out and get the mail, she thought, *and then have something to eat before I pass out.* The air outside was sweet and pleasant as she went to the mailbox. She stood sifting through the stack of envelopes and mailers.

"Anything interesting in there?"

The deep, husky voice startled her. She had not seen the hulking figure until he was nearly beside her. But she relaxed, immediately recognizing her next-door neighbor.

"You startled me," she said. Then, laughing, "No royalty checks, if that's what you mean. I usually perform this mail-sorting task next to the recycle tub, since eighty percent of it is typically the junk variety. But today I wanted to linger outside and enjoy the dying afternoon. Spring is on us."

She tucked the mail stack under her arm and extended her hand. "Grace Gleason."

"I know. I watch you on the news. I'm Horace Gunter," he said. Nodding toward the property adjoining hers on the north, "I live over there."

Grace gave a teasing smile at the man whose once barrel chest was obviously becoming eclipsed by a spreading waistline. "I know," she said, "I've seen—well, not exactly seen—heard—you and your buddies in the backyard."

Gunter rubbed the salt-and-pepper stubble on his chin and grinned. "Hope we haven't disturbed you too much."

"Not at all," Grace assured. "I think it's great that you and your chums have such a good time together."

"We're all a bunch of retired reprobates," he laughed, a sort of smoke and whisky sounding wheeze. "When we sit around that fire pit and the beer and the stories start flowing, we get a little too loud."

"Don't think anything of it, Horace," Grace said. "I heard you're a retired cop."

He nodded yes. "I was on the force in Charlottesville, Virginia, for too many years than I can remember. Moved here three years ago to be near my two kids. Then they pulled up stakes and moved across the country for their careers. So here I am."

"Well, I have a healthy respect for police," she said. "If you've met any of Atlanta's finest, I probably know quite a few."

"I imagine we know a lot of the same ones," he said.

"And I have one very dear friend who was a detective in the Dallas force before I moved here. Prince of a man."

"What's his name?" Gunter asked. "Maybe I know him."

"I doubt it," she answered. "His entire career was in Texas. His name is Ned Moore."

The retired cop screwed up his forehead in recollection. "Oh yeah, I remember Ned Moore."

"How could you possibly know him?" Grace asked, astonished.

"I met him at a conference in D.C. a couple of years before I retired. We sat in the hotel bar and had a conversation. You'd be surprised how many cops I know from around the country because of those conferences we all attended. You ever talk to Moore?"

She shook her head. "No, not recently."

"Well, when you do, give him my regards." He turned and started toward his house, then turned back. "Grace, you don't need to be a stranger when the boys come over. You'd be more than welcome to join us and tell some of your own stories."

She laughed. "I might just do that."

An hour later, she would have that opportunity. Standing in her kitchen, heating leftovers for her dinner, a flash of light through her kitchen window caught her eye. Grace peered out the window across the back of her lot and saw several figures next door in the gathering dusk, huddling over Gunter's fire pit as he kindled a growing flame. She could make out muffled voices bantering, laughing, sounds that would grow much louder as the night wore on.

Grace felt comforted as she gazed at the embers in Gunter's pit, thinking back to her childhood when neighbors knew each other and routinely visited each other and simply talked. In an age of social media and all-evening television watching, those social interactions all but disappeared. It made her sad. She wished for a moment she could return to those simpler times.

She considered for a moment, and then decided tonight would not be the time to cross the yard and accept Horace's invitation. *But I will soon,* she promised herself.

**

Grace rose early the next morning. Big Six aired a public affairs program on Sunday mornings in the wee hours, hosted by a part-time reporter. The poor time slot guaranteed low ratings, but people with strong interest in the subject matter on a given Sunday tuned in. Grace knew the interview about the Costa Rica missionary trip would air and so set her alarm for five and brewed some strong coffee.

Settled into the couch with her coffee, she watched. *"Reverend Richmond, you and some of your congregation just returned from an annual missionary trip to Costa Rica. Tell us what you accomplished there..."*

She was happy with the result, and she was certain the piece would help meet expectations of her management vis-à-vis her assignment as religion reporter. But as she watched, her mind drifted in another direction—to that of Khalila Noorani and the interview she would do with the woman in the afternoon. She was excited, because this would be an exclusive.

Grace was waiting when Noorani arrived promptly at two, walking into the newsroom smoothly and gracefully. She was alone and glanced suspiciously at Steve Jankowski setting up lights.

"Khalila, I appreciate your coming in," Grace told her. She nodded toward Steve. "He's one of our photographers who will shoot our interview." She motioned toward a chair, and the woman sat down while Grace pulled up another one and faced her. "I can't tell you how beautiful I think your hijab is."

The woman lowered her eyes in modesty. She didn't seem the firebrand Grace had seen in action during protests. "Like all my sisters, I wear it not to attract attention, but to display the modesty required of us. The Qur'an says, 'Tell thy wives and thy daughters and the women of the believers to draw their cloaks close round them. That will be better, so that they may be recognized and not harassed.'"

Grace motioned to Steve, who turned on the lights and started to roll the camera. "That's a good place to begin," Grace said. "Khalila, it is said of you that you adhere strongly to the principals of Islam, not only in your dress but in following all the Qur'an's teachings. Yet you haven't always been a Muslim, have you?"

"My parents were from Lebanon," the woman responded. "My father owned a business that he moved to Miami, so I was raised in Florida as a Maronite Catholic. But when I went to California, to the university at Berkeley, I was exposed to a variety of beliefs and religions. Islam found a special place in my heart, and eventually I converted."

"Was your friendship with Slay T. Jefferson, now known as Aahil Moghaddam, part of that conversion?"

"I was influenced by many people I met there, including a wonderful Imam at the Berkeley Masjid near the campus. I did meet Monroe Jefferson—many called him Slay at the time—and I recognized he was going to be a powerful and righteous leader."

"A leader who is now charged with murdering a deputy sheriff."

"Unjustly accused," the woman responded calmly.

"The surviving deputy identified his photo, didn't he?" Grace pressed.

"The description he gave of the killer did not match the description of Aahil Moghaddam. He later changed it to fit the photo ID."

"If he was innocent, why did Aahil Moghaddam flee from authorities?"

"Ms. Gleason, he has been harassed by authorities all his adult life, because of his struggles to eliminate injustices and oppression of minority races. The warrants those deputies were said to be serving were for made-up crimes, designed to take Aahil as a political prisoner. If you were so unjustly accused, wouldn't you run away?"

"What I would do isn't relevant here, Ms. Noorani. One last question, and I hope you aren't offended by it. You have been a follower and supporter of Aahil Moghaddam since his days as Slay T. Jefferson in California. You have been a trusted adviser to him and have advocated many of his causes. Are you romantically involved with him in any way?"

The Muslim woman's eyes opened wide in the same look of defiance Grace had seen during political confrontations. Grace realized she was hitting a nerve.

Khalila waited a beat and took a breath. Then, calmly, "I am a lawyer and community organizer, and I simply support the Imam as he does the good work of helping his people. He is a married man, and I respect that marriage." Her gaze never wavered from Grace.

Grace nodded. "Thank you. I hope you'll let me talk to you again as this case unfolds."

The woman didn't respond, continuing to hold the stare until Steve turned off the camera and lights.

"Why would you ask me such a thing?" Khalila challenged Grace.

"Because a reporter asks the questions her viewers would want asked," she said. "I can imagine many people wanted to know everything about your relationship with him. Khalila, I've been wondering, why did you agree to come for an interview?"

"You mean why agree to come here, to your station? Or why agree to be interviewed?"

"Both."

"I came here today because I know television stations are quieter on Sundays. And an interview in a public place might have created far too much commotion. I agreed to be interviewed only by you, because I know your work. I don't know the others, but I have watched how you conduct yourself. I believe you are usually fair and objective. But I must say, Grace, plunging into that kind of personal supermarket tabloid questioning disappoints me greatly."

"I didn't mean it to come across that way, I promise. I think it was justified. But you must have seen me cover crimes and criminals. Your friend—colleague—is accused of a heinous crime."

"Even when you have covered alleged crimes, I have noted you are impartial. I believed you would give me a chance to give my side."

"I hope this won't be the last."

"We'll see," responded Khalila Noorani.

**

The next day, Monday, at morning meeting Lateisha went down the list of stories in the works. "We got a report early this morning that Aahil Moghaddam was apprehended in Knoxville, Tennessee. He is being held pending officers from Georgia picking him up and bringing him back. Obviously, security is extremely tight. The district attorney has set a press conference for this afternoon at two, to update everyone."

"Bannister and Scott will both cover the press conference," Buck Lohmeyer said. He looked directly at Grace as if expecting a reaction. She smiled back at him, making no comment. The sooner she got out of these meetings without prolonged debate, the better she felt.

Back at her desk, Grace caught up on some research until time to watch her interview with Khalila Noorani as it streamed on her computer.

The noon anchor, Christina Cruz, led it off. "Yesterday our religion reporter, Grace Gleason, interviewed a representative of the mosque headed up by accused killer Aahil Moghaddam. The suspect has been apprehended in Tennessee, making this interview particularly timely. Here's Grace."

Immediately after the interview ran, Grace got a call. It was her news director. "Come in and see me now," Buck Lohmeyer ordered. "My office."

He was waiting with fire in his eyes, his neck deep crimson. He motioned toward the chair across from his desk, but she slowly shook her head and remained standing.

"Gleason, you've stepped way over the line of your assignment," his voice was a sharp knife. "First, there's this child beating story—this interview with a disgruntled mother. Then this...this dialogue with a rabble-rouser Muslim woman who you allowed to plead the guy's case publicly on our station. You're getting out of line."

Grace tried mightily to speak with composure. "Mr. Lohmeyer, we have a minister, supposedly a man of God, beating children and making them marry ex-cons. It seems to me that's within the realm of religious reporting." She paused. "And I've been past Moghaddam's mosque several times. I've seen boys not quite yet men hanging around there, no doubt absorbing whatever messages are being delivered during prayers. Slay T. Jefferson was a strong influence on young radicals in California, and we have no idea whether or not he's helping radicalize some of these young Muslims in Atlanta. I need some leeway to examine if religion is being used to recruit children who serve at the whim of their leader. I've only scratched the tip of this iceberg. Give me some room."

Lohmeyer glowered. "I agreed with Harvey Silver to cut you some slack, but you've run that leash right out to the end, Grace."

She stood looking down at him, clenching her fist, fighting against the urge to explode. "All I'm doing is what I was assigned to do—reporting on religion in the greater Atlanta area. If that leads down some paths you're not comfortable with, Mr. Lohmeyer, I'm sorry."

"God damn it, Gleason. I said no more."

Grace recoiled from the harsh words, and then arched her eyebrows in mock surprise. "Mr. Lohmeyer, you took the Lord's name in vain."

"So?"

"In the presence of your religion reporter!"

She abruptly pivoted and exited his office, hurrying down the hallway toward the newsroom. A bevy of emotions followed her. Embarrassment at mocking her manager that way. Regret at not keeping her composure. Most of all, disgust with her current situation at Big Six News.

Grace sat sullenly at her workstation, fighting for calm. She expected Buck Lohmeyer to follow her and keep the argument going. Or worse, fire her. But he did neither.

She spent the rest of the afternoon doing research, taking notes, mapping out ideas for follow-up on both stories, determined not to yield. She would need to plan carefully to keep her new boss off her back.

Daylight saving time had already kicked in, so she was astonished when she turned her computer off and realized despite the longer daylight hours, dusk was already falling outside. The clatter of the newsroom had slowed to a low rumble, and many of the staff had taken off. *Time to go home,* she thought.

Driving toward Morningside, she remembered several things she need to pick up at the grocery store. Her cell phone rang and she answered as she pulled into the darkening parking lot.

"Grace Gleason?" the deep, muffled male voice at the other end inquired.

"Yes. Who is this?" She pulled into a space and waited.

"Gleason, you're poking around where you're not wanted. You need to back off on that story."

"What story?"

There was no response.

"You mean the whipping preacher story?" She didn't even try to mask her annoyance. Still, there was no response. "Or is it the Muslim murder suspect's lawyer friend?" she added, trying to draw him out. She had received many calls like this one over the years, and it was usually a prank. Or, when the moon was full, one of what she called "the viewing crazies."

"You know what I'm talking about," the caller continued. "I'm warning you straight out. Back off or things could get very uncomfortable for you."

The caller hung up. Grace knew she should probably be more concerned than she was. Years of covering dangerous people had inured her to empty threats from offended viewers.

She handled her shopping chore quickly—she jokingly called it power shopping. She had all the aisles memorized and could navigate them with speed while tossing this box or that can into the cart. As Grace laid her bag in the back seat and climbed behind the wheel, she didn't notice the black seventies muscle car sitting beside her little sedan with its motor quietly rumbling.

Pulling out of the lot, she paid little attention to the headlights in her rear-view mirror. Only when they stayed glued behind her as she turned this way, then that way, did she begin to eye the vehicle with suspicion. She wheeled a sharp right around a corner as a test, and here it came, only a few yards off her back bumper.

Grace's heart began to race. This encounter was far too similar to a time years earlier, in Dallas, when an accused killer she was covering tailgated her for miles, even jarring her rear bumper at one point. She could feel the perspiration on her upper lip as this mysterious car riding her tail dredged up the memory.

Grace merged into heavy rush hour traffic on one of the major four-lane streets leading into the Morningside area. She changed lanes several times, attempting to shake her pursuer. Finally, after deftly positioning in traffic with the chaser far behind, she wheeled a quick right turn down a quiet side street. No one pursued. She pulled over at the curb, turned her lights off and watched, laboring to catch her breath. Still nothing.

She exhaled a massive sigh of relief at having lost the stalker. Yet her disquiet over the incident remained. She knew she would be watching for that black car every time she turned a corner or pulled into a parking lot or ramped off the freeway.

Not only do I have a news director nipping at my heels, she thought, *but there's an attack dog trying to intimidate me, and I don't even know what for.*

CHAPTER SEVEN: Holy Matrimony

The drive to her destination in Alabama took less than three hours, but Grace disliked it just the same. The landscape on the way was boring, and the heavy flood of semi-trailers traveling the four-lane route, speeding up and slowing down as they negotiated the hills combined with the clatter-clatter of the uneven concrete to jar her senses.

Grace had traveled to Montgomery, the Alabama state capital, several times to cover stories. This Interstate 85 highway was the route she took. She recalled major road construction delayed every trip, and today was no exception. Rebuilding of an overpass slowed traffic to a crawl and created a two-mile-long caravan of restless drivers, many of them freight-hauling truckers.

She listened patiently to music until the traffic finally broke free, then moved well above the speed limit as she and other travelers raced to catch up from the delay. Soon she passed the gigantic manufacturing plant a Korean carmaker operated near the border, and in twenty or so minutes she sailed past Opelika and Auburn. Halfway from there to Montgomery she veered off the highway and within minutes found herself driving down Georgia 81 and into the middle of Tuskegee.

This was Reverend Dontell Freeman's hometown, Grace learned from Shaniqua Forrester. His family were descendants of slaves in this county who had worked the short-staple cotton fields. After emancipation, many freedmen remained, continuing to work the land. Freeman attended Tuskegee Institute, later renamed Tuskegee University, before getting his degree from the Claxton School of Theology in Montgomery. He returned to Tuskegee for five more years before moving to Atlanta and establishing his church there. But even after leaving, the preacher maintained his close ties with many of the pastors and politicians in his hometown.

Tuskegee seemed a typical community for that of a population just under ten thousand residents. As she drove into the heart of town, she watched as scattered, modest homes on the outskirts gradually gave way to the kinds of businesses that line the main drag of tens of thousands of similar places throughout the country. Fast-food restaurants, auto body shops and gas stations lined the road. And then, closer to town center, an occasional strip mall with a dollar discount business or drug store.

The only thing that amazed Grace was the lack of diversity. She knew Tuskegee was a historically African-American community, with a black population of more than ninety-five percent. But she wasn't prepared to see so few whites traveling through, or engaging in commerce, or visiting the many historic sites made famous by the likes of Booker T. Washington, Georgia Washington Carver and Rosa Parks.

Approaching downtown, she identified the only high-rise building as a well-known chain hotel. From there, she relied on her GPS system to find the Probate Judge's office. Given Tuskegee's small size, she assumed it would be in some sort of modest office building. Instead, as she turned the corner of Northway Street, she was astounded by the impressive, looming brick edifice whose Romanesque Revival architecture of arched entryways and octagonal wings was topped by an impressive clock tower.

Inside, the building showed its age, as did the furnishings. It housed many different judicial offices, and Grace followed the signs to her destination. A pleasant woman with a motherly smile, stylishly dressed, sat behind the counter sporting a small sign, "Thornton Martin, Judge of Probate."

"You must be Miss Gleason," the woman said in a friendly, clear alto voice.

"I am," Grace answered. "As you obviously know, I have an appointment with Judge Martin."

"He's over at the city council meeting," the woman explained. "But he knows you're coming. Won't be there long, if you don't mind waiting."

She ushered Grace into the judge's office and gestured toward a coffee pot. "Help yourself," she said. "I'll text him that you're here."

Grace nodded and wondered how people ever got along without smart phones. She sat gazing at hers, picking up the latest news, until the judge arrived.

"Hope you weren't waiting too long," he breezed in and shook her hand with a bear-like grip. He was a large man. His hair and beard of white were a stark contrast to his ebony skin. His voice thundered when he talked. "Damned council meetings, always got something I need to check out or they'll go right around me."

"No problem," Grace said. "I appreciate your seeing me."

"Don't have much time," he said. "You're a reporter? Working on something about Tuskegee?"

"I'm following the path of some Atlanta girls who came over here to get married," she said. "I don't really know if it's a story or not, but I thought I'd drive over and talk to you, at least."

"Okay," he said, settling into his office chair and straightening his tie. "Shoot."

"Judge Martin, there's a sort of history of young girls coming from Georgia to Alabama to get married, and I'm trying to learn why they do. Are Alabama's marriage laws more lenient—that is to say, more tolerant of under-aged girls, than those of Georgia?"

"Used to be," he answered. "At one time, girls as young as fourteen were able to marry here without many requirements. In more recent years, that's changed due to legislation passed in the state legislature. Even that was a fight, raising the age of consent from fourteen to sixteen. Now, a girl of sixteen who wants to get married has to have her parents' consent."

"In every case?"

He hesitated. "There can be exceptions. For instance, if a girl is pregnant. Or if she's been sexually active and there's potential for abuse if the girl seeks her parents' permission. Or of course, if the parent can't be located for some reason. In such cases, a court can consent if it's deemed in the best interest of the child wanting to marry. It's very much dependent on an individual situation, and we have pretty broad discretion as long as we stay within the law."

"Judge Martin, when you marry a couple…"

He broke in, "Not me. I don't perform marriages."

"Really!" she responded, surprised.

"Used to. But the demands on probate judges these days are growing, with the number of estates escalating, wills becoming more complicated, and the like. Many of us don't perform ceremonies anymore. Just don't have time to take hours away from other probate duties to do something a minister can do. We issue licenses here, but someone else marries them."

"All right. So who can marry a couple in Alabama?"

He grinned. "Truthfully? Just about anyone who claims to be a minister. And there's no waiting period like in some other states. So as soon as they get their license, they can hightail it down to the Baptist Church, or the Unitarian Church, or the front room of someone who's licensed as a minister of the gospel or a pastor of some religious society. It's a pretty easy threshold to cross."

Grace stayed another fifteen minutes, digging deeper for material she could use. When she left, she felt a bit mind-boggled by the baffling lack of clarity about the marriage laws of Alabama versus Georgia and the various nuances of when a young girl can and can't marry. Her conclusion was the requirement that both parents accompany minors might be easily sidestepped if the child was homeless, or the parents unknown or unable to be located. A minister could appeal to the court in the extenuating circumstances. Or, she thought, falsify documentation.

She wondered if the Reverend Dontell Freeman might have stepped over such a line. Were documents fabricated about the girls' parents? Were birth certificates tampered with? Was Judge Martin simply looking the other way when these girls came across the border? Or being paid off?

The main question that dogged her was, did the ministers involved feel the end justified the means? And was pressure of any kind involved? She had managed to dig up the name of one of Reverend Freeman's minister friends here through court marriage documents. That would be her next stop. But not until after lunch; she was famished.

The town center was dotted with places to eat, but they were mostly chain chicken and burger fast food joints, or Chinese buffets. She searched diligently for someplace more original and authentic. Finally, turning the corner off North Main onto George Carver Road, she pulled into the parking lot of a small, tidy building with a neatly lettered sign on front that said, "Lulu's Grill." The small lawn and shrubs in front were well manicured. Several late-model cars were parked in front. She would give it a try.

Inside, two rows of booths beckoned, with padded seats and polished wooden tables. The open kitchen lining the back wall appeared well organized and maintained. Grace laid her computer bag on the table as she sat, and a young waitress approached promptly with a glass of water and menu. "I'm Kimberly. Can I get you anything else to drink?" she asked politely. Grace immediately noticed her well-designed crochet braids and the bronze-toned makeup that gave her olive complexion a nice glow. *What a beautiful girl,* she thought. *I'll bet she's breaking some hearts.*

"Iced tea," Grace ordered. The girl nodded and retreated toward the kitchen. Grace glanced around. She was the only white person there, but the pleasant surroundings and good-natured greeting from the server made her comfortable.

She turned on her computer and scanned her news sources. One immediately caught her eye. Reverend Dontell Freeman had finally raised bail and was being released. She imagined Bannister Walker, Buck Lohmeyer's attack dog, or perhaps Scott Matthews, would cover it.

The lunch plate of barbecued meat loaf and vegetables was just passable, she thought, but still better than the hot wings and fries she might have had at one of those cookie-cutter places.

"You must be here doing some kind of work," the waitress said, pointing at Grace's open computer.

"Catching up on some things," she replied. "I'm a news reporter."

Kimberly's almond eyes opened wide. "Oh, wow. That's what I'd like to do."

"How old are you, Kimberly?"

"Seventeen."

Barely older than the youngsters Reverend Freeman is marrying off to ex-cons, Grace thought. "Well, if you go to a good communications program at a college or university, and apply yourself, you can do it. Like Robin Roberts." She could tell from Kimberly's expression the name drew a blank. "She's a famous newswoman on one of the big networks. Did you know she was born right here, in Tuskegee?"

The girl's eyes lit up even more. "No, but I'm going to look her up."

Grace grinned inwardly, recalling how important to her burgeoning news career were certain reporter pros who encouraged her. She hoped perhaps this small gesture, in this tiny town, would light a fire under Kimberly. *Maybe someday I'll establish a scholarship at my alma mater,* she thought. *It would be a terrific way to give back.*

Grace packed up her computer, paid her check and left Kimberly an oversized tip.

Driving through the middle of town, Grace had noticed many churches clustered on the southwest edge of the historic district. She noted the names as she drove toward her destination— Messiah Baptist, Zion Miracle Mission, Faith in Christ Ministries, Second Baptist of the Redeemer.

Reverend Mercedes Humphries' church, Mount Ararat Baptist, was farther down George Carver Road toward the southern outskirts of town. She had pulled a photo of it up on her computer during lunch and now recognized it immediately as it came into view. The white brick structure with a massive cross in front was a true contrast to the more conservative, traditional brick structures of most of the churches she had passed. Its irregular shape hinted it might have been built in phases, over a period of time, with sections added as needs arose.

Stepping inside, Grace was impressed by the sanctuary. The pulpit and choir loft were polished wood with brass rails, flanked by throne-like chairs for the ministers. Red carpeting throughout the room matched the deep cushions on the thirty or so polished mahogany pews.

From the back of the sanctuary, Grace saw a lone figure seated on the front row, his balding head bowed. She approached, and the reverend looked up from his Bible, smiling. "I was waiting for you," he said, and patted the pew for her to sit on space next to him.

He was elderly, slender, with a fringe of salt-and-pepper hair lining his shiny skull. Rimless glasses sat gingerly on his broad nose. Although soft-spoken, Reverend Humphries exuded an air of poise and confidence, like an old war vet who had been through all the battles and emerged unshaken. She noticed a slight age-created tremor in his hands.

"I thought you would be in an office," she admitted.

"This is where I write my sermons, up here," he said, pointing to his head. "Looking up at that figure of Jesus on the cross, and referring to the Lord's book from time to time, I get my inspiration right here in this seat, every week." He closed the Bible and turned to her, serious. "You wanted to speak to me about marriages."

"That's right, Reverend Humphries. As I told you on the phone, I'm covering the story about Reverend Dontell Freeman over in Atlanta. I believe you know him?"

"I do," he nodded. "Known Dontell many, many years, from his days here in Tuskegee. In some ways, he was almost like a son to me, after he joined the ministry and seemed to consider me a mentor. Terrible thing, him getting locked up like that. Do you think what he did was wrong?"

Grace shrugged. "It seems to me he crossed a line. I'm here to report, not to judge, but what they were doing in his church seems a bit—shall we say, misguided?"

"Have you spoken with him?"

"No. I received information about an hour ago he has been released from jail. So I hope to interview him when I get back. At least, someone at our station will."

Reverend Humphries shook his head. "Dontell is a good man, Miss Gleason. I wasn't there, to see what went on in his services of course, but I know he can give you a strong argument for what he does. Spare the rod and spoil the child."

"Spanking the children isn't why I'm here, Reverend Humphries."

"Of course not," he answered. "You came about the marriages."

"According to county records, you presided over at least some of the weddings of young girls he brought over here."

"That's right."

"Some of them were as young as fourteen, many others no more than sixteen?"

"Yes."

Grace was a bit flustered at the directness of his terse responses. "Well, sir, you're aware many of those girls were matched up with convicts out on parole, with Dontell Freeman doing the matchmaking?"

"I am."

"Well, sir..." she groped uncharacteristically for the right question, "...how can you justify helping them get licenses and marrying them, knowing all along Reverend Freeman set it up?"

"They call it holy matrimony, Miss Gleason. That's what it is, holy. Dontell helping those girls and those wayward young men get their lives back on track. Getting them right with the Lord." For the first time, his voice began to rise, as if he were cranking up a sermon. "Plenty of arranged marriages in the Bible, you know? Think Mary and Joseph found each other on an online dating service? No Ma'am. They found each other through their God, and that's what Dontell is doing. He came asking me to help him, since Georgia laws are stricter. I have no problem helping Reverend Freeman save souls, Miss Gleason."

She paused. "Reverend Humphries, saving souls might be one thing. But do you think any of those girls were forced into their marriages?"

He peered at her over the glasses rims, his shriveled lips pursing as he grew angry. "Never spoke with one girl who said she was coerced. Never heard one of them complain. Now, it seems to me you're a little off base, if you report he made them come over here and marry those men. Have you asked the girls?"

"Not yet, Reverend Humphries, but I plan to."

"You do that, Miss Gleason. You go back and ask them if Dontell Freeman, or Mercedes Humphries, or Probate Judge Martin who issues licenses, ever once forced them into anything. You'll find out you came over here to Tuskegee, Alabama, on a fool's errand. Now, good day."

With that, Reverend Mercedes Humphries rose and left the sanctuary, leaving Grace to sit there, alone, aghast, not knowing if his outburst was one of outrageous indignity or from pangs of guilt.

Grace drove slowly back through town and sped back onto Interstate 85, stunned and confused. She had spent hours on this trip, and she was no closer to answers than when she left Atlanta.

Three hours later, she was happy to get back. It had been a long day, and she was growing tired. Even so, she knew it wasn't over. An hour outside of the city she called photographer Steven Jankowski.

"Steve, can you break free to meet me? I'm going to try interviewing one of the girls on this marriage story."

"Tell me where and when," he answered. Immediately she became invigorated. Not only was Steve her favorite cameraman, but she also felt his mature, burly presence added a measure of safety when she ventured into dicey waters.

They met at a rundown strip mall not far from the neighborhood where the lawyer, Bruce Newton, told her one of the young girls lived.

"Thanks for meeting me," she said to Steve as she climbed into the station truck.

"No problem," he nodded. "Does this girl know we're coming?"

She half-grinned at him, all the answer he needed. She handed him a small slip of paper with an address, and he entered it into the GPS.

Steve steered the vehicle down Moreland Avenue and turned onto Glenwood, through the old Basswood Park neighborhood. As they drove, Grace realized they were an easy fifteen-minute drive from the site of the Imam murder. A slight shiver found its way down her spine.

Grace had been here before, once reporting on the many 100-year-old houses left vacant in the wake of the 2008 recession. She remembered seeing how ruthlessly thieves had scavenged anything of value in the abandoned properties, and set fire to some. Real estate agents she interviewed told her houses were selling for less than $10,000 each. Now it appeared the area was clawing its way back. Despite seeing some homes still abandoned, she also noted many newly built homes constructed in the same craftsman style as the originals. The city had demolished some of the public housing projects that had fallen into disrepair and crime. And the advent of the Atlanta Beltline project, the city's most comprehensive transportation and economic development effort ever undertaken, was beginning to make a difference.

"You have reached your destination, on your right," the GPS voice informed them.

Grace carefully surveyed her surroundings. It was the long-time habit of a reporter, but also a reaction to being followed earlier.

Looking around, she could see this block still needed a lot of work. Ramshackle frame houses cried out for paint. Unkempt yards needed to feel the blade of a good mower. Here a rotting, leaky roof sported a blue tarp. There a front porch sagged, its lower step almost on the ground. They had just passed through several blocks of restoration hope, and now they were in post-recession hell.

Jankowski pulled the truck to a spot where a curb once had been, now a series of broken concrete chunks, and turned off the engine. "That's it right there," he nodded toward a modest brick house with two front windows boarded up. "You sure that was the right address?"

There was no garage, and on the gravel driveway running the length of the house to a walled back yard sat three vehicles. The farthest back was a rusted-out pickup Grace was sure could not possibly run. The second, an old compact car, sat up on concrete blocks, three of its wheels missing. Closest to the street sat a fifteen-year-old sedan with a dented fender and a sheet of plastic taped over the broken passenger window.

"This is it, I'm sure," Grace answered. "Getting cold feet?"

Steve frowned. "Let's go," he said tersely and hopped down from the driver's seat. He opened the back of the truck and pulled his camera out, trudging toward the house as Grace hurried to catch up.

Before they could reach the porch, the front door flung open and a young woman sprang out wearing shredded-knee blue denims and a frilly top that revealed her bare midriff. Her oversized thighs and stomach bulge hanging over the jeans waist made Grace wonder if she was pregnant or merely fleshy from hamburgers and fries and sugared colas.

As she slammed the front door, bounced off the porch and turned toward the car, the young woman stopped short at the sight of two people with a camera coming toward her. "Wha—who are you?" she demanded in a firm but hazy voice.

"Ms. MacCauley? Jamica MacCauley?" Grace asked.

"Yeah. Who are you? What do you want?" Jamica questioned, pulling self-consciously at her yarn dreads.

"I'm Grace Gleason from Big Six News. Jamica, I was over in Tuskegee and talked to the minister who presided over your wedding there. I'd like to ask you some questions about your marriage."

Immediately, the front door flew open again. "Hey!" a baritone voice shot out at them. "What the hell's going on, Jamica?"

The man who stepped out displayed an angry expression, eyes narrowed, brow furrowed. He wore no shirt or shoes. His low-slung blue jeans looked grimy. He hopped off the porch and charged at Grace and Steve. His torso, obviously ripped from lifting weights, was completely covered with tattoos. His neck also sported various ink designs, as did his forehead except for a few areas that revealed the pasty-white complexion of someone who had spent too many years cooped up in a cell.

"I said, what the hell do you want?" he said. "Jamica, get back in the house."

Jamica retreated to the front porch but lingered there, watching.

"Sir, we would like to ask Jamica some questions about her marriage. Are you her husband?"

Jankowski turned on the camera and hoisted it onto his shoulder. The tattooed ex-con stepped forward, held a meaty hand up to the lens and then balled it into a fist, staring menacingly at Steve.

"Okay, okay," Steve responded to the implied threat. "I'll turn it off."

"Damn right you will," the man said. Then turning to Grace, "Missy, I seen you on the TV news. You been going after Reverend Dontell Freeman, ain't you? You've got no story here, so you might as well git."

"Are you Floyd MacCauley?" Grace asked.

"None of your business who I am."

Grace arched her neck. "I know you're Floyd MacCauley. Now tell me, did you and the good reverend conspire to force that girl to go to Alabama and marry you?"

MacCauley's glare turned to smoldering rage, and he fixed it squarely on Grace. Her heart pounded, but she was certain he wouldn't get physical. Not now, in the daylight. Not here, in his own yard.

He stood staring, his neck muscle bulging. "Now, I asked you nice to…"

"That was nice?" Grace interrupted. She felt Steve tugging at her arm.

"I asked you nice to git," her antagonist continued. "Next time

I won't be so polite."

Jankowski's grip on Grace's arm grew tighter, and she could feel him urging her away from the scene. She sighed inwardly, in resignation. It was obvious the situation was so volatile there would be no interview. She nodded and motioned Jankowski back toward the truck.

As they pulled away, Grace could see MacCauley leading Jamica by the arm back into the house. Just before he pulled her through the door, he looked back at Grace and Steve with a menacing scowl. Grace knew she would never forget his name nor that threatening glare, punctuated by the hideous facial tattoos. And she could only imagine what would come next, after Floyd and Jamica were inside.

"Jesus, Grace," Steve chastised as they drove back toward the station.

"I know, I know. But Steve, I kept thinking how horrible it would be for my own daughter to be caught up in that predicament." Grace paused. "It's just—sometimes I get so wrapped up in getting the story I kind of forget a situation might be risky."

She smiled at her photographer, and he grinned back.

"You're a real piece of work, Grace Gleason," he said.

"Come on, you like it when I crawl out there on the ledge," she laughed. "Gives you a chance to be a hero by talking me back off it."

He shook his head, continuing to smile. "Someday maybe I'll let you jump."

CHAPTER EIGHT: Judas Priest

For several days, Grace's reports were a mixture of positive community stories and an occasional update on the Aahil Moghaddam murder charges or the trial of the preacher, Dontell Freeman. She was itching to dig deeper into both, and to segue the child beatings into the marriage of girls from the church to cons on parole. She was determined to make the most out of the religion beat by pursuing the meat of these issues and intermingling them with feel-good stories to keep her news director happy.

Two days after her confrontation with Floyd MacAuley in his yard, she found herself downtown late in the afternoon. She was doing a remote from a soup kitchen. Jankowski hadn't been available, so she enlisted Cassandra Barrett to photograph the story. Grace had worked with Cassandra before, especially once on a scary mass murder in Midtown carried out by a berserk day stock trader. Although Steve was numero uno in Grace's book, Cassandra was good and Grace was happy to work with her.

"These spiritual leaders from across the metro area have formed a coalition to demonstrate their support for helping the homeless get at least one square meal a day," she heard Jackson Davis drone into her ear piece. "Grace Gleason is on hand to tell us about it. Grace?"

"Jackson," she said into the camera, "more than a dozen clergymen have already signed up to support this effort. Each of them will spend some time down here at Soup for the Souls every week, passing out meals, listening to problems, doing the good work they preach about to their congregations."

After interviewing one of the homeless persons and then the pastor from an inner city church, she closed out her report. Driving back to the station with Cassandra, she began to feel she was living a double life—trying to hold onto her job while still going after stories that seemed to churn constantly in the background.

Barrett parked in the back of the station as dusk set in. Walking across the dimly lighted lot, Grace thought she saw a shadowy figure a few yards away from the walkway. She grasped Cassandra's arm. "Do you see that guy?" she asked.

"Yes," the photographer answered. "Startled me for a minute. But he's probably just waiting for someone to get off work. Sorry, Grace, but I have to go. Need to pick up my kids." Cassandra disappeared into the building. Grace turned to follow her, but the figure of the man approached closer.

It can't be the guy who followed me, she thought. *He wouldn't be crazy enough to wait for me here.* Still, she knew unstable people had done crazier things than that. Her pulse pounded, and she picked up her step toward the door. Yet the man continued to move toward her until she could finally make out his features. He was dressed in khakis and a button-down shirt, probably in his forties, a little portly, with a neatly trimmed brown beard. Hardly the appearance of a loony.

"Grace Gleason?"

"Yes?" She felt her heart in her throat. She was ready to crash through the door in the building and scream for help, but her instincts fought against it, told her to wait.

"I'm not—I'm not trying to bother you or anything. I just—I

have something you might want to do a story on."

Relieved, Grace caught her breath. "Why not come inside and we can discuss it?"

"No," he answered, his voice quavering nervously. "I don't want anyone to see me. Look, Grace, I feel like I know you. I've been watching your series on religious issues, and I might have information you can use."

"Okay, what's this about?"

He hesitated. She noticed his hand trembling a little. "It's hard to talk about, but it needs to come out. It's about a law they passed here in Georgia a couple of years ago. It's called the Georgia Victim Fairness Act."

Grace's mind sprang to alert. "I remember," she said. "It opened the door for cases to be filed against accused child abusers."

"That's right," the man said. "Cases that were already past the statute of limitations. Abusers can't be criminally charged, but they can be brought into court and answer to claims of abuse."

"What's that got to do with me? And you?" Grace asked.

The man paused again, staring at the ground. "Years ago, I was molested by the priest in my parish," he said as Grace listened intently. "I don't want to go into details, but the priest was sent to a so-called treatment center for troubled priests."

Grace was stunned. "What's your name? Completely off the record, I promise. I won't ever reveal it without your permission."

"You promise?"

She nodded firmly, connecting her eyes with his for emphasis.

"Max Morrison," he said.

"Max, I understand your not wanting to go into the news-room. But let's not stand out here. There's a little cafe two blocks down the street. Let me buy you a cup of coffee and I'll hear you out."

He agreed to follow her there. The place was fit snugly into the middle of a small strip mall. Hardly anyone was inside, and Grace led Max Morrison to a corner booth. Settling in, she fumbled for a note pad in her purse. "Okay if I write some of this down?" she asked.

"Write down anything you want," he responded, sliding in across from her. "I'm not going into much detail. I just wanted to make sure somebody knows all of this. The priest was here in Atlanta, and I know I wasn't the only boy he messed with. I'm not giving you chapter and verse about my story. But I can give you enough to follow up on this guy. I've had a lot of therapy and other kinds of help to get past it. Maybe you knowing about it—possibly doing some kind of story—will help some of the others.

"His name was Father Anthony Bianci," he went on. "He came to Atlanta in the seventies and was assigned to Annunciation Catholic Church in Marietta. Several years later, he was trans-ferred to my family's parish in Cherokee County. I grew up less than a mile from the church."

"So this was long before major allegations of sexual abuse in the church came to light."

"Right. I was eight when it started, and it lasted for about two years before he was suddenly transferred to Rome, Georgia, when allegations arose that he had abused three boys. I was one of them. That's ironic, isn't it, that an Italian-American priest who studied at the Vatican would end up in Rome?" He laughed and shook his head. "As I grew up I stayed informed about his where-abouts. In 1988 he was transferred to a treatment center in Wash-ington, D.C. I lost track of him after that, and frankly, didn't care. I got some professional help and moved on with my life."

He sat back and studied her face, which registered shock and dismay.

Grace scribbled a few more notes and put the pad in her purse. "Max," she said, her voice shaken, "I don't know what to say. I grew up in the church, in Chicago. Despite our problems as a family, we were devout Catholics. I've reported on everything in my career, from bribery and murder to drug gangs and rape. But this horror shakes me to the core."

They sat silently for several minutes. Finally, she said, "Thank you for your courage in coming to me. I promise I'll treat your story with the utmost confidence. But I will pursue it through other sources."

He nodded. "Morgan Staton."

She cocked her head, trying to recognize the name.

"He was an assistant district attorney my parents talked to once. He was trying to go after this guy," Morrison explained.

"Of course," she said, remembering. "He was the Chero-kee County district attorney before he retired. I talked to him sev-eral times, working on various stories."

"He became a sort of expert on child abuse cases," Mor-rison told her. "Prosecuted several hundred of them, I think." He paused a beat and looked at his watch. "I have to go."

She nodded. Max Morrison had given her all she needed to pursue this story.

As she watched him drive off from the parking lot, Grace felt a sickness in the pit of her stomach. Offenses involving predatory authority figures weren't new to her. They were all over the media every week. But this was the church of her childhood, a refuge she always regarded as sacrosanct. When she reached the newsroom, she sank into the chair of her workstation, opened her desk drawer and stared at the Saint Anne holy card she kept there.

CHAPTER NINE: Morgan Staton

Grace remembered a few details about the former district attorney for Cherokee County from news reports when he was trying an accused murderer. He had a reputation as a straight-shooting kind of guy. A native of Auburn, Alabama, he attended the university there and was in the Army ROTC program, run by the father-in-law of Vietnam war hero General Harold Moore. She remembered reading quotes from fellow cadets that he was diligent about his appearance and drill precision, and he made excellent grades.

That was all she could recall, and she had no time to research the man. But she needed to know why she should trust him. She would have to probe his background, interview-style, face-to-face, and rely on her well-honed instincts.

They sat on his patio sipping tea as Staton answered her questions. He didn't seem to mind the grilling; it was almost as if he had expected a probe of his authenticity. He seemed to enjoy telling her his story.

"I was pretty lucky," he said. "Auburn didn't have a law school, but I took all my pre-law classes there and completed the ROTC program. The Vietnam War was winding down when I graduated, and I got an Army Reserve assignment. So I was able to take care of my military obligation and finish my law degree at the University of Alabama."

"Then what?" Grace asked eagerly, reflecting her natural interest in people's progression through life.

"That gave me a great path into the JAG Corps."

"So you were an attorney in the Army Judge Advocate General's Corps?" Grace responded.

"Right. It was an eight-year obligation. I learned a hell of a lot, as you might imagine. I would have stayed through retirement, except I got a call from an old friend, Patrick Neal."

"The district attorney for Cherokee County."

"Pat and I were close buddies—fraternity brothers and ROTC classmates at Auburn. He wanted me to come out here and be his Chief Assistant DA. Patrick was several years away from running for Congress, and he thought I might want to try for his job when he moved on."

"I vaguely remember covering a trial you were on up here," Grace said. "Everybody told me you were firm but fair."

He smiled but didn't respond. Grace decided she was talking to a solid character.

Staton took a sip of tea. "When you called, you said you're thinking about a story on Father Anthony Bianci. Why him? And why now?"

"I got a tip from someone close to a boy who was abused by him," she stretched the truth. "I'm working on some stories about religion in the Atlanta area, and thought I'd look into it, that's all."

Morgan took a long swig of his tea and wiped a paper napkin across his broad chin. He sank back into the lounge chair, showing a paunchy belly. "Man, that goes back a ways. What do you want to know?"

"I was told you were once pursuing him on behalf of some victims. What did you learn? Why didn't you prosecute? Why has the church not taken more responsibility? Where is Father Bianci now?"

"He's dead," Staton answered flatly.

Surprised, Grace paused for a moment and thought. "I hadn't heard that. I haven't had time yet to do any kind of internet search. Well, he would be in his eighties now, wouldn't he? How long since he passed away?"

"Just a couple of months," he answered. "An internet search might have turned up an obituary, but then again, maybe not. He kept very private the final years of his life. I understand he was in poor health the past two or three years, living in Tucson—nearly blind and needing to walk with a cane. Still smoked like a chimney and chug-a-lugged supplement drinks, relied on a few neighbors to help him get around when he needed to."

"So, about my questions," Grace probed.

Staton took a deep breath, remembering. "Let me give you a rundown of what I recall. I handled dozens and dozens of child abuse cases, and it's been a few years, so some of it might be a little muddy. But a lot of it became permanently etched in my mind when I went to see him after he was transferred to Rome."

"Rome, Georgia," Grace confirmed. "How long ago was that?"

His gray eyes narrowed as he calculated. "Nearly thirty years ago. I remember the statute of limitations on any cases that might have been filed had already passed. But for the sake of the families, I wanted to confront him and find out what I could, see if he would acknowledge any wrongdoing. Odd thing was, he didn't seem very surprised about why I was there. Almost like he expected someone to show up and question him or something. Of course, he denied he did anything untoward."

"Did you believe him?"

"No. The victims' stories were too compelling."

Grace took a sip of tea and sat forward. "Morgan, would

you be willing to let me interview you for my newscast on religion? We could set up a date later this week and I'll bring a cameraman with me. Now that Father Bianci is dead..."

"Former Father Bianci," Staton interrupted. "He gave up his collar after moving to Arizona."

"Okay, now that the former priest is dead, you couldn't get sued for defamation for anything you said."

"Why wait?"

"What?"

"I don't see any reason not to do it today. Give me fifteen minutes to change and comb my unruly gray hair, I'll follow you down to the station and we can do it there." He grinned. "Hell, Grace, it would kind of be like old times."

"Sure," she smiled back.

The drive to Big Six took thirty minutes. "Lateisha, get me a photographer, will you?" Grace said to the assignment editor on the phone as she drove in, keeping an eye on Staton's car behind her. "And find me a quiet spot, please, in the production studio. I'm going to do an interview that will roll your socks down."

Lateisha met her in the newsroom. "Grace, Cassandra Barrett is all set up and ready to go. I'm a little concerned we're all going to get our butts chewed out when Mr. Lohmeyer comes back, though. You know what he's been saying about you over-stepping your assignment."

"Lohmeyer's not here?" Grace felt a measure of relief.

"No, he's out of town for several days."

"Where's Jenny Kim?" Grace asked, referring to the assistant news director.

"She went out to Gwinnett County. She had to deal with some trouble Steve Jankowski got into."

"What trouble?" Grace's face registered surprise.

"He was photographing an apartment fire story out there and was arrested for obstructing a police officer. The cop apparently told him to move his video equipment away from the scene and Steve didn't move fast enough to suit him. Believe it or not, the policeman hauled him down to the Gwinnett County jail."

"Lord, what else can happen?" Grace exclaimed. "Don't worry, I'll take the heat for doing this interview, if there is any when Buck comes back. You're the best, Lateisha."

Ten minutes later, Grace was face-to-face with Morgan Staton, covering a story that excited her and broke her heart at the same time.

"Mr. Staton, you said the archdiocese transferred Father Bianci to a parish in Rome, north of Atlanta. That's when you interviewed him?"

"That's correct."

"What happened then?"

"The hands of any families wanting to press charges were tied," he answered. "The four-year statute of limitations had already come and gone. But the pressure on the church to take action was immense. They sent him to a treatment center in Washington, D.C., and some time after that to a similar center in Tucson."

"Did he continue in the priesthood?"

"No, he turned in his collar in the mid-nineties and moved into an apartment. He lived out the rest of his life there."

"What's the significance of his story coming out now, after all of these years?"

"About two years ago, the state legislature passed a law that would permit civil suits to be filed in certain instances, opening a two-year window. There could be no criminal findings, but accused child molesters would have to face their alleged victims, and their families, in a court of law. One case had been filed and was pending when Bianci died."

"Did the archdiocese ever acknowledge a role in protecting accused priests like Father Bianci?"

"There was a cash settlement in one instance I'm familiar with," the retired DA said, "but it was kept hush-hush. In several others I learned the archdiocese paid for some clients' psychological treatment. But the accuser in the case filed under the Georgia Victim Fairness Act didn't get his day in court. He is angry about that."

Grace turned toward the camera. "Understandably, this highly charged subject is difficult for everyone, especially alleged victims, many of whom have undergone years of therapy to overcome their sense of loss and shame. Tomorrow we'll attempt to interview one such person, although to protect his identity we will disguise his face and alter his voice. I'm Grace Gleason, with 'Religion Today.'"

Grace walked Staton out to his car. "Can't thank you enough for coming down, Morgan."

"Happy to do it, Grace. So you're going to do some follow-ups, huh?"

"I guess so. This is an important story, but even so, I don't intend to make it a prolonged part of my newscasts. The priest is dead, and I don't know how to make it more meaningful to my audience than the interviews I have set up. Besides," she went on, "the arraignment of Aahil Moghaddam is scheduled for tomorrow morning. I'm not covering it, but I want to be there for it just the same."

"Oh yeah," he reacted, "the Muslim cop killer. That'll be a damned circus, won't it?"

"I imagine it will be. The judge denied bond, of course, so after he pleads there'll be all sorts of fireworks trying to get him released."

"Ever get plain old tired of all this legal chaos?"

She shrugged her shoulders. "Sometimes. Did you?"

"Now that I'm retired, I miss it once in a while. Then I think about what we did today, and what you'll be doing tomorrow, and I'm glad I hung it up when I did."

"I think about retiring sometimes," Grace said. "Especially when I get threats or hang-up calls, or some yahoo tailgates me home."

"Really? You get a lot of that?"

"Oh yes. I'm not making it up. It gets pretty daunting at times."

"Grace," he said, his eyes dead serious, "if I can ever help you with any of that, don't hesitate to call. I still have a lot of friends on the force and at the DA's office. You always treated me with respect, and I appreciated it."

"Thanks," she said, feeling a new level of comfort.

After Morgan Staton was gone, Grace returned to her desk and sat there a long time, pondering. She was exhausted. But an idea ginned in her mind. She was running from story to story—not the good-works reports, but serious controversies with religious leadership at the center of them. An Imam, the spiritual leader of a neighborhood mosque, accused of murder. A minister arrested for beating children of parishioners. A former priest who allegedly molested boys. What if she could clearly describe a common thread to all of this and challenge an entire community to think about it through a series of commentaries? She had done so, to some degree of success, with the Atlanta drug wars. Why not in her newly assigned role as religion reporter?

Would Buck Lohmeyer permit it? Would Harvey Silver back her up? Grace didn't know if she had the energy or resolve to carry it out, and that worried her. It was such a series, after all, that drove her to Savannah. But her search for truth and fairness, and her ambition for responsible, meaningful reporting, wouldn't let her stop thinking about it. It wasn't the positive subject matter Mr. Silver originally envisioned for her.

She knew her management might balk at this departure from her assignment.

But she knew she had to try.

CHAPTER TEN: Buck Returns

The interview with Morgan Staton ran on the evening news, and Grace stuck around to watch on the newsroom monitor. She was pleased with the way it turned out.

Almost immediately, Mrs. Nicholson delivered a small stack of message slips. From her experience, Grace could guess the reactions from regular viewers—just names, no titles or explanation—would be split about fifty-fifty. Some would thank her for finally bringing the story to light, while others would chastise her for attacking their church without more proof or corroboration.

There was a request for a callback from the spokesman for the archdiocese, obviously wanting to make a statement. She would call him in the morning. By then, Buck Lohmeyer was scheduled to be back from his trip, and she would be able to gauge what her response should be.

But a more pressing message, unrelated to the priest story, caught her eye. It was from Shaniqua Forrester, the woman she had interviewed in lawyer Henry Newton's office about the child-beating minister.

Grace returned her call immediately. "What's up, Shaniqua?"

"Miss Gleason, thank you for calling back. I was wondering if you'd like to talk to another woman whose kid was whupped."

"Well, maybe," Grace said. "Is her story pretty much like yours?"

"You know, the pastor and his muscle guys been saying I just spoke out to get some publicity," Shaniqua's voice smoldered. "He's out on bail now, and he's bustin' for a fight. Well, today I had to console another mother, and this is awful serious. Her boy got some bad bruises, Grace."

"Can you give me her location and meet me there first thing in the morning?" Grace responded.

"Sure can."

Grace had barely hung up when Steve Jankowski stopped by.

"Heard you got in trouble with the law," she half-grinned. "Everything okay?"

"Tempest in a crock-pot," he said, smiling back. "Cop got a little too aggressive and I got my hackles up. Jenny came out with the station lawyer and we got it worked out. No biggie. But Grace, we've got more problems than that."

"What do you mean?"

He motioned for her to follow him. When they left the newsroom and entered the front lobby, she could see the cause of Steve's concern. A small crowd was gathering outside, on the front lawn. The station's night security guard, Jimmy, locked the door and stood watching them with a scowl. Mrs. Nicholson was wide-eyed at the reception desk, frantically dialing the phone.

Grace pulled Steve back through the doors to the newsroom. "Is that what I think it is?" she asked.

Steve said, "Several Catholic groups got together and decided you were a little rough on the archdiocese. We could see them streaming onto the property just as we arrived from my little set-to in Gwinnett. Since Buck's gone, Jenny high-tailed it to Harvey Silver's office and they're huddling there now, trying to decide how to handle it. If I were you, I'd get out to my car and see if you can slip away before they become belligerent. So far it seems all they've done is massed together and tried to figure out a course of action."

"I can't run away from a story I did," she protested.

"Go. This is management's problem, not yours. All you did was deliver an interview."

"He's right," she heard station manager Harvey Silver's voice approaching from down the hall, with assistant news director Jenny Kim in tow. "Grace, I heard what Steve said. I think you should go home. Jenny and I will go out and talk to them. If they have a spokesman, we'll get a camera out there and give them a chance to say their piece."

She nodded, gathered her purse and briefcase and slipped out of the side door to the parking lot. It was growing dark, and she welcomed the chance to get away unnoticed. At the same time, she felt a little cowardly, running from viewers reacting to her report.

Within fifteen minutes, she was in Morningside. She turned up her street, comforted by the sight of her home. But as Grace entered the kitchen from the garage, she immediately felt a shudder run down her neck. "Oh, no!" she shouted.

Her kitchen window had been smashed. Glass was scattered all over the room. On the floor lay a brick with a note tied to it. Nothing else seemed to be disturbed.

Stop the story or be sorry! the amateurish scrawl spelled out on the note.

Shaken, Grace frantically hurried through the house, turned on lights, searched every room, opened and closed closet doors, even peered behind drapes. There were no intruders; nothing was bothered except the broken window.

Returning to the kitchen, she looked out of the glassless opening and saw her neighbor, Horace Gunter, walking from his fire pit toward his back deck.

"Horace," she screamed. "Horace!" He stopped and peered in her direction. When she waved desperately at him he came running.

"My God, what's going on, Grace?" he puffed, entering the kitchen. "Jesus Mary. What happened?"

Grace was too panicky to answer, so she handed him the brick with the note still tied to it. He read it as she quietly gasped for breath.

"Who could have done this?" he asked. "I've been rummaging around in the back yard. I didn't hear a peep. Let me get you some water."

Finally she found her voice, although it was shaking. "I'll get it," she said. "Somebody upset with my interview about a wayward priest must have done this. It was on the air today. Horace, would you mind looking around outside to be sure nobody is there? I need to figure out what to do about this broken window."

He put a hand on her shoulder. "You sit down, drink your water and try to calm down. I'll look around and then we'll figure out how to clean up this mess." Horace disappeared out the back door and was gone for five minutes. He returned carrying a thin piece of plywood, a hammer and some nails. "I had this wood left over from a project I was doing. Let's board this thing up until you can get someone out to replace the pane."

Grace swept up the broken glass as Gunter covered the damage.

"I can't thank you enough for your help, Horace," she told him. "It's great to have a neighbor like you."

He nodded. "No problem. Do you have to work tomorrow?"

"I have an interview bright and early, and then an arraignment I need to attend."

"Tell you what," Horace said. "I know a good handyman who charges unbelievably cheap prices. He's the guy who was helping me install the plywood in my garage, to seal in some insulation. If you trust me with a key to your house, I can get him over here tomorrow and he'll replace your window."

"Of course I trust you," she said in a preposterous tone. "You came running when I screamed bloody murder, didn't you?" They laughed. "I'd be grateful if you'd do that, Horace."

When he was gone, Grace glanced at the clock on the wall.

She had lost all track of time. She wanted to tune into the final newscast and see if anything ran about the protest crowd, but she was too tired. A quick, hot shower and then bed was all she could see in her immediate future. It would be hard to get to sleep, she was certain. *Who could be doing such things? And why?*

**

The next morning, Buck Lohmeyer was in his office early. His assistant news director was nervously nibbling at her fingernails in the chair across his desk as he berated her.

"Jenny, what in the hell went on here yesterday? I get back and check out the last two days' newscasts and discover you've been letting Grace Gleason run amok with provocative stories. And then I get an earful from my boss about a protest group outside the station."

Jenny Kim was twenty-seven. This was her first job in news management after working the other side of the camera since earning journalism and business degrees. Flustered, her cheeks turned red, contrasting with the hue of her shiny black hair. She fought back against the tears glistening in her dark brown eyes.

"Things got a little out of control, Buck," Jenny protested, her chin quivering. "I was tied up all afternoon yesterday trying to get one of our photographers out of jail. Some overzealous cop cuffed him when he didn't move his equipment away from the scene of a fire."

"We'll deal with that issue later. Right now I want to know what happened with the mob that showed up. And why in God's green earth you let Gleason roam so far away from her assigned beat. Kim, you know she's supposed to be reporting on the positive side of religion, not calling all sorts of rogues into question."

Jenny nodded understanding. "I know."

"So? Where is she? I checked, and she's not in the newsroom."

"Right now she's out on an interview."

Buck squinted his eyes. "Let's have it."

83

"Another mother of those kids who were spanked in church. Buck, this one is even more serious than the first. And we've got the exclusive. I couldn't just let it go."

The news director exploded, rising from his chair. "Damn it, Jenny. We have other reporters. Did you think about that? Any one of them could have taken that interview."

"These people trust Grace," she objected. "I don't think she would have talked to anybody else."

"This crap has been going on too long around here. You'd better get on board with me or get off the frigging boat. Now get out of my sight before I really get mad." The frightened woman jumped from her chair and slipped quickly toward the door. Buck sat back in his chair, his face crimson with anger. He bellowed after her, "If Grace Gleason goes Jenny, you go with her."

CHAPTER ELEVEN: A Spanking Shame

Shaniqua Forrester was there, waiting, just as she said she would be. It was a cool morning, still early, and Shaniqua pulled her coat tighter around her as she watched Steve Jankowski park the station van.

"I was afraid you might not show up," she said to Grace as the newswoman and her photographer approached the shabby old apartment building on the near-west side of the city. "Shoulda known you'd keep your word."

"You remember Steve," Grace said. "He's going to photograph the interview. What's the name of the woman?"

"Miranda Young." Grace's face registered surprise at the middle class sound of the woman's name.

Forrester led them inside where they were met with graffiti on the walls, doors and windows and railings in utter disrepair, and the faint smell of urine everywhere. Grace knew this area was considered "in transition." Its history was one of crime and poverty, but in the past ten years developers had discovered a market existed there. They bought up the decades-old houses a block at a time, renovated or replaced them, and sold them at nice profits to young singles and couples wanting affordable housing within easy driving distance of their work downtown. Yet there were pockets of the old neighborhood, like this one, that hadn't yet been touched.

"This apartment building is one of the last standing from the past," Shaniqua told them as they went inside. "Been tearing them down to put up more expensive places. I hear they been trying to re-zone this whole block, make it commercial. With all the people itching to get into the new subdivisions around here, these businesses can't wait to get their hooks into 'em."

She stopped and knocked softly on a rotted, paint-peeled

door. It opened a crack, and a brown hand went up to slide the chain lock off. Grace was pleasantly surprised to see a nicely furnished room, neat and tidy. She nodded at her interviewee. The woman smiled back politely, then took a long, concerned glance at Steve's camera.

Shaniqua said, "Miss Grace, this is Miranda. We talked last night and she's a little concerned about doing this. I told her we all got to stand up to the man, otherwise nobody going to be able to protect their young ones. If we don't speak out, tell people what's really going on, the bullies are going to have their way."

Miranda Young was soft-spoken and respectful. "I appreciate your coming out here to my house," she told Grace. "But word's getting around that we're spreading information about this, and plenty of people in the congregation are angry about it."

"Have you been threatened?" Steve asked.

"Not in so many words," Miranda responded. "But I had several calls—people asking 'What you up to, Miranda?' or 'You're not going against the reverend on this, are you Miranda?' One man who's close to the pastor came out yesterday evening. I went to Spellman College with his wife, so we've been friends for years. He said, 'Miranda, now you know when you make trouble it has a way of doubling back and finding you.'"

"That sounds like a threat to me," Grace told her. "Listen, Miranda, Steve is going to photograph you in a way that your face isn't revealed. We can even alter your voice if that will help. And your boy will not be photographed except for the markings on his body. Shaniqua said he has visible marks up and down his legs and buttocks and back."

"All right," the woman appeared to relax. "Let's go ahead."

Grace interviewed Miranda Young who then called her son into the room. The six-year-old appeared obediently but stared at the floor self-consciously. As Steve's camera rolled, Miranda pulled the boy's shirt and pants away to reveal large, purple bruises and ugly yellowish flesh from the beatings.

Turning to Jankowski, Grace instructed softly, "Turn it off, Steve. I'll do the cutaways when we get back to the station." He shut off the camera but furrowed his brow, appearing not to understand Grace's departure from her usual routine of completing the story on site.

Grace shook her head as she turned back to the mother. "Miranda, what I just saw is horrifying. This boy needs to see a doctor immediately."

"I don't want that kind of trouble," the woman answered. Grace could hear agony in the mother's voice.

"You can't let these wounds go untreated," Grace argued. "We need to get him to the emergency room right now, Miranda. If it's a matter of cost, don't worry. I'll help you get Medicaid coverage, or maybe the hospital will even write it off."

Miranda stalled. "I don't have transportation, Miss Gleason. I take the bus to work, and Maurice here gets the school bus."

Grace looked at Shaniqua who nodded yes. "Steve, go on back to the station. I'll catch up, and we'll finish cutting the story there. Miranda, go ahead and get your things," Grace insisted. "Shaniqua and I will take you to Southbend."

Southbend Hospital was the butt of constant jokes about being the repository of all the Saturday night shootings, stabbings and rapes in the thirteen-county metro area. It was an exaggeration, Grace knew. But at the same time, she was aware this facility had a top-flight emergency ward, often overrun because of its proximity to downtown and its weekend nightlife.

There would be no Saturday night chaos in mid-morning on a weekday.

Still, the wait was much longer than she hoped. As they waited, she kept in constant touch with Scott Matthews who had already gone to the Federal district court where Aahil Moghaddam was to be arraigned. *Lawyers not here yet,* he texted. *Delay in the previous cas-*

es. Will let you know when they arrive. Grace became edgy and irritable, waiting. Shaniqua promised to deliver Grace at the court building after they finished here, but now it appeared Grace might miss the proceedings.

Finally, Miranda's name was called and they all were permitted through the door to the examining room. "Hello, I'm Doctor Khatri," the woman announced with a heavy Indian accent. "Let me see what's going on with this young man."

She examined the bruises without reaction or emotion, then turned to Miranda. "These are serious injuries, Ms. Young. Several deep contusions, and there is also a small cut. How did he get them?"

Miranda hesitated, glancing at Shaniqua and Grace. "He was playing with other children at the church we attend, and their rough-housing got out of hand," she lied.

Grace was aghast, but she said nothing. This was Miranda's son and Miranda's problem. She had probably interfered more than she should.

"I don't think you're being truthful with me, Ms. Young," the doctor said directly, impassively. "I will treat these wounds and give you a prescription to help him with the pain. But I have to inform you this must be reported to the police."

Miranda's hand went to her mouth, her black eyes glistening.

"I promise you, you will have a visit from the Child Protective Services people," the doctor added.

Miranda cried in the back seat, holding her son's head in her lap as Shaniqua drove her home. "I knew I shouldn't have spoken out," she sobbed. "The pastor and his gang of supporters will surely punish me for it."

Shaniqua turned and shushed her. "We have friends on our side, Miranda. They ain't goin' to do nothin' to hurt you or your son. You just need to cooperate with the protective services folks when they come out. I'll back you up, 'cause they whupped my kid too, remember."

**

When Grace rushed into courtroom B in the federal court building, she quickly scanned the packed room and found Scott sitting in the third row. She squeezed in beside him. The Imam was already standing with his attorney at the rostrum, listening to the judge. Moghaddam looked thin and haggard. His chin whiskers were straggly and unkempt. He wore a prison jumpsuit, and his hands and ankles were shackled. The ankle-length white "thobe" and linen skull cap he was known for were gone, as was the long string of beads around his neck Grace recalled seeing him wear in photos.

"You're aware the grand jury has returned an indictment?" Judge Ronald Thorton asked in a voice so low Grace strained to hear the words.

"He is aware, your honor," Moghaddam's lawyer responded.

The judge ran down the list of charges. "Mister Moghaddam, you are charged with counts of malice murder, felony murder, second-degree murder, aggravated battery, two counts of interfering with the duties of a law officer and fleeing the scene during the commitment of a felony crime. Do you understand the charges against you?"

"Yes I do," Aahil answered in a firm voice.

"How do you plead?"

"Not guilty."

"Because you have already proven to be a flight risk, I am ordering you to continue being held without bail," the judge said. He glanced at the defense attorney and then the lead prosecutor seated at a nearby table. "I will notify you promptly when I have you on the pretrial schedule and ultimately when we have a date for a trial. You have both indicated you have motions and I will consider those and rule on them in a timely manner. Anything else?"

"Not at this time, your honor." Aahil's lawyer said.

The prosecutor shook his head no and stood, gathering up his papers. The judge was already headed back toward chambers.

"Short and sweet," Matthews said to Grace.

"Always is," she answered. "Are you doing a remote from here?"

"No," Scott said. "I'm going live on Christina's noon cast."

"Great. Can I hitch a ride back to the station? Steve Jankowski dumped me."

"Sure," Scott said. "But I might want to let you out a block away." She responded with a curious look. He laughed. "I heard Buck Lohmeyer is on the warpath about your reporting. He jumped all over Jenny Kim this morning, and now she's kind of mad, too. The nerve, letting you out that Catholic priest when you could be interviewing the First Methodist choir leader. Oh yeah, I'm definitely dropping you off down the street. I don't want to take any incoming fire by being in your company."

Grace laughed with him. "I'll duck down when we arrive so he doesn't see me with you." Even though she was joking, the subject matter of their banter—Lohmeyer's obvious and puzzling dislike for her news work—was becoming a true pain.

They returned to the station without incident. Grace hunted down Steve Jankowski in the editing suite where he and an editor worked on the footage of Miranda Young and her injured son.

As they worked, the young, melodious voice of assignment editor Lateisha Robinson floated through the doorway. "There you are, Grace. Christina wants your report on the injured boy for her newscast at noon."

"It'll be ready," Grace said, and Steve nodded concurrence. "What about Buck?"

"I don't know where he is," Lateisha answered.

Grace took a deep breath. "Okay, Steve, let's get those cutaways done and finish the story."

Less than an hour later, Grace had slipped into the outer lobby where a large monitor loomed over a seating arrangement. She was the only person there, except for Mrs. Nicholson at the reception desk. As Grace watched Christina's newscast, including Scott's live report on the Imam arraignment, a wave of apprehension swept through her.

A delivery man came and went. A representative of the Advertising Council approached Mrs. Nicholson and asked for the public service director. The receptionist nodded and took him back to the offices. Other than that, Grace was alone in the space. And she felt profoundly alone—defenseless, anticipating a blitz from her boss as soon as Christina said, "Here's Grace Gleason."

Just then, much too soon for Grace's liking, Christina said into the camera, *"Here's Grace Gleason to tell you that story."*

Grace watched her image come on. *"I am here in the home of a member of the congregation of the Church of Faith. She is also the mother of a six-year-old boy. Those two parts of her life combine to tell a devastating story of how a religious leader can cross the line to control the lives of his people."*

On the video, Grace turned toward Miranda Young who was shot from behind by Jankowski so her face was not revealed. Steve had recorded a close-up of Grace asking the questions after she returned to the station, and she marveled at how flawlessly he and the editor inserted them into the interview.

"You became concerned about your pastor when he and some of his flock began spanking the children of parishioners, is that right?" She asked.

"Yes. The spankings got increasingly worse, carried out with rulers and sticks," the mother said. Grace was also happy Steve and the technician had done such a good job of disguising Miranda's voice. *"Last week it all came to a head with me when they held my boy by his arms, pulled down his pants and thrashed him over and over for what they thought was bad behavior. You know, Miss Gleason, we Christians are familiar with the verse that says, 'Suffer little children to come unto me, and forbid them not: for of such is the kingdom of God.' But I don't think Jesus had this kind of beating in mind."*

"Let's see what we're talking about, can we?" Grace said.

The next pictures were of the youngster's backside. *"These are serious wounds,"* Grace was heard off-camera as Steve photographed the boy from behind. *"As a mother myself, I can't imagine letting anyone get away with this."*

"The reverend has many supporters for this kind of treatment," the mother answered. *"They help him with it, because I think they truly believe this kind of punishment sets our children on the straight and narrow."*

"Yet it is the children who are in pain," Grace said into the camera. *"Reverend Dontell Freeman is out of jail now, so he'll be preaching—and presumably spanking— again as soon as next Sunday. Meantime, some mothers, like this one, not only wonder what will happen to them as members of his congregation, but they also must be concerned about the long-term effects on their children. Back to you, Christina."*

Leaning back, Grace felt the satisfaction of a job well done. She had first gone into journalism with a desire to hunt down the truth—to expose wrongdoing wherever she found it. Now that she was a religion reporter, it was increasingly obvious not all the bad guys were drug dealers or murderers or crooked cops. It made her feel good, like the Grace Gleason of old, to put this story out there for her viewers to evaluate.

But her elation was short-lived. The doors from the newsroom to the lobby opened and Buck Lohmeyer stuck his head out. "Come see me in an hour," he said quietly, then turned and left.

She knew. This was to be her day of reckoning.

CHAPTER TWELVE: Showdown

He appeared calm. Whereas Grace expected Buck Lohmeyer to be snorting fire and speaking in tongues, there was none of that. She sat in one chair across the desk from him, and assistant news director Jenny Kim sat in the other. Lateisha Robinson, the assignment editor, was shrinking behind them against the wall, her eyes wide with dread.

Lohmeyer smiled and looked directly at Grace. "I'm not going to yell at you," he said. "I've done that already, and it got us nowhere. You have defied my orders not to cover these controversial news stories when your role is supposed to be exactly the opposite. I have appealed directly to you about it, and you have ignored my wishes. Frankly, I don't quite know what to do about it. I could fire you, but that would only mean a major battle with my boss. That's how highly you're thought of around here. No, Grace, there must be some other way we can solve this problem."

"What are you afraid of?" Grace asked softly.

"What do you mean?"

"We have the number one news station in the city," she explained. "We got it not by being goody two-shoes, but by doing the honest, hard-nosed work of good investigative journalism. Why are you so afraid to keep going down a road that brought us so much success?"

"I'm not afraid of anything," his voice began to crack a bit with aggravation. "We're going to continue doing excellent journalism around here, Grace. We have very good reporters assigned to the stories you're usurping. The issue is, who's the boss?"

"So that's it," she reacted. "You're not angry because I'm doing stories you don't want me on. You're angry because your—I don't know, your bossdom—is being threatened."

She went too far. Lohmeyer's ire built quickly, like a flame in a tinderbox.

"You're damned right I'm the boss, and you are defying my orders," he thundered. "Scott Matthews is covering the Dontell Freeman spanking story. You jumped him on it today." He glanced at Jenny and then Lateisha. "You two aren't innocent in all of this."

"It's a religious issue, even more than a criminal case," Grace protested. "Besides, Scott was over at district court for the arraignment of the Imam. He was there all morning waiting while I interviewed the mother of the spanking victim."

"How do you know?" Buck's eyes shot lasers.

"We were in touch. And I joined him in court after the interview."

"You went to Moghaddam's court appearance? That's totally a waste of resources." He sat silently for a moment, gathering himself, obviously trying to fight off the anger. "Now Grace," he said more calmly, "that interview with the mother is the final story you're doing on Dontell Freeman and his bully-pulpit church. And that's final."

"I'm not so sure that's a good idea," Grace said, fully aware she was now swimming out to sea, far away from the safety of shore. "Tell him, Jenny."

The news director turned toward his assistant, his bushy eyebrows raised in curiosity. Jenny pressed against the back of her chair, sitting straight up, her chin slightly quavering.

"Well?" he asked.

"The abusive pastor story is getting picked up by the networks," Kim answered. She looked quickly back at Grace, seeking support.

"I've been getting calls the past hour from network reporters," Grace chimed in, "wanting to know what I know, asking for permission to use my videos and interviews."

Buck's body seemed to go limp. He stared at his desktop and had no response.

"Mr. Lohmeyer, I'm not at war with you," Grace tried to appeal. "I truly see my role differently than you do, and I know Harvey Silver wants me to have some room to operate. I'm willing to do the stories you want me to do. In fact, I have coverage scheduled for later this week of an interfaith group building a Homes for Glory house. That's the kind of positive trend among religious circles Mr. Silver said he wants me to cover, and I plan to do it. It will be good for us with the community, and believe it or not I actually feel good when I report on those activities. So I don't plan to stop. But I also don't want to let up on calling transgressions to the public's attention if religious leaders are at the middle of them. We have an obligation to do it. I have an obligation as a journalist."

She waited a tick and took a breath.

"In fact, I came to Atlanta and this station because your predecessor pitched me on the idea of doing a series of broadcasts covering the crime and corruptions in the city's underbelly. We uncovered a lot of unsavory activity going on and played a role in bringing some bad guys to justice. I don't see why religious leadership shouldn't be held accountable in the same way, just because they wear a collar or robe or a yarmulke. Mr. Lohmeyer, I can't think of a more meaningful way to address some of these religious issues."

He looked up at her, a disconsolate look in his eyes saying he was tired of the argument. "So what do you propose?"

"I want to do a series on the other side of religion, the face of the church or mosque or synagogue nobody really wants to see—but must see if our communities don't want their places of worship corrupted. And if they don't want their children exploited. I am proposing a week-long series using the stories I've been working on as ground zero."

Buck shook his head slowly—Grace couldn't tell if it was a refusal or resignation. Finally he said, "We'll see. I'll discuss it with Silver."

"I'd like to be in the room," she smiled as sweetly as she knew how.

"Of course you would," he said, the annoyance in his voice telling her the news director wanted this discussion to go away. "You ladies get to work. I have things to do." He dismissed them with the wave of his hand. As they left Lohmeyer's office and walked the hallway toward their workstations, Jenny Kim and Lateisha Robinson wound up on either side of Grace. She could feel each of them squeeze her hand as they walked. She turned to see; they were beaming at her.

CHAPTER THIRTEEN: Jeff, Again

"Hi Mom." Megan sounded ebullient over the phone.

A kind of peculiar shock wave ran through Grace—an unexpected, disturbing mixture of surprise and guilt. All her adult life she had labored to achieve a balance between her need for a career and the responsibilities of motherhood. If anything, since her divorce her protective instincts had pushed her toward a higher sense of obligation to single parenting than to news reporting.

This morning, at the sound of Megan's voice, she immediately emerged from her obsession with the chaotic news stories she was chasing and rose toward reality, like a deep-sea diver emerging toward the water's surface, fighting against the bends.

It had been a week since she had seen or even talked to her daughter. The embarrassment of this realization was practically overwhelming.

"Hi Megan," she managed, swallowing hard. "Sorry I haven't been in touch. Work has simply had me buried."

"No problem, Mom. I've been crashing on my work here, anyway. I just called to let you know Dad is coming through this weekend. He's going to some conference in Florida and has a layover here. He wants me to meet him at the airport for lunch."

More stabs in the heart and gut. The idea of Jeff coming through Atlanta again dredged up an odd sense of trepidation, an inconvenience she didn't want to deal with. Grace's feelings for him had long since ended. Her only interactions with him the past couple of years were to discuss matters about their daughter. But now, the thought of him lunching with Megan introduced an inexplicable sense of distress. Was it jealousy? A sense of space being invaded? She wasn't sure. If so, Grace realized she had no right to feel either. This was the other half of the makers of her precious daughter.

Yet she didn't like whatever this emotion was that flowed through her. It was foreign to her, and distasteful. It made her feel somehow greedy. She knew she didn't want to see Jeff and assumed the feeling would be mutual. This would be his time alone with Megan. She didn't understand why it hurt so much.

"Mom, I'm taking Joe with me. I want Dad to meet him."

Now the stars swam angrily into the skies of Grace's universe. Lightning flashed. Thunder rolled. She felt her forehead burn. Grace had not even met the young man, and now Jeff would shake his hand, sit across the table looking him directly in his Columbian eyes, making small talk about his home, his parents, his life plans. His future with her daughter.

"Megan," she stammered, "I don't think that's a good idea..."

Megan's musical laugh interrupted her. "Don't worry, Mom. He's not going to ask for my hand in marriage or anything. I just want Dad to meet him before we graduate, and this might be the only opportunity. I know you haven't met Joe yet, but we'll all get together soon."

The floodwaters in Grace's mind ebbed a bit as her daughter's explanation began to sink in and make sense.

"Okay," she responded. "But I want to see you. I've been strung out on these stories, but if you can spare some time today I'll meet you for lunch."

"That works for me," Megan said. "My last class gets out at one, and then I have to dive into a project later this afternoon and work through the night."

"You work too hard. I worry about your health."

"That's like the grass calling the frog green," Megan said.

They met at the Magic Plate Diner. It was rainy, and Grace was glad she had brought her purse-sized umbrella. She was sitting, waiting, when Megan swept into the place with the hood of her raincoat up. She smiled widely when she spotted her mother.

Megan was in a cheerful mood, and Grace had managed to put her brooding about Jeff's impending return behind her. They talked and laughed about small things. Their good-natured banter, and the cheeseburgers and fries, made it seem like old times when they would sit and talk into the wee hours.

This time, in less than an hour, Megan had to say goodbye. "Thanks, Mom," she said, grasping Grace's hand across the table.

"You're welcome. Go ahead and get back—I'll stay and take care of this."

"No, I don't mean thanks for lunch. Thanks for understanding about Dad meeting Joe, before you've had a chance to. And thanks for not lecturing me about it."

Grace nodded. "I gave you a hard time the last time we ate here. And I'm sorry. After that, I was determined to let you know I trust you. You're a grown woman, and sometimes your grumpy old mother forgets that."

Megan squeezed her hand again and then whisked away from the booth and out the door, pulling her hood up against the weather.

Grace sat for a brief time, finishing her tea and paying the check. Then she looked at her watch. Nearly two. She would have just enough time to drive out to meet Steve Jankowski and do the interview she finally managed to set up with one of the girls the preacher married off in Alabama.

She wanted to interview this girl at the station, where she could control the situation. She recalled with some anxiety her previous attempt at interviewing one of the newlyweds. An angry husband nixed that idea. But Shaniqua Forrester talked to this one and gave Grace the go-ahead earlier in the day. "The kid is okay with it," she told Grace over the phone. "Her name is Pearl. But Grace, the husband won't bring her down there. Says you have to come out to the house."

"Is her husband going to be a problem?"

"Don't think so. He wants you to interview him, too. Name of Eddie. I talked to him myself, personal. Said he'd never been on TV and got kinda excited about it."

By the time Grace was driving to her destination, the rain had stopped. The little duplex sat on a corner, in South Atlanta, just off Interstate 85. Steve's station van was sitting there waiting when she arrived.

"I already talked to the guy," Steve told her as he stepped down from the vehicle to meet her. "Says it's cool."

"I just hope he's telling us the truth," Grace said warily.

"They want to do it inside. Let's go."

Eddie answered the door. He was forty, portly, bearded, Hispanic. "Hey Pearl, they're here," he shouted toward a back room with little Latino accent, to Grace's surprise. She stepped in and glanced around at the littered room, frowning at leftover meals sitting on the coffee table, cigarette butts smashed into ash trays, empty soda cans strewn around the place.

When Pearl entered, Grace was astounded at how young she looked. Her diminutive size and shy expression added to the impression. Her hair was in corn rows, and a garish shade of red lipstick created an almost comic contrast with her mahogany face.

"Hello, Pearl. How old are you?" Grace asked.

"Fifteen," a baby-doll voice answered.

Grace looked around the room for the least cluttered space. "Well, Mr. Jankowski here is going to set up some lights and his camera. You two stand over here, and as soon as he's set up I'll interview you both, okay?"

Pearl glanced up at Eddie.

"Sounds good," he said, his black eyes glistening with excitement.

Steve turned the lights and held a sheet of white paper in front of Grace as a test. He turned on the camera and nodded.

"You two were married in Alabama, is that right?" Grace led off.

"That's right," Eddie said. "Reverend Dontell Freeman set it up. Helped us get all the paperwork done and went over there with us, himself, as a witness."

"Pearl was fourteen at the time?"

"Right," Eddie answered. "I done a little time, I guess you know. The reverend, he helped me get straightened out after my release, found me this apartment, got me a job bagging groceries down the street."

"So Pearl," she turned to the young girl, "how did you first meet Eddie, your husband?"

Eddie jumped in, to Grace's annoyance. "Pearl goes to the man's church," he said. "She ain't had much home life, and he brought her over to meet me, help us both get our lives together, you know? Don't understand why they put him in jail. He's done nothing but help people like us."

"Now I want to ask Pearl," she said, moving her microphone as far away as she could from Eddie. "Pearl, did you want to marry Eddie, or did Reverend Freeman tell you to?"

The girl looked up at her husband, a puppy seeking permission. "I wanted to, I guess," she answered in a small, hesitant voice. "The reverend, he knows what's good for people. He said me and Eddie would be a good match. You know, I can cook some, and clean and stuff. Eddie, he's got hisself a job, so we doin' okay."

"You've been married for six months. How do you feel now about being a wife?"

"Okay I guess. We fight sometimes." Again, Pearl looked at Eddie and recoiled slightly from his stern expression. "Guess all married couples fight sometimes," she added quickly.

"What do you two fight about?"

"Stuff. Money, mostly," Pearl answered. "I gotta cook meals on however much he gives me. Gets mad when I can't make enough food on it."

"He gets mad? Pearl, does Eddie treat you okay?"

"I treat her good. Don't I, Pearl honey?" Eddie broke in. Grace could see his fist rolling into a little ball.

Pearl paused, staring at Eddie, and then nodded. "He treat me okay," she said to Grace, "'cept sometime he drinks too much. Got hisself a temper and when he gets mad, I just try to keep away, you know. All married people fight, I s'pose."

"So Reverend Dontell Freeman didn't force you to marry Eddie, Pearl? You're happy in this marriage?"

"I love Eddie," she said, her face lighting up when she saw Eddie smiling down at her. "Reverend Freeman, he doing the right thing by helping us get our husbands, giving us a good home life. And helping them out when they get paroled, you know? I ain't got no complaint about the reverend."

Outside, as she watched Steve load his equipment into the truck, Grace exclaimed, "My Lord, did you hear that? That poor little girl is praising that preacher for forcing her onto a man who's controlling, if not borderline abusive. How does he get away with it?"

"Don't know," Jankowski said, shrugging his broad shoulders. "You want to follow me back to the station?"

She shook her head no. "I'm going on home. I have an appointment with a clinical psychologist from Emory University. He's going to help me understand about the Stockholm Syndrome."

"I've heard of it," Steve acknowledged. "The Patty Hearst thing."

"Sort of like that," she said.

"What? You think it figures into this story somehow?"

"I'm not sure. Maybe I'll find out after I talk to the shrink."

She turned toward her car, parked behind the van, when something caught her eye and stopped her cold. Rounding the corner and creeping slowly toward them was a car that looked eerily familiar. "Steve, don't move," she exclaimed with urgency in her voice.

"What?" he followed her eyes to see a black muscle car inching past them. Its heavily tinted windows concealed whoever was inside. "What is it, Grace?"

"It's that same car, I'm sure," she was trying to catch her breath. "The one I told you tailgated me that night after we ran my interview with Khalila Noorani."

"Oh yeah, the woman who served as adviser to the Imam," he recalled. "You sure it's the same car? They made quite a few black Trans Ams back in the day."

Grace watched in horror as the car slowly passed, its muffler rumbling, and crept around the next corner out of sight. "I was parked right next to it that night before they followed me," she told him. "I was scared to death, but that didn't shut down my reporter's training to remember details. That car that just passed us had some gold pin-striping down the side and along the back, did you see it? So did the car that followed me that night. Steve, it has to be the same one."

"Well, he's gone now," Steve said. "I'll follow you home if you want."

She shook her head. "It's still light. I'll be all right. If he's trying to get me off the Imam story, it won't work. But how did he know I'd be here?" Her eyes opened wide, as if she had just discovered a secret. "He must have been watching me at the diner and followed me here."

"Damn, Grace. Check out your surroundings wherever you go from now on. Hard telling if these people are playing around, or if they're the real deal," Jankowski warned. "I'd like to have Grace Gleason around to keep working with."

CHAPTER FOURTEEN: Stockholm Syndrome

Grace was surprised at how young he looked. She expected a professor of psychology at a major university, especially a nationally recognized expert in a given subject, to be a doddering old silver-haired man. As she walked into the Fusion Grill in Buckhead and scanned the bar area, there was nobody matching that description. No wrinkled, withered gentleman in a tattered sweater with leather elbow patches.

She saw two small groups of millennials crowding the front of the bar, laughing it up after a day at the office. One trio of middle-aged women, smartly dressed, sipped martinis while they visited. And on the very far end of the bar, a lone, pleasant-looking, middle-aged gentleman stood and nodded her direction as she approached.

"Hi Grace," he said, extending his hand. "I'm Dillon McAfee. I knew I'd recognize you right away since I've seen some of your television news reports."

"I thought you'd be—I don't know—a lot more mature, shall we say? You've written so many books and articles and won so many awards. I thought..." she hesitated, searching for words.

"...I'd have a foot in the grave, dragging around a ball and chain or carrying one of those scythes they depict father time with?" he chuckled.

"Something like that." She nodded at his glass. "Is that red wine?"

"Merlot. Would you like a glass?" She nodded, and he ordered it.

"Dr. McAfee—"

"Please," he interjected, "Dillon."

"Okay, Dillon. The truth is I was also surprised by your name. Irish, right? I thought all psychiatrists and psychologists were Jewish.

We Irish Catholics are supposed to be on the couch getting analyzed, not getting rich listening to other people's troubles."

McAfee roared with laughter. "Now, isn't that a little preju-diced?"

"Not really. Maybe slightly biased by my upbringing, though. My alcoholic mother and domineering father would have been perfect patients for one of your psychiatry colleagues. But I want to hear more about you, doctor. You have accomplished so much in so little time."

"Not much to tell. I was on a fast track when I got my PhD at the University of North Carolina."

The waiter brought her wine, and she nodded thanks. "A tar heel, huh?"

"It's a well-kept secret that one of the best grad schools for clinical psych in the U.S. is right up the road in Chapel Hill," he con-firmed. "I wrote my dissertation on the Stockholm Syndrome and to my surprise, it was published in nearly every country in the civilized world. That propelled me onto the lecture circuit and into a dizzying schedule of magazine articles, interviews, expert panels, you name it." He took a sip of his wine. "Problem was, I missed the classroom. Emory called one day with a great offer. I answered without hesitat-ing. I have no regrets about getting back to the teaching I love."

"You've been in Atlanta for how long?"

"I'm in my tenth year here," he said. There was a brief silence between them. "This is the point," he said, "where I would normally return the favor—you know, probe you about your background. But the thing is, I already know all about you."

"Really?"

"When you called, I took the liberty of doing a little research. You're all over the internet, of course. And the station's website and Facebook page go to great lengths to extol your virtues, brag about your talents and skills, and chronicle your long list of awards."

"Well, that probably took about five minutes of reading," she laughed in false modesty. "So you turned the tables on the reporter.

The truth is, I would normally have researched you much the same way. Except that my reporting schedule has had me running crazy these past two weeks."

"Working too hard?"

She grinned and took a drink. "Don't diagnose me, doctor. I've worked my tail off all my life. That's because I love my job. I also get knee-deep into a story that concerns me, unlike some of these young puppies coming into the business these days who bob on the surface like a cork on the ocean."

He laid some money on the bar. "Let's adjourn to the dining room and have a bite, shall we? I took the liberty of reserving a table."

Grace glanced at her glass, nearly empty. She didn't realize she had been drinking so fast.

"Leave it," he said. "I'll order us a bottle when we get in there."

Grace nodded agreement but was already beginning to feel the effects of the wine she had drunk. She would switch to tea.

She followed him into the main restaurant and watched as he spoke to the hostess. Dr. McAfee was not tall, but he carried himself like a bigger man. He likewise wasn't stocky, but his mid-sized frame appeared to be rock-solid, as if he worked out regularly.

What attracted her most to him, though, were his deep, intelligent blue eyes and the square cut of his firm jaw. He seemed to have a gentle, courteous, almost elegant nature about him, but his physical appearance made him seem to her every bit a man in control. She had not had a relationship in a long time, and she had no intention of starting one. But if she were so inclined, she thought, this might be the kind of man she could fall for.

Over small plates of crab cakes and lobster rolls, Grace told McAfee about her interviews with the parents of the spanked children and the girls coerced into marrying parolees.

"What I don't understand," she told him, "is that the followers of this preacher appear to support him even when it's to their detriment—or worse, to their childrens'. They seem to put all their power into his hands. So naturally, I'm curious about what compels them to do that. And how he can command such respect even though the activity itself might not be respect-worthy. Dillon, is that the Stockholm Syndrome at work, or something else?"

Dillon had finished a glass of wine from the bottle and poured another. He gestured toward her with the bottle, but she shook her head no. She had permitted him to pour a half-glass when it was first delivered, and only took a few sips before asking for iced tea.

He pushed his plate away and answered, "Maybe, maybe not. Do you understand what it is?"

She said, "I've read a little. But give me the abbreviated version, you know, as if I were cramming for one of your mid-terms."

He laughed. "I'll try. Here goes. It first got widespread notice in hostage situations. Received its name when hostages in a Stockholm, Sweden, bank robbery developed a strong bond with the captors who abused them. They refused to testify against the robbers after being released. A woman hostage even married one of the criminals.

"In that same timeframe, Patty Hearst changed her name and denounced her family while she was held hostage by the Symbionese Liberation Army. She participated in their bank robberies and expressed support for her captors publicly. She later tried unsuccessfully to use the syndrome as part of her defense. She was sentenced to prison, but it was later commuted.

"Boxcar loads of research have been done on the subject. The Stockholm label was broadened over time to collective reactions to traumatic situations, not just individual cases such as Hearst's. The truth is, emotional bonding with one's captor or abuser was not new when the Stockholm story came out. Many studies of various kinds of abusive situations had already uncovered countless situations in which this bonding is a strategy for survival of abuse or coercion."

Grace asked, "So are the members of this pastor's congregation bonding emotionally with him when they support him and refuse to cooperate with police? Or with other church members who oppose him? Same thing with the girls he marries off to those ex-cons?"

McAfee smiled. "It's possible, even likely. Without some psychological study of the people involved, it would be speculation. But the elements are there. Support for his rationale and behavior. Continuing to stay engaged in his church despite his bullying behavior. Negative reactions by many of them toward the authorities who arrested him. In the case of the girls, their refusal to resist being coerced into marriage or being abused by their husbands. Those sound to me to be classic descriptions of the syndrome."

"Dr. McAfee—Dillon—would you let me interview you for my stories on this?"

"Of course," he responded.

"Tomorrow?"

"I have classes in the morning. Could we do it in the afternoon? I can come by the station."

She nodded agreement. "I have another interview in the morning, anyway," she told him. "A group of people building a Homes for Glory house."

"I'm familiar with that organization," he told her. "It's a truly great cause. So you don't just do what they call hard news?"

"Well, that's a long story," she answered. "I'm having a battle with our news director about my role on the staff. It seems he only wants me to do what we call puff pieces—you know, charity events and church choir concerts. I have a history of hard-nosed crime reporting, and we disagree about my continuing role on such reports. I cover enough feel-nice stories to keep him off my back."

"Ah. You're cooperating with your captor, are you?"

She laughed, astounded. "I guess."

"Grace Gleason," he announced wryly, "It's very possible you're exhibiting Stockholm Syndrome behavior. I think you might need a good psychologist who can help you deal with that."

The professor walked her out to her car, they said their goodbyes and she drove off as he watched. *Amazing, I had never thought of that,* she thought as she drove. *Stockholm Syndrome behavior, indeed. I need a good psychologist, do I?*

Well, I could do worse than Dr. Dillon McAfee!

CHAPTER FIFTEEN: Homes for Glory

The sun was dazzling, and Grace was ecstatic. She and photographer Cassandra Barrett were in Smallville, a northeast suburb, to cover the dedication of the Homes for Glory house. Weather forecasts were predicting a forty percent chance of rain, but not until late afternoon. Grace had covered plenty of stories in wind and rain and icy blasts. So when she and Cassandra stepped from the van and the warmth of the sun hit her face, it lifted her spirits.

An unusual crowd was gathering, unique because it was comprised of members of many faiths. Grace noted an impressive assortment of yarmulkes, hijabs, ministers' collars, broad black hats of Hasidic Jews and several thobes—long, robe-like garments—worn by Muslims. Those symbols of religious dress were sprinkled among a gathering crowd of family members, politicians and workers. Their attire ran a gamut from suits and ties, to blue jeans and baseball caps, to shorts and tee shirts.

"This is the most remarkable assemblage of people banded together for a single cause you could witness," Grace spoke into the camera. She swept an arm toward the front of the house where the crowd congregated, and Barrett followed the gesture with her camera to capture the scene. "At a time when faith-based conflicts and political tensions exist all over the world, these people—Christians, Muslims and Jews—are working together for the good of a cause. They have completed the first of five planned houses, and today they are here to dedicate it."

Grace motioned a woman to join her. "With me is Valerie Cohen, the executive director of Homes for Glory. Ms. Cohen, how did this interfaith build come about?"

Valerie was slender and pretty, about thirty, with long, auburn, wavy hair. "Grace, our wonderful participating organizations and sponsors built dozens of houses for people in need of a helping hand over the past decade," she said. "But it seemed to me each one had only the imprimatur of a single organization or religious group. I thought, 'Wouldn't it be especially meaningful if the three Abrahamic faiths would work together as one, pounding nails side by side?' Our board discussed it with several representatives of Jewish, Christian and Muslim organizations, and they eagerly accepted the idea. So here we are."

"And where we are," Grace reported, "is standing next to the three-bedroom, two-bath house where Ida Ramirez and her three children will live, starting today. They will accept the keys from one of the Gwinnett county commissioners in about five minutes. Ms. Ramirez, who helped in the construction of the house, will pay it off over thirty years from her salary as a receptionist, at zero profit and zero percent financing."

She turned again toward Valerie. "You expect to build more of these interfaith homes?"

"We hope to. All of the parties say it's a good idea—to spread the concept that all faiths believe fundamentally in helping their fellow human beings. Their participation sends a powerful message."

"In a few minutes, we'll watch as leaders of these three faiths conduct a dedication of the house," Grace concluded. "After Mrs. Ramirez receives the keys, I'll have a chance to visit with her and see this event from the viewpoint of a very happy family."

After Grace wrapped up the story, she said her thanks and goodbyes to several people while Cassandra loaded her equipment into the van. Climbing into the vehicle, as Cassandra waited behind the wheel, Grace was surprised to see tears running down the photographer's cheeks.

"What's wrong?" Grace asked.

"Nothing," Barrett wiped at her face with the back of her hand. "It was a moving experience being there, that's all. There's so much hate going on all over the world, and in this one small spot, in a little Georgia suburb, these people are working together and making a difference."

Grace smiled to herself as they drove. Cassandra's words had a strong, positive effect on her. She wondered how many of her viewers would feel the same way. Her resentment at having to cover these stories while Bannister Walker and Scott Matthews chased hardened criminals and corrupt politicians, embarrassed her a little. She decided she would approach her coverage of the good side of religion with greater appreciation and respect.

Back at the station, Grace sorted through notes on her computer. She decided she should try to do more to flush out information on the Imam accused of murder, Aahil Moghaddam. Given her increased emphasis on how religious leaders were impacting the lives and belief systems of young people, she needed to know what was going on with the youth of Moghaddam's masjid. Years ago, before his conversion, Slay T. Jefferson preached a brand of hatred toward authorities. Somehow she needed to find out if the man who converted and became an Imam brought his revolutionary attitudes to his mosque, most especially to the young people attracted to him.

The question was how to approach it. Though Scott Matthews was young and less experienced, Grace often used him as a sounding board. He was smart and sometimes thought of an angle she hadn't considered. It had been a while since she visited with Scott. Grace missed talking to him.

She found him in his cubicle, huddled over his computer.

"Working on anything exciting, Scott?" Grace asked.

Startled, his concentration broke. "I am," he answered. "The abusive pastor and the parents who were arrested with him are out of jail and feisty as ever. Reverend Freeman is apparently back in the pulpit, vowing he won't stop the spankings."

"Are you setting up anything with him?"

Scott looked up at her, a quizzical expression on his face. "You mean an interview?"

"Of course."

"Grace, are you joking?"

"No, why? What do you mean?"

"Don't you know? He's telling everyone he's only going to talk to one reporter. You."

Grace felt her mouth drop open. "Where did you hear that?" she asked, dumbfounded.

"I called the guy up last night. He told me point blank. 'Gleason's the only interview I'll do.' I couldn't believe it—you've been on that guy like a bug on a windshield. It blew me away that he would even want to talk to you, much less do an exclusive."

"Why didn't you tell me?" Her voice rose in frustration. "Why am I the last to know?"

Scott's face grew crimson. "Grace, it was discussed in the morning meeting. You were out on that house dedication. I swear, I assumed Lohmeyer, or Lateisha, or someone, would have told you."

She stormed from the newsroom, double-timing to the news director's office. He wasn't there. She tried the assistant news director, Jenny Kim's workstation with no luck there, either. Lateisha Robinson was at her desk but embroiled in an animated conversation on the phone.

Upset, Grace decided to cool her jets and get back to work. After all, she thought, this wasn't the first time, nor would it be the last, that things around the newsroom fell through the crack. She only hoped the lack of communication wasn't intentional.

She found Steve Jankowski in the editing suite. "Lunch?" she asked.

"Sure, Grace. We can decide how you want to do the interview."

"That's right," she exclaimed, "the Emory professor, Dillon McAfee." She was embarrassed she had forgotten him in her pique over the Dontell Freeman snafu.

Grace rarely lunched with her co-workers. She preferred to use her time doing some research on her computer or catching up on her reading. But Steve was the exception. Every two weeks or so, they stole away and hunkered down with takeout in tiny Fairmont Park. Only ten minutes from the station, it was tucked back into a vintage neighborhood, not far from Midtown. Hidden from the busy traffic routes, not many people seemed to know about it. A three-court tennis facility that had seen its better days bordered one corner of the park. Usually, several players were there, and Grace and Steve sometimes sat and watched the back-and-forth of the game while they ate.

More often, though, they would walk down one of the winding trails, back through the trees and bushes to Marlo Creek. They would sit on one of the wooden benches overlooking the stream, munching on burgers and fries, watching the slow rivulet of spring water meander its way through gravel and mud and sand along the backyards of adjoining fifty-year-old houses.

And they would talk. Like today.

"There's no better time in Atlanta than spring," Grace inhaled the sweet air and gazed beyond the treetops at a blue-blue sky.

"Maybe. But I'm a summer guy," Steve said.

"It gets so hot."

"Never too hot for me," the photographer said. "Plenty of places to strip down and get in the water, let the sun beat down on you. Get a nice tan."

"And skin cancer," she poked his arm. "I hope you lather up when you do that."

"Don't be so bossy," he teased and she returned his smile warmly.

"I've always wondered what it would be like to be on the other side of the camera," he said.

"It's not so hard," she answered. "Just takes experience."

"I couldn't do it. I watch you in hairy situations—you know, like the drug bust we covered that day last year—and a lot of reporters would've freaked out. You stay so cool. How do you do that?"

"Festina Lente," she answered.

"What is that?"

Grace grinned. "It means make haste slowly. I learned about it from my news director when I worked at a station in Dallas. We used to watch video of my news reports so I could improve my on-air delivery. We were reviewing my coverage of a murder, and he could see I was in a kind of frenzied fury on camera. That's when he said it. 'Festina Lente. Proceed without wasting time, but take a moment to act prudently.' He said if I internalized it, if I worked at it every time the news came at me headlong and breakneck, it would become my best friend. He was right. I'm not always so calm underneath, Steve, but it helps me calm things down—to make haste slowly."

"Oh, then it's sort of like sports," Jankwoski said. "They say players don't become good until they learn to slow down the action in their mind. It helps them see everything that's going on."

"Same thing, I guess," Grace said.

Steve smiled. "So, the interview. Think you're onto something with this Stockholm Syndrome?"

"He thinks there could be something to it. We'll see what he says for public consumption."

"You two had dinner, right?" he teased. "Think you're onto something with the ol' prof?"

She poked his arm again. "You know me, Steve. I'm all business. I have enough complications in my life, trying to get a daughter through college, without going down that road."

"I'm just saying maybe you need to relax and enjoy life, let a little bit of the outside world in."

They started back toward Grace's car. "Yes? You know so much about the outside world, do you? Jankowski, you got married to your high school sweetheart. How many kids do you have now?"

"Five," Steve laughed heartily. "Yeah, well, when you've got a good thing going, you don't want to mess it up, know what I mean?"

She nodded. "I agree wholeheartedly, my friend."

Driving back, Jankowski said, "We got so much into food and banter, we didn't even discuss the interview with the professor."

"No worries," she responded. "Steve, we've done so many stories together I have no doubt everything will fall right into place."

Dillon McAfee was already there when they returned. Mrs. Nicholson ushered him from the lobby to the newsroom and deposited him in the side chair at Grace's workstation to wait.

"I finished my last class early," he explained to Grace. "So I thought I'd come on out. I hope you don't mind."

"Sorry I wasn't here," she said after introducing him to Jankowski. "You should have called."

"You know, I would have, but I didn't have your cell phone number. We need to fix that."

Grace pretended not to see the look on his face that said there was more to the comment than a business request.

She cast a sidelong glance in Jankowski's direction and winced at his droll smile. "Let's get started," she said. "Steve, we'll set up back in that corner of the newsroom, okay?"

Steve grinned again but went to work.

The interview went smoothly, mostly following the line of questioning she had asked the previous evening over dinner. But an idea struck her as she neared the end of the questioning. "Dr. McAfee," she asked, "you said it would take a professional evaluation to help determine if the Stockholm Syndrome is at work with those affected by activities at the Church of Faith. What is the possibility of that happening? Might the authorities, or the court, who are trying to sort out the prosecutable crimes, order such a review?"

McAfee appeared surprised by the question, tipping his head back and narrowing his eyes. "I'm not a prosecutor or judge, Grace. Just a college professor. You'll need to ask the lawyers that question."

After the interview, she walked him out to the parking lot. A light mist was beginning to fall, but it felt refreshing as it cooled on her face. "I didn't mean to put you on the spot," she said.

"It took me by surprise, I'll admit," he answered. "But Grace, it's fine. You did what I imagine any good reporter would do by asking it. After all, it's an unusual case."

"It is," she agreed. "Dr. McAfee—"

"Dillon," he interjected.

"Dillon. Thank you for lending your expertise to this story."

"It was my pleasure. I hope you won't take this the wrong way. We have a professional relationship now, sort of. But I'd like to see you again."

Grace hesitated. "You mean socially?"

"I do."

She paused again, searching for a response. "Well, Dr. McAfee, that's an extraordinary request. Let me give it some thought, okay? I have so much on my plate right now."

"That's the very reason I'm prescribing some down time," he laughed. "You get so wrapped up in your work, I wonder if you ever have fun at all."

"My work is fun," she said. "And being a single mom was, too, until my daughter Megan got into college and became so independent."

He reached out and rested his hand lightly on her arm. "Let's leave it an open question, shall we? You have my number. If you're ever in the mood to relax, have some lunch or dinner, or just take in a movie—you do know what a movie is, don't you?"

"Yes, professor, I know what a movie is," Grace fired back in mock agitation.

"Well, pick up the phone and call. Grace, I'd like to spend some time with you, without a story hovering over us."

"We'll see," she responded.

"Fair enough."

It was raining harder as Grace drove home, but her mind wasn't on the weather. She hadn't gotten over the Dontell Freeman situation at the station. *Buck Lohmeyer should have told me the reverend wanted an exclusive with me. I wonder if he kept it from me intentionally.*

She was still smoldering about it as she poured a glass of Pinot Noir and retreated out her kitchen door. The rain had cleared as quickly as it had started. Final remnants of the setting sun peeked through thinning clouds.

This back porch was becoming her best friend. From the first day back after Savannah, and all the times since when things got dicey, sitting here in her rattan rocker and watching day turn to dusk, calmed her. She sipped at the wine and let the drama of the past few days drift through her mind. The interview with a girl who might have been coerced into marriage. The uplifting story of a housing project that brought together people of several faiths. The prospect of exploring what went on at the Imam's community mosque.

Dillon Mcafee and his invitation.

Even the idea of someone violating this private, important space, smashing her kitchen window, didn't detract from the solace she felt here.

"Hello over there!" The voice was familiar. It was Horace Gunter waving from his fire pit. "Come on over, Grace."

She really wanted privacy. But she had turned him down on several occasions, preferring to be alone with her thoughts, winding down. Yet her neighbor had been so gracious, getting her window fixed. And he seemed to be an interesting sort. She left the porch and crossed to his yard, carrying her half-finished glass of wine.

"So you've decided to check out the old guy's outdoor man-cave, have you?" he chortled in his low, husky voice. "Sit down, take a load off. I've got some guys coming over to swap lies in an hour or two."

"I won't be here," she said, sliding into one of the padded lawn chairs ringing the pit. "It has been a long, long, long day. I just wanted to come over and say hi."

"Glad you did," he said, taking a swig from his longneck beer bottle. "You're about empty. What's that you're drinking?"

"Oh, some cheap Pinot Noir," she answered.

"I don't have Pinot," he said. "But if you want to switch to white, I have a couple of bottles of Chardonnay in my supply chest here." He opened a small portable cooler and held up a bottle.

"I guess that would be okay," Grace approved. "I rarely drink more than a glass, but with the week I've had, I think I've earned a second."

They settled back and gazed at the fire, watching its sparks rise into the darkening night.

"What made it such a hard week?" Horace asked.

Grace recounted her trip to Tuskegee, the interview with Pearl, married to ex-con Eddie, and the flap over who would handle the Dontell Freeman story.

"To top it off, I think I'm being stalked."

"Stalked? What makes you think so?" he asked, holding out the wine bottle toward her glass. She shook her head no, but Gunter ignored her and topped off her wine. She didn't object. "Don't think you're being a little paranoid, do you, with all the controversial stories you're involved in right now?"

She cringed slightly. "I'm not imagining that black car that keeps showing up, Gunter," she fired back at him in an unusually combative manner. "And who are you to be skeptical? You saw what they did to my window, for God's sake." Her speech was becoming slightly slurred. She was losing track of how much wine she drank, and Horace poured more into her glass.

"Yeah, I guess that's true," Gunter yielded. "Funny, I almost forgot about that. Oh yeah, I need to return your key, too."

She waved the comment off. "No, you hang onto it," she said. "It's a spare, and I can't tell you how much I appreciated your getting that guy over so fast to fix the glass. I might need to call you sometime to come over and fix the plumbing."

His laughter roared across the yard. "I might have to bring the handyman with me," he replied. He emptied his beer and popped the top off another. Horace's voice became more solemn, serious. "Listen, Grace, if anything like that happens again, I want you to call me. I know from my police days how to scare the living hell out of someone who stalks or harasses. Just say the word and I'll come rescue you."

She finished her wine. She felt gratitude, as she had that day when the retired district attorney, Morgan Staton, offered his help. She stood up unsteadily. "I gotta go, Gunter," she muttered, feeling woozy. "Long day tomorrow."

"Aw Grace, stay at least until the gang gets here. I'd like you to meet 'em."

"Another time," she said. "Thanks for the wine." He watched her walk unsteadily toward her back porch. She stumbled a bit on the top step.

Grace felt relaxed and mellow, but also out of touch with her senses. Inside, in her bedroom, she felt the room spin. Unable to stop it, she plunged into bed with her clothes on. The room continued to swirl, even after her eyes were closed. She wanted to get up and change, to wash her face, to shake off this awful feeling, but uneasy sleep overtook her.

CHAPTER SIXTEEN: Penance

The garbage men outside were setting off nuclear explosions. Birds in the back yard were warbling at the decibel level of a rock concert. Grace tried to open her eyes, but some alien power was streaming laser beams far more intense than morning sunlight through her bedroom window.

She squinted, groaned and rolled over onto her back. Her head pounded. Perspiration soaked the hair matted on the back of her neck and stuck her top to her underarms. Her queasy stomach and throbbing pulse propelled her up out of bed and into the bathroom where she debated between aspirin and sodium bicarbonate. The bicarbonate won.

She could only recall once, in college, when a hangover made clinging to the bathroom porcelain necessary. It was after a University of Texas football game, when she and then-fiancé Jeff let their hair down at a party and drank large quantities of beer. She didn't ever want to have that experience again, so something to calm her stomach had top priority.

And, she reasoned to herself, the bicarbonate has aspirin in it anyway. It took several minutes, but she felt the effervescent ingredients working. *They must be storming through my bloodstream,* she thought, *waging world war three against the excessive amount of alcohol I guzzled last night. What was I thinking?*

Leaning against the bathroom sink, still fighting the urge to convulse, she stared intensely at the mirror, a judge examining a hardened criminal. What she saw was not pretty. She cringed at having slept in her clothes. She shrugged her shoulders at her own stupidity.

Grace dragged herself into the kitchen and made coffee.

Usually, she had it ready the night before. A touch of a button in the morning would start that reviving liquid bubbling into the pot. Today of all days, when mere movement seemed to hurt, she had to measure it out, pour fresh water from the refrigerator door, and wait. It seemed to take hours.

Meanwhile, she pulled two slices of bread from the cupboard and set them by the toaster. Dry toast and coffee might help what ailed her.

But a hot-hot shower appealed even more. She stumbled back into the bathroom.

Grace felt fresher, somewhat recovered, as she returned to the kitchen from showering and dressing in clean clothes. She made the toast and poured her first cup of hot coffee. Sinking into the love seat on the porch, she looked out across her yard. She winced at the memory of sitting in this very spot the previous evening, accepting Horace Gunter's invitation to his fire pit. She couldn't remember the last time she had drunk so much. She promised herself it would be the last.

Thankfully, she was feeling nearly human when her first call of the morning rang on her cell phone. It was the assistant news director.

"Grace, are you on your way in?" Jenny Kim asked.

"Not yet. I was—well, kind of delayed."

"We need you in here, Grace," Jenny's voice took on a tone of urgency. "We just learned an Atlanta State College student has been held in custody by the FBI on suspicion of terrorism. That's all we know. Buck wants you to cover it."

"Me? Why?"

"We're shorthanded down here. Everyone is out on assignment. We thought you'd be in by now."

"So now that you're short-staffed, Buck thinks it's okay for me to handle hard news, right?"

"Please, Grace. Don't give me a hard time. He didn't want to go this route, but I told him it's as much a story about religion as it is about the arrest. I made your argument. I thought you'd want to do this story."

"Jenny, I'm sorry. I didn't mean to give you a hard time. I had a rough night and morning, that's all. Give me what you have, and I'll go cover it."

She rushed, but she was too late. People were already filing out of the courtroom, including rival news reporters. Grace spotted an old friend, Rick Dent, a veteran radio newsman she once worked with, and collared him. She was still fighting for breath from the sprint from the parking garage when she grasped his arm going by.

"What went on in there, Rick?" she asked Dent.

Rick shrugged, smiling wryly. "What happened to you, Gleason, oversleep again?"

"Something like that," she blushed. She felt as if she had missed a mid-term final. "So, you were about to tell me, what?"

"Since it's you, Grace—and considering I already filed my story from the courtroom—I'll share. As always, it only took three minutes. Magistrate reads him the charges, asks if he understands them and then 'how do you plead?' Not guilty, of course. End of story. All exactly as expected."

"At least I didn't miss much," she said. "Thanks for nothing, Dent."

The newsman flashed a goofy, put-on smile. "Always happy to help the TV rip-and-readers. Gotta go," Rick said, pulling the strap of his ever-present sound pack onto his shoulder. "Big robbery down at the Union National Bank. I think they got all of a few hundred bucks. The FBI doesn't tell amounts, 'cause they may want to add."

She teased, "You're still chasing cop cars and ambulances

and fire trucks?"

"Yeah?" he joked back. "I heard you're chasing preachers and choir directors." He guffawed and hurried down the hall. "Let's do lunch, Gleason."

She nodded at him, knowing she would call. It had been far too long since they sat and swapped stories. Grace always enjoyed the way they gave each other a hard time. She made a mental note to get in touch soon.

Grace hung around the doorway, waiting to see who else emerged. After a few minutes, a group of business-attired lawyers appeared, and she recognized one of them. Grace interviewed assistant U.S. attorney Janice Robertson several times in a Federal wire fraud case, and they developed a mutual respect.

"Janice," she called out. "Can we talk a minute?"

Robertson was young for her position, attractive and polished-looking in a beige business suit. Rumors followed her around that someday she would be headed for something big in Washington, D.C.

The assistant DA split off from the group as they headed toward the elevator and walked toward Grace. "I'm surprised to see you here, Gleason. I thought your new boss—what's his name, Lohmeyer? I figured he would send his shining star from South Carolina to cover this Hussein Bejan guy." She peered over her fashionable glasses like a librarian questioning a noisy teenager.

Grace persisted, "Janice, I'm not up to speed. All I know is this suspect was indicted for some kind of terrorism plot. Help me out?"

The attorney glanced around, making sure everyone else was gone. "Let's walk down the hall and find an alcove or something," she advised. "We're not unsealing the indictment until tomorrow, and even then not revealing details. But maybe I can help a little bit. We need the same agreement we've had before on cases like this. No attribution. Anonymous source. Are we clear about that?"

"Agreed."

"I mean it, Grace. Don't get me in trouble."

Grace gave her a reassuring nod. The woman turned and walked down the hallway. Her thin, well-toned body glided at the pace of someone nearly late for court. Grace hurried behind her, feeling some hair envy as she noted Robertson's lustrous, shoulder-length auburn locks. It served to remind Grace she was beginning to show tiny streaks of gray in her own shiny blond tresses. It might be time to start doing a little color magic.

Negotiating a turn into a deserted courtroom, the attorney sat on the back row bench. "What do you know so far?" she asked Grace.

"Only that Bejan is an Atlanta State engineering student, a naturalized citizen from Syria. And that he's in trouble for aiding and abetting a terrorist plot to bomb Washington, D.C. buildings. Do I have it right so far?"

"Pretty close. Here it is in a nutshell," Janice told Grace. "The FBI arrested him about a month ago for sending information about potential targets to this jihadist who's in jail in Great Britain. Two days ago, the Bureau arrested another Syrian-American, Parveen Mustafa, in Beirut. The Lebanese government turned him over, and he was brought to New York where he'll face charges in Federal court, either here or there, not sure yet."

"What's their connection?" Grace asked.

"Our guy and Mustafa were friends ever since meeting in a mosque in Atlanta.

"Which one?" Grace broke in eagerly

"I can't say," Robertson answered.

"Does that mean you know and aren't allowed to say, or

you don't know?"

Robinson flashed her an annoyed look. "I can't say," she repeated tersely. "At any rate, the two traveled to Canada last year and the FBI says they asked around about how to hide there if anything came down in the United States. Tomorrow my boss will issue a news release saying the charge against Mr. Bejan is serious and involves national security, and that he will be prosecuted not for carrying out terrorist acts, but for providing material support."

Janice Robertson rose quickly and started toward the door. She turned for a moment. "That's all I can tell you, Grace. You'll have to wait for the rest, or dig it out from other sources. Good luck." Robertson left Grace sitting all alone, wondering what she really had that could be put on the air.

As she arrived at the station, Grace had two hours to pick up anything else she could and write the story for the noon newscast. She called everyone and anyone she thought might be able to provide even the tiniest piece of the puzzle. The clerk of the Federal judge whose hearing she had missed. A friend at the Atlanta FBI office. The public affairs officer for the Federal penitentiary where Bejan was being held.

After exhausting her resources, Grace sifted through the notes on her computer and began to write. The time flew, and Grace had barely enough time to finish her report and get it put on teleprompter.

Christina Cruz anchored "Big Six News at Noon" and led with Grace's story. "An electrical engineering major at Atlanta State was indicted this morning on terrorist charges in Federal court," she said. "Grace Gleason was there. Here's Grace with the story."

Grace was seated at the adjacent desk, and the camera light went on. "Christina, Federal authorities charged the student, Hussein Bejan, with material support for terrorist acts. Although they have yet to release details, here is what I've learned through my sources."

A year-old photo of Hussein Bejan flashed onto the screen as Grace continued. "Mr. Bejan was arrested nearly a month ago and indicted by an Atlanta grand jury. He has been held in solitary confinement in the Federal Penitentiary here ever since. Earlier this week, another man, Parveen Mustafa, was arrested in Lebanon. He was taken to New York and is held there. The U.S. Attorney in Manhattan told me Mustafa faces charges in Federal court. Some sources believe Bejan might have implicated Mustafa in the half-dozen or so interviews the FBI conducted with him."

The camera returned to Grace as she went on "The two men, Bejan and Mustafa, reportedly attended the same mosque here in Atlanta, and took trips together to Canada and Syria. We're still awaiting details about their alleged activities and who else, if anyone, might have been involved.

"As for Mr. Bejan, a naturalized U.S. citizen, his defense attorney pointed out the indictment does not constitute any imminent threat. He added he's confident his client will ultimately be cleared of the charges. The judge did not set a trial date this morning, and Hussein Bejan will be held without bail."

Christina asked, "Grace, is there any information regarding what mosque these two young men were connected with here?"

"Not yet," Grace responded, silently wishing she knew.

"Will the two be tried separately, or is it possible they will be tried as co-conspirators?"

"That's hard to say," Grace answered, "until more details are released about what the charges involve, and the extent to which the two are accused of working together. Christina, we still have a lot to learn. I will keep you updated."

"Thank you, Grace Gleason," Cruz said. Then, turning to the camera, "We will have more on this story. As soon as we have it here at Big Six, you will have it. In other news, another Atlanta metro bank was hit by robbers this morning. Here's Scott Matthews with the story…"

Buck Lohmeyer was waiting for her at her desk. "Good job, Grace. Sorry we had to throw you into the fire that way." He tried his best to smile.

She flashed him a curious look in response. "I'm a newswoman, Mr. Lohmeyer. It's what I've done my entire career. No apology necessary."

"I know. I just wanted you to know I appreciated your flexibility, since this hearing wasn't exactly in your bailiwick." She watched him walk away, wondering if this was a move of conciliation on Buck Lohmeyer's part or a subtle signal that Hussein Bejan wouldn't continue to be her story.

Grace sat silently staring at her desk for several minutes after he left. Her headache had returned, and her spirits began to sag. After so brutal a morning, the physical pain mixed with the personal humiliation over her previous night's behavior, were taking their toll. She was flagging. She needed to get away, have something to eat, drink some tea, rally and rejuvenate. Or call back in sick, go home and dive into bed.

Mrs. Nicholson ruined those thoughts. "Grace, there's a man out there," the receptionist said, nodding toward the door to the front lobby. "He wants to see you."

"Who is it?" Grace asked wearily.

Mrs. Nicholson shrugged, holding her palms up as if to say, "who knows?" "All I know," she told Gleason, "is he appears to be from somewhere in South America or the Middle East and speaks with an accent. I asked if he had an appointment, and he said no, but he wanted very much to meet you."

Grace's first instinct was this stranger might be related to previous attempts to intimidate her. She doubted it; whomever that was constantly sneaked around instead of confronting her. And the security guard at the front door scrutinized anyone coming inside the station. Still, she thought about living in an era when crazy people shoot up workplaces and schools and malls with regularity. She wanted to rush out the back door and flee to her car. But she didn't.

The first thing Grace noticed about the visitor was how strikingly handsome he was. His face was smooth and olive-toned. His wavy hair was thick and black as midnight. But it was his eyes—dark, shiny, seeming to smile all by themselves—that drew her in.

He sat so erect in one of the lobby chairs, it made him appear tense and nervous. As she approached, he stood and smiled widely, extending his hand. "Thank you for seeing me, Ms. Gleason," he said, exuding politeness. "My name is Behram Quershi."

"How can I help you, Mr. Quershi?"

He motioned for her to sit next to him. As she did, he pointed at the large monitor overhead. "I saw your report just now, about the young jihadist. Your coverage on this young man fits the reason I came down here to see you in the first place."

"Wait a minute, Mr. Quershi," Grace protested. "Did you call him a jihadist? We don't know that. All we know for sure is he has been charged with sending information to some unnamed terrorist organization. No one has called him a jihadist. I certainly didn't."

"Ah, but they will, and you will, because that is what he is."

"And you know this how?"

"He fits the pattern," Behram said. "I have seen many of them all my life, Ms. Gleason. I can tell just by looking and listening to what they say." He shrugged. "But that is not why I am here."

Grace was uncomfortable with this conversation. Ambiguity and gamesmanship were not her strong suit. "Why are you here, Mr. Quershi?"

"First let me tell you a little about me. I am a United States citizen. I came here from Pakistan many years ago. I intended to return home, but I fell in love with America and got my citizenship. After working for ten years in the restaurant business, I changed my career dramatically and became a documentary film maker."

"That's quite a switch," she said.

"I had friends in the advertising business, and I always worked with them on my commercials. So I was no stranger to film. I had an opportunity to bid on a promotional series for a non-profit, and won it. A full-time film career was no big leap of faith."

"Mr. Quershi, I don't have a lot of time," Grace was growing impatient. "What does any of this have to do with me?"

"Your reporting is showing the ugly side of my religion, Ms. Gleason, the players who do not represent the true values and beliefs of Islam. Aahil Moghaddam. Hussein Bejan. Parveen Mustafa. These are not the true Muslim faces. They are imposters. I saw the same sort taking over my native country, radicalizing it. It was once modern and economically vibrant and positive. Then the extremists took over and turned it into a place of hate and fear.

"Ms. Gleason, when you report only the terrorists, I worry that your public will believe all Muslims are haters. I have been a taxpaying, voting American for many years. My son attended the Air Force Academy and served honorably in Iraq and Afghanistan in the war on terror. I am currently making a documentary about my love for this country and hatred for those who are destroying my native land—and hope to destroy the U.S., as well. Ms. Gleason, I'm asking you to keep in mind there are many of us who feel the way I do, not the way of the Aahil Moghaddams and Hussein Bejans and Parveen Mustafas."

"You are aware," Grace responded, "our station ran a piece giving Moghaddam's protestors in our front lawn a chance to have their say?"

"I am. I saw it, but it's not the same. I don't know if Moghaddam sponsors jihad in any way or not. But I do know he is charged with murdering a policeman. He is being tried for a felony in the country I love, a crime I would not ever commit, nor would any of the people I know or pray in mosque with."

Grace shook her head as if to discourage him. "Mr. Quershi, you're talking to the wrong person. I'm a religion reporter, not a political commentator."

"Ah, but you see, these days it's difficult to separate the two, don't you think? Look at the activities in my own native land, where a religious party—Jumaat-ud-Dawa—is accused by the United States government of being a terrorist front. Many believe this group is a jihadist organization, yet it has registered in Pakistan as a political party. Do you not think politics and religion are discussed side-by-side in the mosques in Lahore?"

"Mr. Quershi, I don't pretend to be an expert on Middle Eastern politics. So what are you asking me to do?"

"Respectfully, two things. First, I would like it if sometime next week you would go with me when we film, to see what we are attempting to do. We are showing the positive side of American Muslims and the life they love in this country. We only wish to help Americans of Islamic faith to see the benefit of assimilating. And second, I am inviting you to come to dinner at my house with me and my wife, and several friends. Maybe if you see who we are, and how we live, you could include one or two of my friends in your newscast—to let your viewers see the real Islam."

Grace closed her eyes and sighed. "I have a very trying schedule right now, Mr. Quershi. I don't have the time to spare." She watched him frown and quickly added, "I only report the news, but I do see where you're coming from. I will promise this. When a story comes up that might cast a negative reflection on your religion, I'll see if it would make sense to invite you or your friends to come give your reaction. It seems to me, if more Muslims would speak out against the extremists, it would serve to balance the story. I promise to stay in touch."

He nodded understanding and glumly watched Grace return to the newsroom. As she approached her desk, she kept on going. Not only did she desperately need to put something in her stomach, but she also needed to get away from this madness.

Her queasiness, a leftover from her hangover and her trying morning, nagged her as she approached the parking lot exit. Suddenly, her weary mind had a violent jolt. Speeding away from the station lot, onto the street and veering around the next corner, she spotted the black Trans Am with the gold pin-striping.

Despite her sinking physical and emotional state of affairs, the sight of her tailgater leaving the station just ahead of her shook her senses wide awake.

CHAPTER SEVENTEEN: Absolution

Lunch didn't set well. Grace thought a bowl of chicken soup and a cold glass of sweet tea would revive her. To the contrary, as she sat in a booth at the Magic Plate Diner gingerly spooning in the hot liquid, the nausea of this morning returned. She imagined she was feeling fatigue as much as illness, but either way, she knew she couldn't finish the food, much less return to work. She munched one of the saltine crackers, but even that couldn't quell the unsettled feeling.

"Mrs. Nicholson, I've taken ill," she called in on her cell. "Please let Mr. Lohmeyer know I'm on my way home, to bed."

"Can I do anything else for you, Grace?' the receptionist asked, registering concern in her voice.

"Yes. Make this go away," Grace groaned.

The ten-minute drive to Morningside seemed like an hour. Grace fought against dizziness as she turned up her street and into her driveway.

She had already slept in her clothes once today, and she was tempted to do it again as she dropped her purse and computer bag on the kitchen counter. Yet as she trudged into the bedroom, she knew she would be sorry later if she didn't change. She managed to get into a soft cotton nightgown she knew would feel better to wake up in. Grace ignored setting her alarm and slid under the cool, wonderfully luxurious sheets. In less than a minute, she was out.

Her sleep was fitful, invaded by strange nightmares. When she opened her eyes, the clock said four. Now as she lay staring at the ceiling, only half-awake, Grace tried to piece together fragments of the dreams. She remembered something about a child being severely beaten with bamboo rods, a deadly bombing in some country already laid to waste, and a courtroom where someone in a burka was screaming at the judge. She could make sense of none of it, and as she sat up on the edge of bed, the memory scraps disappeared

like wisps of smoke into the stratosphere. She was happy the disturbing images were gone.

Her stomach was more settled. Yet rising to go shower, she
still felt as if a ton of bricks were sitting on her shoulders. Because of
its erratic nature, the nap did little to erase her fatigue.

Hot water helped, and she stayed in the shower a full fifteen
minutes. As she toweled down, she felt serious hunger pangs. No
wonder; the only solid food she had eaten all day was the dry toast in
the morning and a few small bites of cracker with the soup she had
forcibly swallowed.

After hurriedly dressing in blue jeans and a sweater, she went
to the kitchen and peered into the fridge. Nothing appealing appeared.
Grace grabbed her purse and keys. The salmon salad at the Fusion
Grill might be just what the doctor ordered. It wasn't her normal dinner
hour, but the odd events of the day made her oblivious to routine.

Grace wouldn't normally have worn denims to this place. It
wasn't considered upscale, but it was frequented primarily by young
professionals who lived and worked in the business district of Buckhead. Today she would sit at the end of the bar, as she had many
times before, and no one would know the difference. It was still early,
so the large after-work throng that usually frequented the bar area
had yet to congregate.

"Let me have the salmon salad," she told the bartender, "and
the biggest glass of iced tea you can find."

"Half-priced martinis today until seven," the bartender chirped
happily. He shrugged at the disgusted look she gave him and went to
get the tea.

Grace was nearly finished with her meal when the after-work,
pre-dinner crowd streamed in—slowly at first, then with furious momentum. Soon, the bar was stacked three-deep with millenials sipping the discounted martinis and chattering raucously. Sitting as she
was at the bar's end, Grace thought she might be spared the on-
slaught of happy hour craziness. But the corner space beside her
became a popular place for incoming traffic to squeeze in and wave

at the bartender for attention. After being jostled several times by this in-and-out human circulation, she knew it was time to leave.

She paid her check and rose to leave. She watched with amusement the rush of people battling for her bar stool, like ants scrapping for bits of food.

The evening air at dusk should have been rejuvenating. Yet Grace barely noticed it as she climbed wearily into her car and drove onto the street. She couldn't remember when she had last been so bushed. Maybe just before Savannah, but this fatigue might rival what she experienced that time. After everything she had been through, it was no wonder she felt wiped out.

Grace looked forward to getting back home, but an alarming, memory-jogging sight rudely interrupted her thoughts. It pumped adrenaline of apprehension through her system and opened her eyes wide with surprise and panic. The blue flashing lights in her rear-view mirror reminded her of a night not so long ago, when a policeman with a devious plan to scare her off a story about dirty cops pulled her over and set her up on a phony drug charge. *No!* she thought. *This can't be happening again.*

Grace stared at the mirror, shaken, unbelieving. The cop popped the siren briefly and left his lights on. Trembling with exhaustion, fear and aggravation, Grace slowed the car down, pulled it slowly around a corner off the main street and stopped. She waited stark still as the cruiser sat behind her, its headlights on high beam, nearly blinding her as she watched for the policeman to emerge.

She knew it would take at least several minutes while he ran her plates. Grace had the station's lawyer, Hank Hamlin, in her cell phone. Waiting, shakily, she sent him a quick text: *Just pulled over for who knows what? Fulton County cop. Have not been drinking, no traffic violation. Help. Film at eleven.* She was certain Hank would react. He pulled her out of a scrape once before when those crooked cops tried to frame her. He would take this situation seriously.

Finally, she watched in her mirror as the patrol car's door opened. The officer left his car and walked toward hers. She rolled down her window and placed her hands on the steering wheel where he could see them.

"License and registration please," the young cop requested politely. She looked at his badge, noting his name, and handed him the documents. He barely glanced at them.

"Ma'am, you were failing to maintain your lane. Have you been drinking?"

"Absolutely not," Grace answered. *At least, not tonight,* she said to herself.

"I'm going to ask you to step out of the car please," he said, handing back her license. "Keep your hands where I can see them." Grace did so, unsteadily, wishing she were in the comfort of her back porch or sitting in her den watching *Jeopardy* reruns. Her tired body struggled to obey her silent commands to appear coordinated.

"I'll ask you once again, are you sure you haven't been drinking?"

"No, officer, I have not. You can smell my breath if you want."

Grace's attempt at levity didn't seem to sit well with the cop. His deepening frown said it all. She knew better, was told by Hank Hamlin in the previous incident never to joke, or be sarcastic, or volunteer information not asked for. But the fact she had not been imbibing made this encounter seem a little silly to her.

"Ma'am, I'm not joking," he responded stridently to her comment, "This is serious."

Serious? This is getting ridiculous, she thought.

"I observed your car weaving across the yellow line," the officer told her. "I'm going to ask you to take a couple of simple tests." He held up a pen and instructed, "I want you to follow this pen with your eyes. Do it as smoothly as you can." Grace could feel panic building up inside. She knew her gaze was jerking, and she realized from stories she had covered this erratic eye movement was one of the things police look for in a DUI.

"Now walk down that way," he ordered, pointing away from her car. "Take nine steps, heel-to-toe, along a straight line. Turn on one foot and return in the same manner back to me."

I could do this in my sleep, Grace reasoned silently. *But I'm so tired, so utterly exhausted, I don't know if I can manage or not.*

As she walked back to the officer, wavering as she did, she realized this field test was going badly. She wondered silently why she had not refused to do it.

"Ma'am, I want you to stand on one foot for thirty seconds, with your other foot about six inches from the ground." She lifted one foot and struggled to keep her balance on the other. She battled as her leg turned to jelly. She wobbled back and forth, trying mightily to hang onto the one-foot stance. But after about fifteen seconds, her attempts were futile. Nearly falling, she landed both feet down, hard.

"Officer, I'm not drunk. I haven't even been drinking anything but tea," Grace protested. She realized now she was breaking all the rules. Never argue. Never volunteer. But she had to convince him she was telling the truth. "I'm just totally exhausted from work. We can go back and you can ask the bartender if I had alcohol. Wait, I think I have the receipt in my purse. You can see for yourself."

She reached for the car door to retrieve her purse, and the policeman held his hand out, stopping the door with force. "Ma'am, I'm only going to tell you this once, or I'll have to take you in. You stay right here and do as you're told. Do not make any sudden movements. Do not get back into your car. Are you willing to take a breathalyzer test?"

"Do you mean a roadside test? Here? Now?"

"Yes Ma'am."

Despite her exhaustion and the stress of this encounter, Grace remembered interviewing a DUI attorney once in a case involving such a test. He told her roadside breathalyzers were not reliable, and his advice to his clients was to decline. "The police can't force you to do it," the lawyer told her. "Of course, they can arrest you and require a blood test in custody. But that's often preferable to having to defend a poorly administered test in court, or one done with defective or unreliable equipment. No matter what the test registers, if it indicates any blood alcohol, some police consider you driving drunk."

Grace was conflicted, because she knew she had no alcohol in her system. If she took the test, she should pass with no contest. *Yet if these things are that unreliable, I might be better off refusing and insisting on an accurate blood test at the police station.*

"No, I've been advised not to take the test," she said with finality, feeling her pulse pounding in her heart, her head, her entire body.

"All right, I am placing you under arrest for suspicion of drunk driving. Put your hands behind your back. I am going to put these cuffs on you and take you to the station where a blood test will be administered. We are going to secure your vehicle here at curbside, and I will bring your purse." This young man was all business, procedure to the max.

It was not the first time she arrived at the Grain Street jail in Northwest Atlanta in the back of a cruiser with her hands pinned behind her. She experienced that scary trip previously while working on a story about a rogue band of crooked cops. She was entrapped then, by one of the wayward cops. And now she wondered if this was another attempt to interfere with her investigative work.

But that didn't make sense. The previous story threatened some of the men in blue—the ones who decided to cross the line between protecting the public and enriching their own lives. And even then, the bogus arrest didn't hold up to scrutiny, so she was released. This was much different. The stories she was working on now had nothing to do with the police. In fact, the APD and Fulton County might benefit from the reporting she was doing about law-breakers.

She watched the fourteen-story jailhouse, notorious for its shoddy, crowded conditions, come into view. A shudder went down her spine at the thought of being booked here yet again, of spending even ten minutes in the horrible place. The arresting officer led her into the building, triggering dreadful memories of once having spent the entire night in this institution.

Suddenly, her sagging spirits took an astonishing turn for the positive. Standing next to the desk where she was to be booked was Hank Hamlin, Big Six's in-house attorney. "You got my text," she squealed joyfully.

"I did," he said. "Grace, be respectful, but don't volunteer any information. Answer the questions this booking officer asks, truthfully, but don't add anything else or try to explain. They're going to draw your blood, and if the test comes back negative, you'll be released."

She felt exhilarated. Hank was the lawyer who stood by her, helping her work through the legal system in that last bogus arrest. She was in good hands.

The next time she saw Hamlin, Grace was sitting anxiously in a cell. He approached, accompanied by a cop with keys. "You're all clear, Grace. Not a trace of alcohol."

"I told him," she muttered. "The jerk wouldn't listen to me."

"He was just doing his job," Hank said quietly as the cell door clanked open and she slipped out. "Let's go pick up your things and get out of here. I'll drive you back to your car. The arresting cop said he left it locked on the curb."

Driving back in Hank's luxury SUV, Grace felt too tired to speak. Yet she was compelled. "Hank, you said that guy was doing his job. But I wonder if there's more to my getting arrested than that."

"They cruise past those bars in Buckhead regularly, Grace. Especially during happy hour. You were simply in the wrong place at the wrong time. He had to believe you had a snootful."

"Maybe," she answered. "But there was something—I can't quite put my finger on it—something that felt so familiar having been through that trumped-up arrest before."

He pulled over behind her car. "We're here," he said.

"I can't thank you enough, Hank. What would I have done if you hadn't shown up?"

"You had enough presence of mind to text me. Luckily, I was still at the office. Look, Grace..." He hesitated, stumbling for some words. "...That last time, when I picked you up at the jailhouse and that terrible night when someone took shots at us as we drove away..."

"I know," she said. "It was horrendous. And you were so

brave, trying to protect me."

"No, Grace, you have it wrong. I made a pass at you, remember? I tried to play the big lifesaver, but then I screwed up and tried to kiss you. I don't think I ever apologized to you for my behavior."

"Hank, you did. Everything's okay."

"Anyway, when we talked before you left for Savannah, I thought we made a connection. We said we might get together when you got back."

She cringed inwardly. She didn't want to have this conversation. "Hank, I didn't make any promises."

"I know," he said, "but you left the door open, remember? Grace, I haven't pushed it, tried to be patient, because you've been knee-deep in all those tough news stories. I thought you might need some time. But I'd still like to see if there's something there."

Her heart took on a heavy feeling. This was absolutely the worst time to have to think about Hank's advances. Grace had no desire to start a relationship with him, even as well as he had treated her. She didn't have the time to think about a romance in her life right now, much less actually have one.

Besides, there was still Dillon McAfee. If she wanted to pursue a man in her life, she knew Dillon came much closer to the ideal candidate than Hank. That very thought made her wonder why she hadn't accepted the professor's invitation at least to call him.

She turned to Hamlin and shook her head slowly, sadly, and watched as disappointment washed across his face. "Sorry, Hank, I just can't."

He nodded as she stepped from the car. "Be careful going home," he said tersely.

Grace was sad, but she knew if she had extended Hank even an iota of hope, he would have wanted to follow her home, to ensure she was safe, possibly to collect the kiss they never had.

Grace hadn't felt this miserable in a long, long time.

CHAPTER EIGHTEEN: The Show

The station manager of Big Six came from humble roots in the Midwest. Harvey Silver scratched and clawed his way into the business. Stints as on-air radio newsman, then assistant manager for a number three TV outlet, then ownership of a small-town radio station, pumped a love for broadcasting through his veins. His experience, knowledge and business acumen brought him to Big Six, the top news station in Atlanta.

Because he was battle-tested on both sides of the microphone, Silver was sympathetic with his news staff. But when it came to ratings, he knew what buttered his toast. Maintaining the station's number one position in the city was all-important.

His early-morning meeting with the station's news director was tense. Ratings that began to flag during the latest sweeps period were troubling. He didn't mince words about it as Buck Lohmeyer squirmed in his chair across from Silver's desk.

"We're going the wrong direction, Buck," he complained, leafing through the ratings report and then peering at Buck over his reading glasses.

"Harvey, we're still top station in the market," Lohmeyer offered weakly.

Silver's response was a sharp dagger. "Damn it, numbers two and three are gaining ground on us, and we're standing still. When I brought you in I told you I expect to improve our standing, not give ground. Buck, you know I have a soft spot for the news operation. I've been there. But that doesn't make any difference with my bosses, so it's not going to cut it with me."

Lohmeyer nodded and sank deeper in his chair, silent.

"Buck," Harvey continued, "those corporate suits don't give a tinkers damn about how we turn their profit arrow green. They don't give a flying flip if we score five scoops a week or chase ambulances. They want the advertisers to stay with us and to be willing to pay for bigger audiences. It looks to me like we have two alternatives. We can make some bold moves to restore our viewers' faith in our news operation…" He paused, "…or we can tighten our belts, cut some staff and do more with less."

"Come on, Harvey, cutting staff would mean less investigative work, weaker reporting and ultimately make us look like those other bozos."

"Exactly. So?"

"I've been thinking," Lohmeyer slid to the front edge of his chair, elbows on Silver's desk. "We've been chasing several sensational news stories, all having the potential for religious extremism. A Muslim Imam kills a deputy and raises questions about what's been going on in his mosque. A college kid gets charged with terrorism, and nobody has yet dug up how he got radicalized. A preacher over in the west end gets arrested for beating kids in his church, pushing teenage girls to marry parolees he is trying to rehabilitate, and essentially turning half his congregation against the other half."

Silver pulled his reading glasses off, tossed them on the desk and appeared to listen with greater interest.

Lohmeyer continued, picking up the pace of his pitch. "Now a man comes out of the woodwork and claims a former Atlanta priest abused him years ago."

"All right, I'm listening," Harvey said, curiosity in his voice. "Everyone has those stories, don't they?"

"In one form or another, but we have some clear advantages. Gleason is the only news person in town the spanking preacher—that's what I call him—will talk to. And the guy who outed the priest came to her, because she's our religious reporter. Other reporters as well as some of the national news outlets have sniffed around, wanting to know what we know. But I have an idea that will blow the other locals away and possibly garner us some national attention at the same time."

"I'm still listening."

"Here it is. Gleason and I have discussed the possibility of turning her loose on these stories with a weeklong series. You know, sort of like, how are some religious leaders exploiting the youth of Atlanta? What are the consequences for the community if they aren't stopped? Where do their influences begin and end?"

"Now I'm getting very interested, Buck. Our ratings skyrocketed when Grace did a similar series on some corrupt cops here in the city. But it was really hard on her, physically and emotionally. Do you think she'd even agree to do this?"

"She seems to be agreeable. But I have one condition. I want Bannister Walker to work on it with her. She needs another set of eyes and ears, someone to carry out some of the interviews and do some of the reporting."

"We're talking about cutting staff, and you want to commit two people to do this?"

"Harvey, it's not a one-person job. If we're going to go after all these rogue actors, Gleason's going to need help. And if we promote the hell out of the series, it'll pay off, I'm sure of it."

Silver thought for a moment. "I like it. Maybe it won't cure all our ratings ills, but it's a helluva start. Go do it."

The morning meeting began a half-hour later. Lateisha Robinson ran down the list of stories in the works. "We're covering that apartment fire in Cobb County in both the morning and noon news-casts. Scott Matthews has it. Anything new to report, Scott?"

"We already have interviews with several residents that ran this morning," the young reporter announced. "Christina will include abbreviated versions at noon, plus I'm headed out right after this meeting to get the fire chief on camera. There's some suspicion it was set deliberately."

Robinson continued down the list and then turned the meet-ing over to Buck Lohmeyer.

"Our ratings aren't strong this quarter," he started. "We're all going to have to get out and dig. We're not going down the road of only chasing murders and wrecks, like the other guys, but the truth is they are gaining ground with that kind of reporting. I want all of you—reporters and producers especially—to get creative, think more like investigative reporters for the morning paper. In that re-gard, we've decided to launch a week-long special on the unholy side of religion in Atlanta."

He glanced at Grace. She looked up from note taking on her tablet, her eyebrows arched in surprise.

"You're all familiar," Lohmeyer continued, "with stories Ban-nister, Scott and Grace have been chasing that expose several reli-gious leaders in nefarious activities. We're going to capitalize on our lead position in that kind of coverage by promoting a series to begin in one week. As religion reporter, Grace will take the lead, doing a half-hour that kicks off every evening newscast. Bannister Walker is going to support her with legwork, interviews and some of the studio on-camera reporting.

"Video and live interviews, commentary, little-known be-hind-the-scenes facts about these characters. In-studio appearanc-es by authorities, opponents, proponents—I want us to shoot the works on this. Title: 'Unholy Mind Games.' I'll task our marketing group with thinking up aggressive promotions to run a whole week before kickoff." He turned toward Grace. "Gleason, any comments or concerns?"

She sat listening, stunned, wondering why he hadn't confirmed this with her before announcing it to everyone in the room. Yet it had been what she wanted all along, and how could she be anything but positive now that he agreed to it? She considered challenging the decision about Bannister Walker, much preferring to work with Scott Matthews. Yet she didn't want to nix the whole thing. Then, suddenly, she had an inspiration.

"Only that I'd like to have MaryAnne McWherter produce it," she said. She knew Buck would recognize it as a quid pro quo for not protesting Bannister's participation. She also knew rumors were flying around about staff cuts, and his agreement on MaryAnne would be employment security for one of Grace's favorite producers. She looked across the table at MaryAnne, who nodded agreement.

"Done," Buck said.

After the meeting, MaryAnne McWherter visited Grace at her desk. "Thanks for asking for me, Grace," she said.

Grace answered, "I did it because you're the best."

"And because you've seen me running around here with knees knocking from all the grapevine reports about staff reductions? Knowing I was the last hired so I'd be the first out? Knowing I don't want to be out on the street again wondering how to support my two pre-teens?" She laughed.

"Can't wait to get started," Grace responded.

"Speaking of which, let's sit down with Bannister and map out a plan. We only have a week to put this baby together."

"And a lot of diverse, highly controversial elements to pull together into a single thread," Grace added. "MaryAnne, tighten your seat belt. We have to be sure all our facts are straight, that we put the most significant elements on the air, and that we don't get Big Six sued." She thought about her daughter, Megan, and what she often said about her architecture studies at Georgia Tech. "This next week, we're going to be pulling a lot of all-nighters."

CHAPTER NINETEEN: Bannister

The reporter who came to Big Six in the Buck Lohmeyer package deal was returning home when he and Buck moved to Atlanta. Bannister Walker grew up in Forest Park, a small community south of the Atlanta airport. He got his college degree from one of the most prestigious traditionally black liberal arts colleges in the nation, Morehouse College. None other than Dr. Martin Luther King Jr., filmmaker Spike Lee, presidential candidate and media personality Herman Cain and many other famous and successful African-Americans graced its halls.

Bannister was tall, suave and polished. After graduation, he quickly became a luminary on the horizon at the top South Carolina television station where he worked for Lohmeyer. When Buck offered Walker a chance to return home and work at Big Six, the reporter didn't hesitate. "You'll have to pay your dues as a field reporter," Lohmeyer told him. "But I guarantee you, an anchor job will rear its head at the right time."

Grace Gleason hadn't had much interaction with Bannister. Their reporting assignments took them on different paths. They were cordial in the newsroom and at morning meetings, but Grace hadn't had a chance to get to know the man.

Until now. Bannister Walker was going to work with Grace on "'Unholy Mind Games." She was certain Buck pitched it that way so top management could see how Walker handled himself in the studio. That suited her fine. She could see he was a good reporter, and she was happy to have the help. *If he doesn't turn out to be some kind of prima donna,* she thought. *This program will take tons of legwork and difficult interviews. We can't afford any squabbles about "who does what" or "who's getting all the good stories."*

She vowed to be sensitive about giving Bannister opportunities to demonstrate his talent.

Grace disliked meetings. That was the reason she tried to be out on assignment as often as possible when the morning staff briefings were held. But an initial get-together with Bannister, producer MaryAnne McWherter and the technical guy, David Williams, was necessary. They decided to convene in the staff break room shortly after morning meeting. The space would probably be vacant, and they could get their business done before the news day got out-of-control busy.

"We've already laid a lot of the ground work for this series," Grace started out. "MaryAnne and David, could you pull together a video of all the reports and interviews we've done to date that will be relevant? And it might be helpful to categorize them. For example, there's the Reverend Dontell Freeman story. Lots of reports about his arrest, the protests, and interviews with members of his congregation. On the Aahil Moghaddam murder trial story, there's everything from initial reports of the shooting, his arrest, courtroom appearance and coverage of his supporter, attorney Khalila Noorani. And then there's this priest accused of abuse. We don't have much yet, but there's the initial report and an interview with Morgan Staton, the district attorney who went to see Father Bianci before the man died."

"Ex-father Bianci, right?" Bannister interjected politely. "The DA was quick to point that out."

"That's correct, ex-priest," Grace responded. "We need to keep that in mind. Anyway, if you can organize all that by tomorrow, let's get back together and review it. Meanwhile, we need to decide what our format's going to be."

"I assumed it would be similar to the previous series we did, 'Crime and Corruption,'" MaryAnne said.

"Maybe," Grace answered. "But let's keep our options open.

Bannister and I will map out what stories and interviews we need to pursue to fill in the gaps. For instance, on the ex-priest story, I hope we can get the man who came forward to do an interview with us—anonymously, with his image and voice changed. As we lay out our work assignments, we might come up with some spectacular format ideas. Agree, Bannister?"

"Absolutely," Walker answered, his dark eyes shining with excitement. "I'm ready. Let's get started."

After MaryAnne and David left to pursue their video assignment, Grace sat with Bannister and discussed story and interview strategies. With only a week to prepare, division of labor would be essential. They knew the Reverend Freeman would only talk to her. The same was true of Max Morrison, the tipster who revealed the priest abuse scandal privately to Grace. That meant Bannister Walker would need to work heavily on the story of the Muslim Imam accused of murder. And, perhaps the arrest of the Atlanta State student who became radicalized.

"Let's not forget what brought us to this point," Grace cautioned the younger reporter. "The commonality of these stories is that each has potential impact on Atlanta's youth, past and present. That's the core premise, and I think it will resonate. Don't forget, we live in a city that once tied itself up in knots over the Atlanta child murders…"

Walker interrupted, "Yeah, but that happened long before I and my contemporaries were born."

"I know. And the truth is, I was just in diapers myself at the time, kicking the slats in my crib in Chicago," Grace agreed. "But it's still relevant. I'm only saying, anybody who was around here then, not to mention the news media who never forget a story, are likely to think, 'Here we go again.' The story of those poor dead kids might be dredged up again—more for the arguments about whether the guy doing time was guilty than for sympathy for the children and their families.

"Bannister, we're going to make a case that radical religious leaders with their own agenda can damage our youth, and often do," Grace continued. "To claim justice needs to be done, our reporting has to be spot-on accurate and painstakingly thorough."

Bannister furrowed his eyebrows in mock seriousness. "Is there any other kind?"

"Not really," Grace laughed. She liked this young man and his positive attitude. She pulled out her tablet; she had already laid out a list of stories to cover, and she wanted his input.

For a moment, she contemplated telling him about the anonymous threatening phone call, the brick through her window and the black Trans Am. But almost as immediately, she decided against it. There was no point in worrying Bannister if none of the threats were delivered toward him.

"Let's go to work," she said brightly. "I'd like to show Buck Lohmeyer what real news programming can be."

Walker sat back and furrowed his brow. "Grace, you're pretty hard on the man. I've worked with him a lot longer, and I've always found him to be a stand-up guy. Here he comes up with this block-buster idea, pitches it to his boss, and puts you on the front row. Don't you think that's a little ungrateful?"

Grace fixed a blank stare on her colleague. "Wait a minute, Bannister. You think this series was Buck's idea?"

"Of course," he said. "He convinced Harvey it would do wonders for our ratings. Why?"

"His idea!" she exclaimed. "Bannister, he didn't come up with the concept. I did."

Walker frowned, squinting his eyes at her in skepticism. "Right. Now who's trying to hog the glory?"

"Seriously? He took it to his management as a Lohmeyer concept for the series? Now I'm really peeved." She stomped out of the room, leaving Bannister Walker looking bewildered.

**

Later, Grace met Megan for a quick supper at the Magic Plate Diner. Whereas they used to talk nearly every day, and see each other at least twice a week, their communication had dropped off. Grace understood why. Her busy reporting schedule and Megan's immersion in the architecture program didn't match up well. Yet she felt the absence of contact was carving a chunk out of her existence. She was excited as she waited in the booth she had claimed.

But her heart seemed to drop when she saw her daughter. A young man was with her—Grace assumed it was Joe. Not that she hadn't wanted to meet her potential future son-in-law. But not tonight, when she needed some heartfelt, one-on-one discussion with Megan.

Too late. Megan was her usual sparkling self as she approached, although Grace noted new dark circles under her eyes and the beginnings of lines in her forehead. Walking behind her, Joe looked serious. He hung back as the mother and daughter hugged.

"Mom, this is Joe. I hope it's okay he came with me. He wanted to meet you."

"Of course I don't mind," Grace said, swallowing back her initial disappointment. She gave the young man a semi-hug. He was only a little taller than she but had broad shoulders and muscular arms. "Please, Joe, you and Megan sit there, across from me."

He nodded. "Nice to meet you," was all the shy man could manage.

Grace could see why Megan was attracted to him. He had a pleasant face, framed by a short growth of dark beard. His complexion was light olive, his eyes deep brown. His hair was cut short and was neatly combed. Even though he seemed to hang back in respect, there was a confident and friendly bearing in his appearance.

They ordered quickly. Megan made it clear when Grace called she had projects to complete, requiring plenty of nighttime oil to be burned.

As they ate, Megan carried the conversation, explaining her latest course projects, complaining about the grading system and describing some of her fellow architecture majors. "Honestly, Mom," she concluded, "some of these people are beyond inspired. I had no idea I would be working with some of the most brilliant minds imaginable. Several of them are going to change the world, I'm convinced."

"That's wonderful," Grace told her. "And Joe, you're in architecture too, aren't you?"

He started to speak, but Megan broke in, "Mom, he's one of those great brains I just described to you. This man has visions for urban renewal and community transformation no one has dreamed of yet."

"Well, that's quite an endorsement, young man," Grace smiled at him.

Joe shook his head and finally smiled for the first time. "Your daughter overstates a little, Mrs. Gleason. I'm sure you know that. She's every bit as smart and talented as I am. Her grades are right up there with mine."

"Do you two have any time at all for a social life?"

They looked at each other with amused expressions.

"What's a social life?" Megan laughed.

"We study together, Mrs. Gleason," Joe responded. "And when—if—we eat, we try to eat together. That is our social life. At least, until we finish our degrees. When we get out into the work world, we'll have time for other things."

"That time isn't too far away," Grace said, looking directly at Megan. "I can't believe you're so close to graduation."

"That's one reason I was happy you called," Megan said.

"Joe and I have more plans than just a social life, Mom. We want to get married."

She couldn't tell. Were they pangs of pain or of joy? Was she delighted at hearing the words, or was this adrenalin pulsing through her body the result of hearing from her own daughter's mouth she would soon belong to someone else? Grace couldn't find words, and simply sat staring at them in wonderment as tears filled her eyes.

"I love your daughter, Mrs. Gleason. We hope to find careers in the same city. As soon as that is settled, we want to begin making plans."

"Well, I guess you discussed this with Megan's father when he came through? You two met him at the airport, right?" The words came out, but Grace felt as if she were choking on them.

"Mom, Joe didn't discuss this with Daddy when they met."

"You see, Mrs. Gleason, Megan told me how strong and supportive you have been for her over the years. You are the one, she says, who looked after her and guided her, kept her safe. I came from an old-fashioned culture where you ask the father's permission, but it wouldn't have been right to talk to Mr. Gleason before I asked for your blessing."

Now the tears that had sat waiting in her lids came flowing down. Her cheeks were a river bed. Grace stood and circled to the other side of the table. Her arms went around Joe. "I can't thank you enough for asking, Joe." Grace looked at Megan as tears continued to gush. She always knew the day would come when she would have to let go. That didn't make it any easier. Yet she found the words. "Of course you have my blessing."

Settling back in her place, Grace dug through her purse for a tissue, but immediately a folded handkerchief was thrust at her. Joe had been raised right, she decided.

She laughed. "I guess this is why you've barely touched

your food?" she asked him.

Joe nodded, smiling. "It's the first time I've ever asked for permission to marry," he blushed. Then, looking at Megan, "And the last."

"Well, it'd better be," Grace teased. "Now, you two get busy and finish eating. You have work to do. So do I. That's why I wanted to get together tonight, Megan. The next two weeks are going to be a nightmare. I'm doing another show like the one earlier—you know, the crime and corruption stories? It's a different subject matter, but just as intense."

"Mom, you're not going to be in any danger like before, are you?" Megan's new lines deepened a bit. She turned toward her boyfriend. "She gets into these intense stories and makes all sorts of bad guys mad at her. I worry to death."

"I'll be fine, Megan," Grace said. "I just have to work my tail off getting ready next week, then pulling the series off the following week. It's nothing I can't handle. There's no peril in these stories that will introduce the kind of threat those previous ones raised."

At least, I hope not, she thought.

**

Grace arrived home just as the sun was disappearing. She entered the kitchen from the garage door and heard the sounds. Horace and his buddies were starting early. Their chat and laughter already reached the usual late-night, four-beer level. She looked out her kitchen window and could see the sparks fly and dusky silhouettes of half a dozen men raising long neck bottles in toasts as they told lies.

Slowly shaking her head, she cringed at the memory of her behavior the night she visited Horace's fire pit. How extraordinarily immature she had been, getting so drunk. She wondered how many of those men would drive home tonight just as inebriated.

Grace went into the bathroom and hurriedly took off her

makeup. She wanted to do a little work on the series before she was too tired to think straight. She changed into her nightgown and climbed into bed, propped a pillow against the headboard and pulled her laptop onto her legs.

The first order of business was to lay out a work schedule for the interviews she and Bannister agreed to. He would have the lead on the Imam story. First, a follow-up with Noorani. Then an interview with Aahil in jail, if his lawyers would permit it, even if they insisted on being there. Perhaps most importantly, he needed to investigate the radicalization of the Atlanta State College student still in custody in the Atlanta Pen. What mosque did he attend? Was there a connection with Moghaddam? Bannister could definitely help her with that part.

And for Grace, the much-anticipated interview with Reverend Dontell Freeman—an exclusive. Perhaps more conversations with his parishioners, pro and con. Then try to set up another interview with Pearl, the young girl Reverend Freeman married off to Eddie, the parolee. Maybe she could do the follow-up with Pearl while she was not in Eddie's presence—and influence. Finally, she would pursue a video interview with the judge in Tuskegee who issued the license or the pastor who married them.

She hesitated in her note-writing, astonished at her own omission of the Stockholm Syndrome angle. She had failed to mention it to Bannister. Yet it would become a key element in their investigation. Dillon McAfee would be a significant interview, probably live in the studio.

In thinking of Dillon, her concentration on the programming broke, giving way to personal thoughts about the man. Odd, but she found him wedging his way into her thoughts increasingly these days. She was conflicted about him. She'd had only two brushes with romance since her divorce from Jeff. A brief involvement with a cameraman in Dallas that ended poorly. And a conversation with

Hank Hamlin, the Big Six station lawyer, that first showed promise, then never went anywhere.

The only intimate experience she had permitted herself since her divorce was with Jeff himself, when he travelled through once on business. Even then, in retrospect, she realized she made a stupid mistake.

She remained so dedicated to motherhood and career, Grace hadn't opened the door for anything else. And now here was a college professor, professional, polished, sophisticated, who wanted to explore a relationship. *I'm not old,* she reasoned to herself. *I haven't even had a hot flash yet. Shouldn't I at least give the man a chance and see if there are more sparks in this world than those stirred up in Horace Gunter's fire pit?*

Sitting with her computer in her lap, Grace nearly laughed out loud. What mental gyrations she put herself through sometimes, just trying to figure out her life and future. Dillon McAfee would remain a distinct possibility, she decided. But first, she needed to approach him as a news professional, asking him to help make some sense out of the religious chaos she and Bannister were about to explore.

Grace made a brief note, *"Stockholm Syndrome,"* on her list and then forced herself to dismiss thoughts of Dr. Dillon McAfee for the time being.

This next part of the planning was the most vexing for her—how to treat the Father Bianci story. She couldn't avoid it, for it represented perhaps the most dramatic example of the whole point of the series. On one hand, she hoped the alleged victim, Max Morrison, would permit an interview, possibly live from the studio. On the other hand, she hoped he would refuse. The former came from her dedication as a newswoman, the latter from a lifetime of belief in the sanctity of the only church she had known since childhood.

She would have to set the stage for all of this on the first night. She sat for a long moment, thinking. Then she began writing.

As Big Six's religion reporter, I have been privileged to bring you awe-inspiring stories of faith and belief, hope and good will. And love. For that is what religion means to many of you, and to me as well.

A church carries out an incredible mission trip to Costa Rica, raising the spirits of people in that country who have little, but who believe big. In our own city, Muslims, Jews and Christians unite to build the first of many multi-faith Homes for Glory, tearing down walls that separate their religions. Ministers demonstrate their devotion by putting in time at soup kitchen for the homeless. A youth choir from a small church in the inner city is invited to participate in a program at Carnegie Hall in New York. Children from a north side Sunday School give backpacks full of school supplies to disadvantaged grade schoolers.

These and many other stories we have brought you inspire us all. They make us want to be better people.

And yet there is another side to religion. A dark side that manipulates the positive messages of faith and forces us to ask if some misguided religious leaders take advantage of their positions to the detriment of others, especially the young, the impressionable, the defenseless.

For the next week, Unholy Mind Games will explore that question and attempt to answer it. Make no mistake, some of what you will see in these half-hour evening segments will be disturbing and controversial. It is our fervent hope, however, that at the very least we will make you think. And, when appropriate, act.

Grace sat back and stared at the screen. She would edit in the morning, but she was pleased with what she had. It would kick the programming off with the right tone and, she hoped, make viewers want to see the entire series.

Yet she knew how divisive this newest chapter in her news

life might be. Someone was already upset with at least one phase of her reporting to the point of threatening her. Someone from that crowd of protesters supporting Aahil Moghaddam? An irate member of the spanking preacher's flock? A protective adherent of the church—her church, the church in which she had grown up—who questioned the priest abuse reports?

There was no way for her to know. She couldn't stop now. Promotions had already begun. Tomorrow she, Bannister, Mary-Anne and David would begin building what they hoped would be a blockbuster news event. Grace pushed her laptop aside, turned out the lamp and lay back. Her mind was a whirlwind of ideas and plans. Yet exhaustion pushed them all farther and farther away until they dispersed gradually like clouds in the summer breeze. And sleep came.

CHAPTER TWENTY: Parveen Mustafa

Normally the reporters for Big Six stayed arms length from management. Not that they disliked their bosses, but the managers were still the brass who could hire and fire, order and criticize. They could dole out best assignments to their favorites and send perceived troublemakers out on disagreeable stories. And they had the power of the purse, meaning they could cut budgets as needed so resources were sometimes slim.

Despite a newsroom's lofty objective of separation from the business end of things, a television station is a corporation. Its owners' primary interest is profit. Some might say its managers, intensely interested in job security, often operate like a political organization.

When Buck Lohmeyer moved to Big Six News, rumors swirled that the man could play politics with the best. Most notably, some staffers in hushed conversations accused him of treating Bannister Walker more favorably than the other reporters. Yet he conversely could sometimes be seen nit-picking the work of the young man he brought along from South Carolina.

On one occasion, in morning meeting, he was particularly harsh in discussing Walker's coverage of a story while Lateisha was going down the list of active stories.

"It appears the mayor is stonewalling our open records request for info on airport contract bids," Lateisha said. "I spoke with our lawyers, and they say the city has missed two deadlines to turn over records. Bannister, you've been covering this. Is there light at the end of the concourse?"

The reporter chuckled at Lateisha's play on words. "I'm trying to get some answers from the mayor, but his communications director is stonewalling. They won't respond to my questions about when they can deliver the required documents. We'll probably have to appeal to the court again before I can get anything out of them."

Lohmeyer exploded, "Damn it. We've been talking about this story in these meetings for a week, and we still don't have any answers. Bannister, why can't you get the man on record?"

"I'm trying, Mr. Lohmeyer. But if he won't answer to the court, I don't see how I can force him to answer my questions."

The news director turned crimson. "That's not good enough. We're a news operation, for God's sake. I expected you to break this logjam. I'd better not see Blake Stone with the story tonight on Channel Thirteen's Next Minute News." Lohmeyer rose and strode toward the door. "Lateisha, keep going. I have work to do."

As Lohmeyer left, Grace felt empathy for Bannister. She was getting to know him through their work on the series, and she knew how hard he worked. She felt the news director's tirade was unfair. Everyone was aware how adept the mayor was at dodging news bullets. Further, Grace wondered why they hadn't pulled Walker off the story. He was supposed to be focused on Aahil Moghaddam and Hussein Bejan. Getting those interviews for the series would be a tall order.

After the meeting, she walked out of the room next to Bannister. "Not fun in there," she muttered to him.

"Not at all," he said. He shook his head and sprinted up the hall toward the news director's office, not back to the newsroom. Grace watched in curiosity as Bannister ducked into Lohmeyer's office.

"Buck…" the reporter's dark brown eyes burned into his boss.

"So now it's Buck, is it? Strange, I was 'Mr. Lohmeyer' in there during the meeting," he said curtly, motioning toward the conference room.

"That was for public consumption. When we were drinking beer together in Columbia, or barbecuing on my patio, you didn't hold me to such formalities."

"I know," Lohmeyer admitted. "But things were a little more casual in South Carolina. Look, maybe I'm harder on you than the others because they expect me to treat you better. They know you're my guy. I understand the mayor's being an ass on this. Besides, I probably should put someone like Scott Matthews on it since you're digging into the Gleason series."

Bannister heaved a sigh and sank into the chair across from his boss' desk. "That's really what I came back here to talk to you about. I'd like your permission to travel to New York."

"What for?"

"I've been trying to get an interview with the Atlanta State kid, Hussein Bejan, while he's incarcerated. But the warden won't hear of it. I tried getting his lawyers to put a little pressure on, but they're opposed, too. They say the Feds have been interrogating the hell out of him, confusing him, making him cough up information, and they don't know what he'll say for public consumption, not to mention they worry about how it might impact jury selection.

"Besides, they're pretty pissed about our coverage of the arrest. We made constant headlines out of something they claim is no big deal. They believe they can sway the judge on some issues, maybe even a change of venue, based on some of the press."

"Okay, so what's in New York? The accomplice?"

"Alleged co-conspirator," Bannister corrected.

"New York's prison system is probably more rigid than Georgia's. You'd never get an interview there."

Walker smiled. "There's more than one way to skin a rabbit. Parveen Mustafa's lawyers are open to an interview if it's off-camera and off-the-record. They say if I don't show up with any equipment and promise to use it as background only, they can get me on the visitor list. Some prisons might balk at having journalists come in, but if the prisoner has them on the visitor list, there's not a lot they can do about it."

"Off the record, huh? Don't see how that would be worth the expense," Lohmeyer said.

"I think it could be. For one thing, he knows as much if not more than Hussein does. They supposedly travelled together and hung out with the same people."

"But if you can't do a story…"

"…I'll have the information in my hip pocket," Walker finished his boss' sentence. "I'll know where the bones are buried. I can use that a hundred different ways—maybe turn up some other sources who will go on record. Maybe use it to convince Hussein's lawyers I should be allowed to interview the guy. Maybe find out where Hussein and Parveen heard talk that turned their path toward jihad. Buck, I need to know what those guys know. Parveen is the key."

He paused, watching Lohmeyer's reactions. The man sat still, pensive, mulling the idea over.

"One more thing, Buck," Bannister said, pressing the issue. "I've been told Parveen's cousin visits him as often as authorities will allow. I noticed the cousin made a statement to the press out in Michigan, where they're from, right after the story broke. Haven't seen anything since, but he reportedly was saying Parveen's trip to Syria was simply a family matter—that he was going to visit his fiancée and get married there. If I can get his cousin talking, that wouldn't fall under my agreement with Parveen's lawyers. It could turn into a great story."

Lohmeyer nodded. "I'll talk to Silver.

Bannister smiled. "Thanks. You won't be sorry. I'm going to start packing."

"Slow down," Buck admonished. "I didn't say okay. I said I'd discuss it upstairs."

"You'll get me the trip. I've seen you in action."

The next morning, Bannister deplaned at LaGuardia Airport in Queens, New York. It was his third time to New York, and each time he stayed at the Hyatt hotel at Grand Central station.

His first trip came shortly after graduation from journalism school, a gift from his parents. For three days, he and three of his Morehouse buddies wandered the Manhattan streets to take in the sights, found half-price theater tickets at the booth in Times Square, took a sight-seeing tour and had a great dinner at Carucci's.

On Walker's second trip there, he travelled alone, for business, a job interview with a major network's flagship station. His contributions on their coverage of a major hurricane caught their eye, and they wanted him. Although he was offered the job, Bannister turned it down. "I just don't think I'm cut out for New York City life," he told the disappointed news director. "I'll stay in Columbia and watch for an opportunity at a large Southern city I'm better suited for."

He moved to Atlanta with Lohmeyer less than a year later.

Now he was here on assignment, but on a shoestring. "Just get up there, stay overnight, get your business done and head right back home," the news director ordered. "Silver won't even pop for an extra day."

There would be no fancy dinners or Broadway plays. Just an overnight stay in Manhattan, subway ride to Brooklyn the next morning and interviews with Parveen and his lawyer. Perhaps his cousin, too. He would have stayed in Brooklyn with easy access to the deten-

165

tion center there, but Lohmeyer agreed to the Grand Central location Walker was more familiar with.

A brisk wind swept in across the airport circle drive as Bannister pulled his carry-on out of LaGuardia and into a taxi. The cacophony of car horns, workers yelling, luggage carts clattering and planes taking off and landing just on the other side of the terminal, told him he was back in the Big Apple.

"Grand Central," he told the driver. "Take the Fifty-Ninth Street Bridge." From the previous trips, he knew the drivers hated that route. But though it was often slower, it was also much shorter and less expensive.

He ate dinner in the hotel coffee shop, watched a Yankees game in his room and went to bed early. The subway ride would take well over an hour, as would the processing routine at the detention center. He needed to get up early and get going.

The next morning, the wind raced in from the East River, carrying with it a stinging mist, as he walked to the subway. Gusts swirled down from the tops of massive concrete structures, forcing him to hunch down deeper into his jacket. He pulled his rolling bag with him; he would head directly to the airport from Brooklyn after his work there was finished.

Bannister had learned the subway on his previous trips here, understanding how to circle the edge of the crowd pushing toward the door and edging through it before it slammed shut. He yanked the bag inside while balancing a go-cup of coffee from the hotel breakfast bar in his other hand. He slipped into the side seat between two bored commuters who frowned at this interloper squeezing between them. But sitting in this crowded arrangement, rather than hanging on a strap, left him hands-free to sip his coffee. After three stops, the other two riders were gone, and there was room to breathe.

The train to Brooklyn made multiple stops, and it was an hour-and-a-half later before he stepped out onto Twenty-Fifth Street, several blocks from his destination.

As the reporter arrived, he stopped and stared up at the Metropolitan Detention Center in Brooklyn's Sunset Park, a multi-story structure near the waterfront, sitting in the area known as Industry City. Bannister read on-line the facility, operated by the Federal Bureau of Prisons, can hold over two thousand male and female detainees of all security levels. It has housed some of the most notorious criminals in U.S. history, including drug dealers, embezzlers, murderers, con artists and terrorists. Some do their time there while others await transfer to another part of the country, as was Parveen's case.

A guard escorted Bannister to the visiting room, surprisingly sterile and high-tech in appearance, all stainless steel and tile.

"Wait here," the guard announced gruffly. Within minutes, he returned, accompanied by a short, bald man in a rumpled polyester suit, followed by a dark, swarthy younger man.

"Bannister Walker? I'm Mustafa's lawyer." Bannister recognized the attorney's heavy New York accent instantly as the voice he heard on the phone, setting up this visit.

"Right," Walker answered, shaking the attorney's clammy-cold hand and glancing at the second man.

"This is Parveen's cousin," the lawyer explained. "He has permission to sit in. Mustafa insisted on it. We're going to meet him in one of the private rooms reserved for attorneys and their clients."

"Let's go," the guard announced gruffly and led them out of the large visiting center to a small room equipped only with a metal table and four chairs. "Wait here," he ordered.

"I expected this place to be a hellhole," Bannister said.

"We got lucky, we're in the new part," the lawyer answered.

"It's not bad here, even though everyone says the food is shit. The older part, the original building, is a different story. It's filthy and stinks like a sewer. One guy, a politician who got his hand caught in the cookie jar and is serving five years, has sued the city over the conditions, it's so bad. Can you imagine that? A politician who could have spoken up about conditions here, but now he's suing the prison system as an inmate. It's a crazy frigging world."

Bannister was about to address his next question to the cousin, but the door swung open and the guard escorted Parveen Mustafa in. "I'll be right outside that door," he droned. "Let me know if you need anything. You've got twenty minutes."

The lawyer nodded and turned to Bannister as Mustafa sat next to his cousin, opposite Bannister. "Just a reminder. Everything said in here is off the record. No pictures or recordings. Agreed?"

Bannister nodded and turned to the prisoner. He had seen photos and a little video footage of Parveen, but in person he looked far younger and less sinister. A short black beard framed his thin, dark face. A white skull cap topped his short-cropped black hair, and a pair of frameless glasses gave the prisoner an almost professorial look.

"Mr. Mustafa, I came to speak with you about the charges the federal government has filed against you. The prosecutors who charged you said you are guilty of providing material support and resources for the purpose of jihad. I assume you will plead not guilty?"

Mustafa broke into a huge, friendly grin. "What they accuse me of is of no matter to me," he responded as Walker's face registered surprise. "Only Allah can inflict vengeance on anyone who does not follow his will. My crime, Mr. Bannister, if you want to call it that, is being on my computer, communicating with others, all of us wanting to learn more about Islam and to speak out against U.S. violence in the Middle East. Which, I might point out, is my first amendment right to do."

He paused, in thought, and suddenly launched into a sermon-like rant about the true meaning of the Islamic faith. He quoted the Qur'an with fervency. He broke into Arabic several times. He sang. Finally, he ended with, "...I answer only to one authority, Mr. Walker. What they say I did, whether or not I did those things, is of no consequence."

Parveen sat back, smiling.

Walker sat listening to all of this, a nearly ten minute verbal rampage, with a rapt stare of disbelief. Glancing at the lawyer, who said nothing, Bannister held up his hand. "Mr. Mustafa. Wait, please. Let me ask a question or two." Parveen nodded. "You and Hussein Bejan, the charges say, travelled together, took video of potential jihad targets and made them available to known terrorists."

He paused, but Mustafa's only response was an intent gaze at him through the glasses.

"Do you deny going to Canada to plan a potential escape?" Walker continued. "Planning to go to a paramilitary training camp in Syria conducted by known terrorists? Discussing attacks on American oil facilities to disrupt the economy? Do you plan to address all these charges in your trial?"

Parveen smiled again, his voice still calm. "They kidnapped me less than two weeks after my wedding, did you know that?"

His cousin spoke for the first time. "His poor mother didn't know what was going on. She doesn't speak much English, you know. She fasted so long she fell ill. I told her Parveen's only crime was sharing vacation videos on line with his friends. Those are the videos that are supposedly material support of jihad?" His voice grew louder, became harsher. "They told Parveen they had telephone tape of his mother giving him permission to travel for jihad. This is a lie.

She only gave him permission to go see relatives, and to get married."

Bannister continued, "Hussein Bejan has reportedly told authorities..."

Mustafa interrupted him. "The FBI has Hussein Bejan holed up in some secret place, I'm sure under constant interrogation. They might make him say certain things to suit their purpose. But we are just a couple of young guys, naïve and immature, talking about things going on in the world. I am not a terrorist, and he is not a terrorist. We worship our God at prayer in the mosque, and we sometimes travel together and visit mutual friends. That's all there is to it."

The reporter sat straight up in his chair. "You and Hussein attend the same mosque?"

Parveen nodded. "Of course."

"Which mosque?" Bannister asked, then, lying, "I have it somewhere in my notes but I forget..."

"Masjid Al-Emaan of Atlanta," Mustafa confirmed. "It's no secret we pray together there and discuss the state of the world. It is there we learn more about the true nature of Islam and the ultimate authority of Allah."

"Time's about up," the lawyer leaned in.

Bannister turned toward him. "Will you represent Mr. Mustafa at his trial?"

The lawyer shook his head no. "He'll likely be moved to Atlanta for trial. Parveen will have a lawyer appointed by the judge, but he intends to represent himself."

"Really? Is that a good idea?" Walker asked, his eyebrows arched in astonishment.

The New York counsel grinned and nodded his head toward Parveen. "Ask him. He has all the answers."

After the meeting, Bannister hurried to the locker where he

was required to store his belongings. Parveen Mustafa's cousin followed, claiming his things from another locker, then walked toward Bannister as the guard eyed him warily.

"Mr. Walker," Mustafa's cousin said, "I ask you to remember one thing when you cover Parveen's trial. His so-called crime is producing literature for a website publication, gossiping back and forth with people he knows online and working on a website. That is all."

"Can he honestly deny he and Hussein talked about doing those things—providing information on buildings to bomb in Washington, D.C., and doing things that would disrupt U.S. commerce?"

"Talking is not a crime, Mr. Walker. As a news reporter, you know well what the first amendment is about. I ask as the trial goes on that you focus on the difference between talking and action. I think you'll conclude Parveen Mustafa is not guilty of any terrorist act."

Bannister extended his hand. "That's not for me to decide, is it?" he said. "I won't be sitting in judgment in that courtroom, only reporting what goes on."

After the guard checked him out, Bannister rushed excitedly out onto the street, yanking his cellphone from his bag.

"How did it go?" Grace Gleason asked on the other end.

Bannister's voice exuded excitement. "Grace, this guy is an incredibly interesting piece of work. The trial is sure to be unusual, putting it mildly. I can't quote any of what he said in there for public consumption, as you know. But his cousin talked to me outside the attorney room, and I don't see why I can't use any of that. He tried to make Parveen's case that his cousin is not guilty of any terrorist activity."

"Can you get the cousin on our show from a remote?"

"I'm sure of it," Bannister answered. "But Grace, here's the bigger news. I may have hit the jackpot. This guy Mustafa and Hussein Bejan attended mosque together, regularly."

"That huge one near the Georgia Tech campus?"

"No, Aahil Moghaddam's mosque in the west end neighborhood," he blurted. "Now we have the two of them connected with the Imam who shot the deputies."

"Omigosh!" Grace exclaimed. "One step closer to making a connection that Moghaddam might have influenced their actions. Maybe now we have enough information to work out an interview with Hussein Bejan."

"And maybe Aahil Moghaddam as well," Walker added.

"Great work, Bannister," Grace said. "Now get your behind out of New York and back to Atlanta. We still have scads of work to do."

"Scads?"

"Technical news term," she joshed. "You'll catch on."

CHAPTER TWENTY-ONE: The Grind

"I have you set up with the spanking preacher."

MaryAnne McWherter was in a nonstop, grind-it-out mode as planning for the show came down to the final few elements. The producer would dash to the workspace of Grace or Bannister or David Williams, barking out the news of her most recently completed task and then move on to the next. This time, she stuck her head over Grace's cubicle panel and announced the latest interview arrangement.

"You're all set for three this afternoon," she continued.

"Where?"

"His church, believe it or not. He insisted, his place or not at all. Jankowski's going to shoot it for you, but take your own car. Steve will come back here, but I need you to get to the airport and pick up Bannister Walker when he gets in from New York." She reached a slip of paper over the panel and dropped it on Grace's desk. "Delta 1845, five-thirty. I'd ask someone else to do it, but there isn't anyone. He could hire a ride, but I figured it would be good for you two to have some time together and talk about his Brooklyn venture. And all the rest of the stuff going on. Okay?"

Grace gave a mock salute. "Okay, general." And MaryAnne was off to fight another skirmish elsewhere.

The tech manager, Williams, was in the editing suite when Grace located him. "David, can we go through the interviews I did with those moms of kids who were spanked? I need to have the right perspective when I question the preacher."

"Easy peasy," David smiled. He began to rummage through his rapidly growing collection of "Unholy Mind Games" videos.

"While you're searching, I'll see if Steve can join us. It might help him get some ideas about how to photograph the interview."

Steve's response to her text was positive; he'd be there in five minutes. After he arrived, Williams played first the video of Shaniqua Forrester, the mother who sued the preacher over spanking her daughter. *"We're alleging the man damaged more than skin on her backside, know what I mean?"* They watched her say. *"That's a harm she might not ever forget, might not ever get over. I won't go back until that man gets removed from our pulpit."*

Next, David played the video of Miranda Young, the other mother of a beaten child Grace interviewed. They all watched with rapt horror as Steve's close-ups showed the boy's injuries, large purple and yellow splotches on his legs and buttocks and an ugly, open wound on his thigh.

His mother was heard over the video saying, *"I cried and cried while they were doing this to him, right there in Sunday service. I begged them to stop, but there are some people with strong bodies and strong opinions supporting Pastor Freeman and his 'don't spare the rod' approach. Nobody would listen to me. I was helpless, and so was my son."*

"That's enough," Grace said as she shuddered in disbelief. "I was there and saw it in person, yet I still get the willies watching the video. Steve, I'm going to put a full-court press on this man. We'll have great footage for the series."

Steve nodded understanding. "Let me know when you're ready to roll," he told her.

The church was in a broken part of the city. As close in as the neighborhood was to downtown, one would expect the area to be a prime target for developers. Businesses and industries would have easy access to the rest of the city's commerce—the huge cola company, major telecommunications firms, the biggest banks—not to mention easy access to the highway running out to the airport.

But instead, the area languished in wasted opportunity. Several parallel streets of poverty and crime striped through the neighborhood. Hookers and drug dealers on the street corners were common. Ramshackle, deteriorating structures housed some of the metro's poorest residents, and property tax bills of less than one hundred dollars on some houses spoke of the region's run-down and neglected condition.

Smack in the middle of this mess sat the modest, brick structure with a huge wooden cross on its roof, called the Church of Faith.

They were waiting for Grace and her cameraman. The Reverend Dontell Freeman and several of his devotees stood rigidly in front of the altar as the Big Six team approached down the aisle. The men waiting wore immaculate dark suits and ties and nodded and shook hands in somber welcome.

"I'm glad you came, Miss Gleason," the preacher said, his large voice echoing throughout the empty sanctuary. "It's time for you to hear the truth about Dontell Freeman. It's time for you to hear how I'm saving souls, not breaking them." The Reverend Dontell Freeman was fire and brimstone. He was a tornado of animation and verve. His strong baritone voice booming out a deep Southern dialect gave sound to the dynamo he was.

"That's what I'm here for, reverend," Grace responded calmly, politely. "I want you to have the opportunity to explain what you do here. Steve, are you ready?"

Jankowski nodded and turned his lights and camera on. He did a quick white paper check with Grace and gave her the okay sign.

Grace looked into the camera. "Today I'm here at the Church of Faith where the Reverend Dontell Freeman is pastor. If you missed the news about Reverend Freeman lately, he was arrested with several of his congregation for allegedly spanking children during church service." She turned to the minister. "Reverend Freeman, do you deny whipping children here?"

"No, Grace, I do not. I and my followers, some of them here today, teach children the consequences of their actions. If they disrespect their parents, they're going to get spanked. If they curse or try some kind of sexual activity, we teach them a lesson. They know when they done wrong. And they know when they do, they got to pay the punishment."

Grace asked, "What about the parents? They don't all agree with your spanking philosophy, do they?"

Freeman yanked off his glasses and pulled a handkerchief out of his breast pocket, wiping them clean energetically. "Those parents are as misguided as their delinquent children," he hissed.

"Spare the rod, spoil the child is what we teach here. If mama-pansy and daddy-pansy don't want their young ones to behave, or pay for being naughty, they don't have to come here."

"Some of them were members here before you came to be pastor. They say they don't want to give up on their church, but they just want you out."

The reverend inhaled deeply and his response spewed like a geyser. "They ain't getting me out, Grace. Ain't getting me out. Look at these men here. They believe in me, in what I'm doing. Hundreds more like 'em. We're living in a world of hate and sin and depraved behavior. None of those things are goin' to take place in the Church of Faith."

Grace paused. "Reverend Freeman, I want to move on to another subject, that of your efforts to marry young girls to convicts out on parole. Some say you take girls with a poor home life and force them into these marital arrangements. What do you say?"

Reverend Freeman slammed his glasses back on his face, stuffed the handkerchief back into its pocket with drama, and huffed out the answer. "I say you got part of it right, Grace. These girls have no home life, no supervision, no role models. They are engaging in sex and running wild on the streets, getting into all sorts of mischief. I show them how being married sets up a stable future for them. These men, many of them undeserving of their jail time, many of them born-again Christians, get jobs when they get out. We help them find a home. They deserve a good wife who can help them get their life back, keep them away from sin."

His black eyes fixed a laser look directly into the camera. "The second part, the part Grace Gleason got wrong, is nobody gets forced into nothing. These girls want to get married, have a good man to come home to. Not running the streets, being whores." He turned toward Grace. "You ask them."

"I have," Grace said.

Reverend Freeman stiffened, eyes wide with surprise behind the glasses. "And? None of them said we forced them into this, did they?"

"No, reverend, they didn't. At least, not while their husbands were standing right there, listening to every word."

Grace helped Jankowski pack his gear into the van. "I guess MaryAnne told you I'm going to pick up Bannister Walker at the airport. Think you can find your way back?"

Steve laughed. "Maybe I'll drive around the neighborhood a little bit, looking for a couple of those drug-taking young hookers."

She slapped his shoulder in mock reprimand. "Steve Jankowski, you're irredeemable," she said, her mouth wide open feigning shock. "What if I told your wife how you talk?"

He chuckled. "She knows I'm harmless. Seriously, Grace, good job."

"Thanks," she said. "Drive carefully."

"You drive carefully," he warned back. "You're the one who's going to be in six lanes of rush hour traffic, trying to dodge idiots who are late for their flights."

Walker's plane was late, but he only had carry-on so there would be no wait for luggage. As they walked to the parking lot, Grace handed him a paper bag. "I took the liberty of picking up sandwiches for the trip in," she told him. "I have bottled water in the car."

"Great," he said. "I only had pretzels on the flight. But hey, you're going to eat and drive? Don't you know that's dangerous? Even against the law in some counties?"

She shot him a reproving look. "You do it all the time, and you know it."

The trip to the station took nearly an hour. They talked about various aspects of the upcoming series and the remaining steps needed to be ready. "You know, Bannister," she said between bites, "I'm really happy Lohmeyer put you on this adventure with me. I had my doubts, just because we hadn't ever worked together. But you've been great."

"It's a pleasure," Walker answered. "You're a real pro. For a girl, I mean."

She looked over at him, eyes wide with surprise. Seeing him trying to hold back his amusement while also trying to swallow a bite of his sandwich, she broke out into laughter.

"The truth is," Bannister's voice turned serious, "I enjoy

working with you, but I don't know anything about you. How'd you get started?"

"When I think back on it, it all seems like some kind of cosmic blur," she answered. "My high school counselor helped me get a journalism scholarship to the University of Texas."

"Hook 'em horns," Bannister laughed.

"Right. I married my college sweetheart, a lawyer. But our careers clashed, for lack of a better description, and we parted ways. I've been trying to balance a demanding career with single motherhood every since."

"If you ask me, you're doing a damned good job of it."

She shot a skeptical look at her colleague. "Tell my daughter that, will you?"

"She knows."

They rode in silence, and Grace finally said, "Almost there. I mean the station, not the program. We still have some serious pieces to fit into the puzzle."

"I know," he said. "Especially the Imam. MaryAnne's working hard, trying to get me in the door."

"Don't let her stop. It's important."

"You're telling me."

"That's what worries me," she said.

"What?"

"I'm wondering what we're leaving out. Do we have what we need to accomplish anything meaningful? I'm worried we'll blather on and on for a week, and then nothing will happen."

"Don't worry," Bannister said. "Grace, I know something's going to result from all of this hard work."

"Oh, sure. I just hope it's not a mass firing."

They giggled together again as she pulled down the long driveway to the station.

CHAPTER TWENTY-TWO: Invasion of Privacy

"Hello. This is Behram Quershi."

Grace immediately recognized the soft and pleasant voice of the documentary maker who visited her in the station lobby. It had a firm but respectful tone, with a hint of accent from his native Pakistan.

"Mr. Quershi, this is Grace Gleason from Channel Six."

"Yes. How are you?"

"I'm fine, Mr. Quershi. I hope you remember my promise when you were here at our station. I told you if ever I thought there would be an opportunity to provide your point of view in any of our stories involving Islam, I would contact you."

"I remember."

Grace felt a bit off-put by Quershi's terse responses, but she knew that might be the nature of his personality, nothing more. "Well, we're going to do a series on several different religions, including Islam, and I'm interested in including you in the discussion. Would you consider it?"

"Yes, of course," Quershi answered. "I would welcome a chance to talk to you about it."

She breathed a sigh of relief. A moderate viewpoint, one telling the positive side of the Muslim faith, from someone who abhorred the radical terrorists, was sorely needed. "That's great, Mr. Quershi. Can you come and discuss it with me?"

Quershi paused a moment. "I have a better idea," he said. "Let me invite you here, to my home. I would like for you to meet my wife and possibly a friend of ours. If you have time, we would like to have you to dinner."

Grace was feeling the time pinch to get everything ready. Yet the refined manner of this man, and his generous invitation, was too compelling. "When?" she asked.

"At your discretion. Tomorrow evening after prayers would be very good for us."

After the conversation, Grace felt extremely positive about this addition to the plan. Given the breakthrough Bannister Walker had in New York with Parveen Mustafa, and with Quershi's agreement to consider an appearance, the aspect of the series that probed Aahil Moghaddam and his mosque was shaping up quickly. But there was still much work to be done on the other aspects of the program—the allegations against the retired priest, and the spanking minister controversy.

Glancing at her watch, she realized she was already ten minutes late for a meeting with David Williams, the young engineer who was working on the technical aspects of the series.

"Sorry I'm late," she huffed into the editing suite.

Williams looked up from a project and nodded. "No problem, Grace. I already have everything set up over there." He pointed toward a desk in the corner with two chairs and a laptop computer.

"You know I don't like doing it this way," she said.

"I agree," David nodded. "An interview with the guy in Tuskegee..."

"...the minister in Tuskegee," she corrected.

"...with the minister in Tuskegee," he continued, "will leave a lot to be desired, quality-wise. But Grace, you said yourself he won't travel to Atlanta."

"I know," she acknowledged, " and the closest television outlets are in Montgomery and Auburn. He won't even go over there to their studios. Unless they have a reason to travel to Tuskegee for a story, I can't persuade them to cover the interview for us."

Williams shrugged his shoulders. "So here we are." He opened the laptop and pulled up the video conferencing app.

Grace sighed. "Yes, here we are. Does he know what to do?"

"I've walked him through it. But he already knew, said he does frequent video conferences with other pastors and even some of his shut-in parishioners."

David worked his keyboard magic and the Reverend Mercedes Humphries' image appeared. Grace leaned into the screen and greeted him. "Reverend Humphries, it's good to see you again."

"Yes," the elderly pastor responded. "Nice to see you too, Grace. I'm afraid we didn't leave things on a very positive note when you were here."

"That was my fault, reverend. Not to worry. As you know, I want to talk to you again about your friend, Reverend Dontell Freeman, this time on the record for our newscast."

"I understand. But Grace, what you will hear from me will be what I told you here in Tuskegee. You know he's a long-time friend of mine."

"Reverend Humphries, I understand, and that's fine. I want your point of view, nothing more. Shall we get started?"

The interview began, and as Humphries predicted, it proceeded along the same lines as their conversation in his Mount Ararat Baptist Church that day. Reverend Freeman was a long-time friend of his. The Atlanta minister had the well-being of the young girls and the parolees at heart when he arranged their marriages. Mercedes Humphries supported what Reverend Freeman was doing, trying to save souls.

But as the questioning continued, Grace felt discomfited. It seemed she was tossing softballs to the preacher, and he was hitting line drives right back at her. This was too controversial a subject to let it slide with a Dontell Freeman endorsement.

As the interview began to wind down, she had a fresh idea, and asked, "Reverend Humphries, a final question or two. I'd like to know, did you ever feel uncomfortable with any of the marriages you performed for Reverend Freeman?"

"What do you mean?" he asked.

"Did you ever, even once, feel maybe you shouldn't be marrying one of the girls? For any reason?"

"Well..." he hesitated, squinting his eyes in recollection, "... there might have been a time or two..."

"A time or two when you were uncomfortable?"

"Possibly," he said. "Some of those men were pretty rough and tough, you know? Some did years of hard time behind bars for felonies. These girls were very young and impressionable."

"So you might have had doubts about the union?" Grace pressed.

"Possibly, once or twice, but it was not for me to judge. I had to trust Dontell's reasoning. He knew them far better than I." He paused for a moment. "Then there was the other thing."

"Other thing?"

"Their age. Now, understand Miss Gleason, every woman in her thirties looks like a teenager to an old man like me." He emitted a small giggle. "But I must say, a few of the girls he sent over didn't look over twelve or thirteen to me."

Grace tried not to sound astounded. "How often did you have those doubts?"

"I wouldn't call them doubts. But once or twice, the question entered my head, 'Is this young lady the age it says on her marriage certificate?' Just a sort of curiosity, you see."

"Then why did you proceed with the weddings in those cases?"

Humphries cleared his throat, groping for words. "Well, I... you know...I had no real reason not to. Reverend Freeman knew them, and they had licenses issued by the judge. It was not my place to second-guess. I just...once or twice, you see...felt like I was marrying a mere child."

At that, Grace wrapped up the interview.

"I feel like I said too much," Reverend Humphries admitted as they said their goodbyes. "I shouldn't have expressed those doubts."

"You spoke from the heart," Grace told him. "That's all I wanted you to do. Reverend Humphries, thank you so much for your time."

David signed them off. Grace sat back and looked at the engineer, her eyes wide. "That was incredible," she said.

"Sounds like the old boy..."

"...Minister..." she admonished again.

"...the old minister might have let his guard down a little?"

"He didn't help his friend's case," she responded. "David, it's getting late. You said you wanted to show me the promotion the marketing department came up with?"

He nodded. "Let me text MaryAnne. She wants to see it, too."

Within a few minutes, the producer rushed in. "Grace, how did it go with the Alabama preacher?"

"Better than expected," Grace said, smiling at Williams. "We'll have more than one side of the story, that's for sure. David, let's see that promo."

Williams switched on a video and Christina Cruz, the anchor, appeared with dynamic choral church music in the background. *Religion. We all know it's good for the soul. But is religion also sometimes a platform for inappropriate dogma? Are some religious leaders crossing the line, using their authority and power for unholy objectives? Are some of today's youth exposed at an early age to improper activity in their religious institutions?* As Christina continued the message, the video switched to images flashing across the screen of Reverend Freeman, Aahil Moghaddam, Hussein Bejan, Parveen Mustafa, then Father Bianci and the shadowy image of a young man with his head bowed. *Big Six News will explore these questions and more next week, when Grace Gleason and Bannister Walker try to find the answers.* Christina came back on. *Watch "Unholy Mind Games" every day next week, Monday through Friday, from five-thirty to six before the evening news.* The music faded as did the image of the anchorwoman and text giving the dates and times crawled across the darkened screen.

"Wow," MaryAnne exclaimed.

"Wow indeed," Grace parroted. "I only hope we can live up to the hype."

"We will," the producer assured.

Grace felt energized by the recent events. Everything seemed to be taking shape. As she drove home, she realized it was dusk and she hadn't eaten anything all day except a protein bar. She was exhausted, but hungry, too. She pulled into the lot of the Fusion Grill.

The usual bartender was there. Odd, she thought, he was always there when she stopped in, but she had never asked his name. She shrugged at the unimportance of this thought.

"Not the martini, I guess," he grinned at her as she plopped down in her spot at the end of the bar.

"Iced tea," she laughed. "And a hamburger."

"Red meat? That's not like you, Grace Gleason."

"Medium rare," she answered, a little embarrassed that he knew her name but she didn't know his. Sometimes she grew tired of being recognized by others, especially viewers driving by who pulled to the curb and yelled, "Hi Grace," as if they were old friends. She knew some other media personalities, such as the pompous anchor Jackson Davis, reveled in such attention. It made her increasingly uncomfortable. Not that she didn't like having a fan base. She wouldn't be human if she didn't. But sometimes the attention could become tedious.

Half an hour later, her appetite curbed, Grace pulled into the driveway and spotted her cross-the-street neighbor, Evelyn Bradshaw, sweeping her front walk. Grace gave her a wave. The woman had greeted Grace so warmly when she first moved into the neighborhood, she felt a brief pang of regret she hadn't sought out the woman's friendship. Sometimes the news business interfered with the normal way of living life, of culturing friendships. She knew it was no excuse, but her constant exposure to the frenetic public side of society seemed to drive her deeper into a desire for privacy.

As she pulled into her garage, Grace experienced an odd impression something was not right. She knew others might dismiss such a sensation as merely exhaustion, or the disorientation of arriving home late. But Grace long ago learned to pay attention to these hunches. She couldn't put her finger on what might be wrong as she climbed out of the car, but the feeling stayed with her as she opened the door. She entered the kitchen warily, but everything seemed surprisingly in order. Then, as she walked by her office to drop off her

185

computer bag, she stopped stock-still, horrified at what she saw. Drawers pulled out and overturned. Binders, papers, books and memorabilia pulled from her credenza and strewn all over the room. Her office chair overturned. A lamp shattered on the floor.

Stunned, Grace dropped her computer bag and rushed to her desk. Everything on it had been ransacked. Her hand went to her mouth as she realized the two electronic tablets she kept there, for note taking and photographing, were gone. She pulled out the lap drawer, the only one the intruders hadn't yanked from the desk. Her contact file and calendar book were missing. Several thumb drives were gone. Her heart was beating at a breakneck pace. Grabbing her cell phone from her bag, she dialed nine-one-one.

Grace sat next to the front door and waited with her head in her hands. Her pulse was a thumping drumbeat and she could feel her eyes burn as they teared up. Who could have done this? The same people who broke her window? The anonymous caller? The Trans Am driver? Her mind was still racing as two police officers knocked.

As the cops entered, Grace was bolstered by what she saw. Behind them, also stepping into the room, were her neighbors, Horace Gunter and Evelyn Bradshaw.

"We saw the cruisers drive up," Horace said. "What happened?" Everyone followed Grace into her office, and she showed them the chaos. Tears of dread and fright streamed down her face. One of the officers began writing down Grace's statement while his partner walked through the rest of the house.

"One of your bedroom windows was forced," the cop told her when he returned. "Any idea who might have done this?" Grace told him about the recent harassment, including a description of the black Trans Am with gold striping.

"Don't touch anything here," one of the officers instructed. "A detective will come out in the morning and dust for prints. We'll file a report and you can pick it up by tomorrow afternoon."

Grace nodded as they left, and waved thanks as Gunter followed them out. As she shut the door, she could hear him say, "... retired from the force in Charlottesville..."

Evelyn remained. "Grace, I'm going to take you home with me. You can't stay here alone tonight. A hot bath and fresh guest room bed will make you feel safe."

Grace nodded, packed a small bag and crossed the street to stay at Evelyn's house. But there would be no sleeping. After tossing for what seemed like hours, she looked at the clock on the bed stand. Eleven o'clock, still far earlier than she imagined. She retrieved her cell phone from her bag and dialed. It would be ten in Dallas, and her old friend and confidante, Ned Moore, the retired detective, might still be awake.

He wasn't. But as Grace unfolded the events of the evening, and the previous threatening encounters, he was sympathetic. "Jeez no, Grace, don't apologize for calling so late. I'm glad you did. Do you want me to come up there?"

Moore's offer was no surprise to Grace. Working as closely as they had on crime stories in Dallas, the detective became a sort of father figure to her. Ned was the one who rescued her when a risky murder suspect attacked her and her daughter. Even after she moved to Atlanta and Moore retired, he accompanied her to Mexico as she worked on a dangerous drug cartel story.

"No, Ned, there's no need for you to come up," she assured. "But thanks for offering. It means a lot to me. You and I went through some real wars together there in Texas. I just needed to hear your voice. The police have all the information, and I have a retired cop living right next door, plus he always has his police buddies hanging around his back yard. I can call on him to help if I need it."

"So who's the cop? The one next door?"

"You wouldn't know him. He moved here from Virginia. His name is Horace Gunter, and he…"

"Gunter? I remember him, Grace. We attended a couple of the same conferences."

"That's right, I forgot. He told me he knew you."

"I wouldn't say 'knew me,' exactly. But yeah, I met the guy and we talked. Grace, you said you could call on him to help. But I wouldn't be too sure."

"What do you mean?"

"He tried to get all buddy-buddy when I saw him at these conferences. You know, popping for beers, wanting to hang around when I was with my own crowd. But Grace, he didn't have such a good reputation back there in Virginia. I inquired around about the guy when he got so chummy. He apparently did some minor un-ethical stuff and nobody wanted to be his friend. Word is he hung around with the wrong people, even got demoted once for some kind of infraction."

"I had no idea," she exclaimed.

"Of course you didn't. And Grace, you said some cops were fraternizing with him there at his house? Don't be too surprised if they're sympathetic with the bad actors from the force you helped put away in Atlanta."

"The ones who ran a robbery ring and robbed and killed that strip club owner!" she said.

"Yeah. You know some of those retired police he hangs with probably worked with those guys. Who knows where their loyalties lie? If it's with the boys you helped catch, those rogue cops might be in jail, but Gunter's visitors are not."

"Ned, do you think Horace might be behind some of the harassment I've been getting?"

"Who knows? I wouldn't trust him. Be sure you keep your security system on, even when you're at home."

"Ned, you're going to kill me."

"No. Let me guess. No security system?"

"That's right. I had one at the townhouse I lived in before, but there wasn't one in this place when I bought it, and I just didn't get around to it. Now I feel like an idiot. And Ned, Horace has a key to my house."

Ned let her sit in silence for a minute, to let her own foolishness sink in. Then, "I shouldn't be surprised. You've always been something of a risk-taker. Okay, Grace, here's what I want you to do. First, is there somebody you can trust to come oversee a locksmith changing your locks and a company installing a security system?"

"Well, my daughter Megan's too busy with her studies. There is this one guy, a professor I've seen a time or two, who's very interested in becoming a bigger part of my life."

"You trust him?"

"Without reservation."

"Than get him over there tomorrow. Do it. Now, here's my next question. When you and I worked together on that murder story here in Dallas, you got a license to carry. Remember? When the perpetrator Udo Holthaus attacked you and Megan before he was caught?"

"Yes," she answered. "I went out and bought a Glock nine millimeter and took shooting lessons. A certain police detective I knew gave me advice."

"Yup, I remember," he said. "Did you keep your carry license and apply in Georgia when you moved?"

"I did," she answered, "I thought I should at least stay current. I still have the pistol, but I haven't been to the range here. I've been too doggoned busy, Ned."

"You're not too busy anymore. Get over to the range and get your aim in shape. Keep the gun with you, even at your desk in the office."

"I can't do that, Ned," Grace said. "They won't allow me to have a gun in the newsroom. If I tried to sneak it in and got caught, they'd fire me on the spot."

"Okay, then keep it locked in your glove compartment. I want you to have access to it wherever you go, got it?"

"I do," she answered glumly, hating this conversation.

"Grace, keep your eyes open. Stay in plain sight of other people. Secure your home base. These people might or might not be deadly, but you can't take that chance." Ned was again silent for a moment. "I lost my wife to cancer. Don't have many of my old buddies around anymore, either. Even though you're hundreds of miles away, you're one of the few people I still have on this green earth. Don't you go and let them take that away from me."

"I won't, Ned. I swear I won't."

CHAPTER TWENTY-THREE: Moghaddam

After his capture in Tennessee and return to Atlanta to face trial, Aahil Moghaddam's publicity machinery went into action. Supporters held daily protests outside the Atlanta Penitentiary where he was held without bond. His lawyers began setting his defense in motion through public statements after his arraignment. His confidante, Khalila Noorani, was widely quoted about his innocence in publications sympathetic to Muslim viewpoints, and she granted on-line video interviews geared to followers of the Islamic faith.

Although many of Atlanta's Muslims counted on those sources for their information, the broader metro population was not widely exposed to news about the Imam. The daily paper and electronic news outlets covered his initial court appearance and then moved on to other news. At the next court appearance, or when jury selection began, they would return to their coverage of the case.

Bannister Walker planned to change all of that. "I'm encouraged by the off-record interview I did with Mustafa in New York," he told MaryAnne McWherter. "We'll never get the judge here to agree to an interview with Moghaddam. But if I can get on his visitor list like I did in Brooklyn, maybe I can learn some things that'll be useful."

"You can't use it," MaryAnne warned as they walked together to morning meeting. "Bannister, I've talked to his lawyers until I was blue in the gills. They won't let him speak on the record."

"Why not? They obviously want to get his story out there—that the cops got the wrong guy, that the deputy's statement about wounding the perpetrator proves it, that his description doesn't begin to match their client."

"Maybe," the producer agreed. "But at the same time, I don't think they'll want to risk a venue change. Won't the jury pool in Atlanta be more sympathetic to his cause than, say, Cherokee County or Rome, Georgia?"

"Could be," Walker said. "But MaryAnne, it seems to me we're worrying about the wrong things. We have nothing to lose by talking to the man. We can decide what to air or not to air, after we hear what his attorneys will allow him to say."

MaryAnne nodded her agreement. "If I can persuade his lawyers, do you think you'll be able to get in and talk to him?"

"I think so, if they'll simply put me on the list. If not, at least maybe I can get him on the phone. From what I've learned about him, he wouldn't want to miss an opportunity for a telephone sermon, at the very least. One way or another, I'm going to talk to Aahil Moghaddam."

"I'll keep trying," she promised.

Shortly after the meeting, one of the Imam's lawyers called Bannister. "Your producer asked us to call you, Mr. Walker. She's a determined young woman."

"And?"

"Look, we're going out there to see him. We have legal business to take care of, but if you promise to stick to a half-hour, no cameras, no recording equipment, we can get you on the list to accompany us."

"When?" Bannister jumped on the invitation.

"This afternoon."

"Today?" the surprised reporter asked.

"Last time I checked, this afternoon meant today," the lawyer scoffed. "Meet us at the front entrance at one. Don't be late."

Immediately after lunchtime, Bannister drove through downtown Atlanta, south past the former home of the 1996 Olympic Games stadium, later converted to an Atlanta Braves baseball stadium. Being new to Atlanta, Walker had never been in this section of town. He had conducted a hurried online search to learn more about the area he'd be driving through.

It was a routine he always followed, thoroughly researching the landscape of any story he was about to cover. "I know I tend to over-prepare," he told Buck Lohmeyer when they worked together in South Carolina, "unlike these young J-school grads who come in and simply wing it. It probably sounds old-school, but I feel like added background knowledge can make my reporting better than theirs. Or at least something I find out might come in handy for a story down the road."

As he researched the route to the prison, he learned a lot about his new city. The old ball park, sold recently as the team moved to a different part of Atlanta, was surrounded by neighborhoods in varying stages of ruin or, conversely for others, revitalization. Avenue Park, Marsh Point, Victorytown, Autumn Hill, Woodstown were names he remembered seeing in his abbreviated search earlier in the day. Even though some of those communities had experienced double-digit vacancies at various times, others became the objects of energetic redevelopment at the hands of active community associations.

Yet even the greatest intentions weren't enough to contend with the ravages of the bursting housing bubble of 2008. Many of the reconstruction projects died, and the tsunami of foreclosures hit this area particularly hard.

Bannister turned southeast past the location of an iconic old barbecue, shuttered five years previously after feeding cornbread and Brunswick stew to Atlanta for sixty-five years.

"It's a shame you can't stop by there today on your way and put some of that great 'cue in your mouth," McWherter told him as she helped him plan his route. "That place was a super treat, although it went downhill some after the owner died, and the new guy finally closed it. There's still some good barbecue in town, but nothing like that place in its heyday."

As he approached the massive prison structure, Bannister stopped at the guard gate. "I'm a reporter from Channel Six News," he explained. "I'm here to meet the lawyer of Aahil Moghaddam, who's being held here."

"He's already gone through," the guard said. "Let's see some ID, please." The guard stared at the card, looked at the visitor list on a clipboard, glanced back at Walker and handed the ID to him. "He's parked in the lot to the right. Cadillac SUV, white. Said he'd be waiting for you and will accompany you in to get your credentials." He nodded. "Have a nice visit."

The lawyer took Bannister through the process and into the section where rooms awaited lawyers needing privacy with their clients. Aahil was already there, pacing slowly back and forth in the tiny space. Bannister immediately recognized the Imam from having covered the initial court appearance, but he noted how much weight the man had lost, and how much more unkempt his personal appearance was, especially his longer, more scraggly reddish beard. Dressed in a prison jumpsuit rather than his customary throbe and skull cap, he walked bent as if incarceration was already taking its toll on him.

The Imam settled gently into one of the metal chairs, across from Bannister, and nodded.

"Mr. Moghaddam, thank you for seeing me today," Walker began. "How have you been treated?"

Aahil smiled, showing a mischievous glint in his eyes for the first time. In an uncharacteristically calm, quiet voice he asked, "You mean are they beating me every day?" He let out a low chuckle.

Bannister smiled and shook his head. "Never having been arrested before, I'd like to know what it's like in there."

"Let me put it this way. I would much rather be in the masjid, leading prayers, studying the Qur'an, teaching, being a devoted servant of Allah. Yet it's not for me to question the wisdom of the Almighty. If I have been put here for a reason, so be it."

194

"You think Allah has a purpose for you here, in prison?"

Moghaddam stretched out his hands. "I am here."

"Your followers protest outside frequently. They say you couldn't have done what you're accused of. Yet your history is one of violence. You advocated violent action when you were Slay T. Jefferson, leading protests for California Lives Matter, is that not true?"

The Imam leaned his head back and stared into Bannister's eyes. "I've never denied that I led a revolution," he began. "Revolution is the tool of those who are oppressed because of their race or what they believe. You're a black man in America. You can't have lived this long without feeling the injustices heaped on us by authorities. What have you done about it, Mr. Walker? Have you stood up for your brothers who have been beaten down by laws we didn't make, by police we didn't hire? Why aren't you locking arms with those protestors you saw seeking justice for me? Because justice for me is justice for all of us who've had their boot on our neck. Sometimes, to right those wrongs, violence is necessary. Isn't that what America was founded on? Hasn't it been a way of life in this country since the beginning? Don't they call it the American revolution? Those who fought it were seeking freedom from their oppressors. Are you getting my point?"

Throughout this speech, Moghaddam grew more animated, his voice more strident. Bannister waited, hoping to ratchet down the emotion. Finally, he said, "Those were views you expressed repeatedly before your conversion to Islam while you were in jail previously. You converted to what many of its followers call a peaceful religion. As a leader of the Muslim faith, do you still feel violence is justified?"

The prisoner returned to his calmer demeanor. "I have not stopped looking for justice. I will never stop seeking it. In fact, as I became more knowledgeable in the truth of the Qur'an, I have grown to love Allah more than the state. Jihad means struggle, and one can only grow through struggle."

"Mr. Moghaddam, you pleaded not guilty to all the charges

against you. Many of your followers profess your innocence. In their press conference after your arraignment, your lawyers said they will prove you innocent beyond any reasonable doubt."

"All true," the Imam answered.

"Then tell me, if you didn't do it, why did you run? The authorities had to track you down in Tennessee."

Aahil looked at his lawyer, as if seeking permission before responding. Then, "I have been dealing with injustice all my adult life. In California, they charged me with so many things of which I was innocent."

Walker broke in, "Innocent? I've read the articles and seen your interviews. You preached a pretty fiery brand of violence to be so innocent, didn't you?"

"Preaching is not doing. If I need to rally people around putting pressure on the authorities who are oppressing them, that's not proof of criminal action, is it? They put me in jail not because of crimes committed but because of the color of my skin. Because I pushed people not to accept discrimination where it exists. And now, ever since my conversion, they have pursued me like a dog for my race and my beliefs."

"You mentioned jihad," Bannister said. "Do you promote jihad in your masjid? Do you preach radical terrorism to impressionable young people?"

Moghaddam sat quietly, pensively for a moment. "I tell my followers struggle is necessary to be free. I promote the search for justice, for freedom from the kind of persecution I've endured for many, many years. Whoever hears my message as the truth eventually understands his obligations to Allah and his duty to society."

"What does that mean, exactly, Mr. Moghaddam?"

"I leave it for you to decide what it means."

Now Bannister raised his voice. "That sounds like a cop-out. Do you promote terrorist jihad or not?"

Moghaddam's lawyer jumped in quickly. "Time is up. You need to wrap it up, Mr. Walker."

Bannister leaned in toward the Imam, still appearing agitated, his hands palms-down on the table in front of him. "Point blank, Mr. Moghaddam, two of your young followers are in jail right now, charged with material support of terrorism. Can you say you had nothing to do with their radicalization?"

Aahil fixed a hard look back at Bannister. "What is radical, can you tell me? Our struggle for freedom and justice cannot be just individual or as a group. It must be both. That is what I tell all who listen. Young or old, man or woman, each must decide what their struggle is about and how they are to honor Allah. That's all I'm going to say about those young men."

"Then let me change the subject abruptly, with one final question," Bannister responded. "As a leader of the Muslim faith, how do you justify some of the barbaric practices taking place in some Islamic countries?"

"Such as?"

"Beheading journalists. Bombing innocent adults and children at weddings and funerals. Binding and half-burying accused adulterers, then stoning them to death."

The Imam paused and then smiled. "Mr. Bannister, do you have a religion?"

"I was raised Baptist."

"You mention stoning. It's all over your Old Testament and even the New Testament."

"It was a method of death penalty for certain sins in those ancient times, that's true. But as you know, Mr. Moghaddam, my faith teaches me that all changed with the New Covenant. Old Testament laws were abrogated."

"Doesn't that make it difficult for a Jew who's loyal to the Torah to justify the practice?"

"I believe modern-day Jews loathe the brutal actions I just mentioned, including stoning. The prevailing thought among rabbis I've read is it's a practice that changed as mankind matured and evolved."

"It's convenient for them to think so," Moghaddam retorted, displaying for the first time in this interview the defiant smirk he often displayed in previous encounters.

**

Driving back, Walker was on his hands-free cell phone relating much of the interview to Grace. "He didn't say anything we haven't heard from him many times over the years. And of course, I wasn't allowed to ask any questions about the shootout or his murder defense. I got one question in about why he ran, but I felt constrained otherwise. And yet..."

"What?" Grace asked.

"...I felt one really important thing came out of it."

"What was that?"

"Hussein Bejan and Parveen Mustafa. When I asked the Imam about them, and about the charges against them, he offered no defense of his mosque. He didn't deny his message might have provided motivation for their alleged crimes."

"He didn't acknowledge it either, correct?"

"That's right," Walker answered. "But Grace, sometimes silence says more."

CHAPTER TWENTY-FOUR: Holy Mayhem

Grace's attendance at morning meetings became irregular. She and Bannister were running so hard to complete various pieces of the show, they had a pass when they needed to be truant. As the days counted down toward their Monday kickoff, they rarely showed up. On such a morning, when Grace was contemplating whether she had time to attend, she noticed Buck Lohmeyer hot-footing through the newsroom.

"What's up?" she queried him over her workstation panel as he passed.

The news director stopped abruptly and took a step toward her desk. "We just got a call. The state senator who sponsored the Victim Fairness bill that died in the legislature is holding a press conference."

"Mr. Lohmeyer, why didn't you say so?" she scolded. She jumped up from her chair and grabbed her computer bag. "Who's shooting it?"

Lohmeyer held up his hand in a halt gesture. "Hold on, Gleason. Scott Matthews is going to cover it."

"No. I'm the religion reporter. I have a vested interest in that topic for our series."

"It's a hot news story, Grace. We'll have it on the noon cast today. Scott is on it, he and Jankowski. They're already on their way."

"I'm going," Grace half-shouted. "I have a right to be there and see how it fits our religion series. Where is it?"

"Outside some law office where the lead lobbyist for the Atlanta Archdiocese works."

"Clark, Martin, Forsythe and Tweedy?" she asked.

"I think that's it," he said. "But I already told you, you're not going." Lohmeyer's pudgy face turned crimson as it so often did when he was challenged.

Grace pushed past him and sprinted toward the newsroom exit. "You can fire me if you want, Mr. Lohmeyer," she tossed over her shoulder. "But I'm going over there. That's an important story for 'Unholy Mind Games'."

She pushed through the exit door and was on her way to her car when one of the station's vans came toward her, headed toward the street. Grace waved it down and peered through the window. Steve Jankowski was behind the wheel, and Scott Matthews rode shotgun.

"What, Grace?" Matthews rolled down the window.

"Open up," Grace said. "I'm going with you."

"What about..." Matthews started.

"Lohmeyer?" she laughed. "He knows I'm out here. He's probably in Silver's office right now, trying to get me fired. Come on, open the door. We don't have time to talk."

As Grace climbed into the vehicle, her boss Buck Lohmeyer was catapulting into the general manager's office, angry and spoiling for an argument. Harvey Silver looked up from reading a report and motioned for his news director to sit. "Come on in, Buck. You look like Jackson Davis set his pants on fire or just knocked over camera three."

"I'm in no mood for jokes, Harvey," Lohmeyer sputtered. "It's that damned Gleason..."

"Okay, what's she done this time that has you doing doubles of antacid?"

"I'm serious, Harvey. The woman's insubordination is out of control. She just defied a decision I made and then dared me to fire her."

Silver listened in patient silence as his news director spilled out the details of the latest act of sabotage by their star reporter. Finally, the station manager said, "Buck, we're on the brink of launching a very risky venture, one you convinced me we should do to shore up ratings. Do you really want me to can the heart and soul of this series just days before we launch it?"

A grim look of resignation crossed Lohmeyer's jowly face. "No, Harvey, I don't. She exasperates me, that's all. I needed to blow off some steam."

**

While Buck Lohmeyer was venting in Harvey Silver's office, his favorite reporter, Bannister Walker, was sitting in a station van near the entrance to the Atlanta Federal Penitentiary. Photographer Cassandra Barrett was at the wheel.

"You're sure he's coming?" she asked.

"When I was here for the Moghaddam interview, I made friends with one of the guards there. I check in with him every day. Talking to someone who's on the air makes him feel important, and you'd be surprised what I can pick up from him. Yesterday he tipped me off that Bejan's lawyer is on the visitor list for this morning. He's coming."

"Do you know what he drives?"

"Cassandra, I do my homework, okay?" he sounded annoyed.

"Sorry. Just asking."

They waited another half-hour, watching cars go in and out of the gate. Finally, Walker reached out and put a hand on Cassandra's arm. "That's him. Third car in line. Grab your camera."

They jumped down from the van and Bannister walked toward the car, microphone in hand. Barrett scrambled to catch up. Walker turned and spoke toward the camera, which Cassandra got running just in time. "We have been unable to interview the 20-year-old student, Hussein Bejan, since his incarceration." Bannister reported. "We are told federal agents have interrogated him several times, however. Today one of his attorneys is about to enter the prison for a meeting with the young man accused of terrorism."

Bannister moved swiftly toward the car of the attorney as it stopped behind another car at the prison entrance gate. As the reporter approached the driver side, the first car moved through the gate. Bejan's lawyer drove to the gate, rolled down the window and showed the guard his ID. Then he peered up at Walker with an aggravated expression pasted across his bearded face.

With Cassandra's camera pointed over Bannister's shoulder and toward the lawyer, Walker questioned him. "Sir, Bannister Walker with Channel Six news. Your client, Mr. Bejan, has declined to be interviewed. But let me ask you, how will you defend accusations he took video of potential terrorist targets in Washington and sent them to known sources of jihad—and that he and Mustafa traveled to Canada to scope out hiding places?"

The lawyer's tone was shrill. "First of all, everything you just said is a false premise. Taking video of interesting places while on a pleasure trip is not a crime in this country, Mr. Walker. Second, many, many people go to Canada from the U.S. every day. That's not evidence of any wrongdoing. We'll vigorously defend against these charges and any others the prosecutors cook up. That's all I'm going to say to you. We refuse to argue this case in the press."

The guard handed the lawyer's ID back and waved him

through. The window went up as the car pulled away from Walker.

**

As Bannister did his best to smoke out the statement from Bejan's lawyer, Grace and Scott helped photographer Steve Jankowski unload his equipment on a downtown street. "You'll each have a microphone," the photographer told them, "so you'll have to keep me posted as to who's going to do what. I can't be in two places at once."

"I thought you were SuperCameraGuy," Grace quipped.

She glanced around at the gathering crowd, immediately recognizing some of the same signs that appeared the night in the station lawn when protestors supporting the archdiocese showed up. She noticed several groups of men wearing Boy Scout uniforms she assumed were part of the local leadership.

"The Boy Scouts and Atlanta Archdiocese actively lobbied against the bill," she told Matthews. "But they weren't the only organizations that did. I assume some of the others who would have to dole out a lot of legal defense fees are in the crowd." Scott nodded.

Several other TV news crews were already on hand, setting up near the array of microphones on the street in front of the law offices. A small unit of police officers stood by as the crowd grew larger, spilling out onto the street and down the block. The police kept herding stragglers out of the street as honking cars inched along, trying to make their way through.

Grace spotted Rick Dent standing off to one side with his usual power pack slung over his shoulder. He was already speaking into his microphone, obviously setting up the scene for his listeners.

State Representative Taylor Wynn stepped from a cluster of people and up to the bank of microphones. Behind him stood a small group of young men and family members, obviously supporters of the legislation.

"Good morning and thank you for being here," the legislator began. "As lead sponsor of the Georgia Victim Fairness Act in this past legislative session, I'm compelled to speak out publicly about its failure to pass. This bill was necessary and right. It would have opened a window of time for childhood victims of abuse to make their case in civil court against individuals and organizations that failed to protect them. These victims, now adults, have never had their day in court because of statute of limitations laws."

As he spoke, the sign-carrying crowd of people supporting the Catholic Church against the legislation grew increasingly vocal. Grace could make out some of their retorts directed at the legislator. Objections of "You'll bankrupt my church..." "Say no to never-ending liability..." and "The legislature has spoken..." rattled through the air.

Wynn held up a hand for silence. "Look, I know many of you believe your organizations aren't responsible for something that happened long ago. But you're also responsible for holding up legislation over the years that prevented these victims of abuse from having their day in court. If you were standing up here with me, as victims or their family members or friends, you wouldn't be so quick to criticize me for helping them get their due process."

Scattered boos rang through the crowd. Grace could see some pushing and shoving going on between those protesting his words and others obviously in favor of the bill. "Let the man speak," one supporter yelled. "This is America."

"Representative Wynn, why are we here at these law offices?" a reporter shouted over the growing noise. Grace shook her head quietly at his lack of backgrounding.

"This law firm employs one of the most active lobbyists against my bill, on behalf of the Atlanta Archdiocese," Wynn explained. "I asked them to come out and meet me face to face, man to man, but they refused. They prefer to work in the shadows over at the capital where they can curry favor with the power brokers. If you want justice for the men who were once helpless boys, blame this law firm and others like them."

Rick Dent stepped forward, pointing his hand-held microphone. "Mr. Wynn, you said on the House floor you talked to many boyhood victims who want to sue not for money, but to finally get justice and closure."

"That's right," Wynn agreed. "The legislature previously created a brief period when charges could be made, but very few cases could be filed in time. That window closed, and we still don't know how many victims still want to face the predators that were sheltered by their organizations."

"That's wrong," a man with a sign shouted from the crowd as cameras and microphones turned to focus on him. "Those are allegations, not proof."

"Exactly why a court should decide," the representative countered.

Another in the crowd pointed his finger. "Don't punish us today for what others did long before we were even around."

A woman pushed her way to the front of the crowd and directly confronted Wynn. "You might mean well, but you want me and members of my church to pay huge legal costs to defend people who are dead and buried or long gone. It's not fair."

Some in the crowd joined in, chanting, "It's not fair! It's not fair!"

At that moment, the front door of the offices opened and a man stepped out, moving toward Representative Wynn with purpose. "Mr. Wynn, this is a business and you are trespassing on our property. If you don't leave, we'll have you arrested."

Now the gathering grew more boisterous. The pushing and shoving gained momentum.

"I have a right to be here, this is a public sidewalk," Wynn shouted over the noise. Then turning to the crowd and yelling into the microphones, "This man is a partner in the lobbying firm that got my bill killed." He turned to the lawyer, nearly nose to nose. "You and your lobbyist who worked so hard to water my bill down to nothing should be ashamed. Send him out here, let him justify his rich client's opposition to the bill."

Over shouts of the mob, the law partner responded, "The archdiocese isn't the only organization hurt by your legislation. There are plenty of people who will go broke defending something they had nothing to do with."

"I know you're not the only one who death-wished my bill," Wynn rejoined. "I'm headed to the regional office of the BSA next." The crowd, and the attending reporters, buzzed with this announcement.

Grace and Scott tried to work their way in close as the throng crowded closer to the two debating men. Glancing over her shoulder, she could see Steve trying to weave his way in for a better shot. She also could see the cops moving toward the unruly bunch. She heard sirens in the background.

As the growing multitude's collective mood built toward frenzy, Grace turned toward Jankowski and motioned for him to focus on her. He fought to hold steady, shooting toward Gleason over jostling shoulders and between waving signs. "As you can see," Grace shouted into the mic as she also fought to anchor herself, "there are hostile sentiments on both sides of this issue. The question of whether a group should be held responsible for others' past transgressions is an old debate. But it's being argued anew as alleged victims of molestation from many years ago seek their day in court. At least for now, their cause has been put on hold—forever for some—because of failure of Representative Wynn's bill to gain passage in the legislature."

Grace felt herself being jostled. "I'm the press," she yelled at people who were getting out of control. "Get back, we're the press." Several men close to her locked into a wrestling match. She saw a fist fly, and someone went down. As more people entered the fray, trying to help their struggling friends, one swung his sign as a detractor came at him. The corner of it caught Grace above the temple and she felt her legs wobble and fail. All she could see as she toppled to the pavement were legs thrashing around. All she could hear were angry shouts. She felt Scott grab her under the arms and help move her away. In an instant, Steve was there to help.

The sirens grew louder, and within seconds a cadre of Atlanta police rushed to encircle the crowd, pulling people apart, restoring order. Grace sat on a curb with blood dribbling toward her eye. Steve pulled out a handkerchief and applied pressure to her bleeding temple while Scott brushed dirt off her cheek.

"Are you all right?" Matthews asked, his voice laced with concern.

"It hurts," she said. "But I think it feels worse than it really is."

An EMT came by from one of the police vehicles, cleaned the small gash the sign made and stuck a bandage over it. "Thanks," Grace smiled weakly at him. Then, to her colleagues, "There's no question religious fervor sometimes brings out the worst in people. I wonder if that will ever change."

"Isn't that what this series you're going to do is all about?" Scott Matthews asked, helping her up from the curb.

"Yes, Scott, that's what it's all about." She turned to Steve. "Did you get any usable footage?"

"Oh, wow, I forgot to take the lens cap off," he teased.

"Some SuperCameraMan," she joshed back.

Walking to the van, Grace began to feel better, stronger. The incident had shaken her, but she was glad her friends were there to help her get through it. She thought about her Glock, locked up in her car back in the station parking lot. What good was it if she didn't have it with her? She had a license to carry. If that protest had turned more violent, or the phantom who was harassing her showed up and used that mob scene for cover, she could be dead instead of slightly injured.

CHAPTER TWENTY-FIVE: Quershi

Nearly everything was in place. All that was left was finding the best way to fulfill Grace's internal commitment to fairness and balance on the Islamic segment. The overwhelming publicity surrounding the arrest and forthcoming trial of Aahil Moghaddam was a constant reminder that some Muslims embraced an extreme, radical practice of their faith. Moreover, the ties of the two arrested students with Moghaddam's mosque that Bannister uncovered pointed toward a possible source of radicalization

And so for fairness, Grace badly needed to introduce the moderate, peaceful view of Islam into the mix. To her, the key was the documentary maker she had met, Behram Quershi.

The Quershis lived in a modest three-bedroom house in a northwest suburb. When Grace pulled into the driveway, she noted another car was already parked there. "I'm going to invite a friend of mine to join us," Behram told her when they agreed to a meeting time on the phone. "She represents an organization that works very hard to gain the public's understanding of Islam, and to assist those who express a wish to convert. Her organization and I have somewhat different viewpoints on the problems the faith faces, but we disagree in a civil manner. I want you to hear their perspective as well as mine."

That Quershi invited the woman, Anna Chatila, to join them said a lot to Grace about the man's fair-minded and inclusive nature.

Quershi's wife greeted Grace at the door with a huge smile. "Welcome, I'm Lorraine." For some reason, Grace expected Behram's wife to be Middle Eastern, olive skinned and raven-haired. Instead, her long, dark blond hair and thin, pale, intelligent face struck Grace as the makings of a former hippie. "I'm happy to have you visit our home. Come on, Behram and Anna are in the living room."

Inside, the home was tidily kept and nicely furnished, though not lavishly. Quershi and Chatila rose from easy chairs in a seating arrangement.

"Grace, this is Anna Chatila. I have to admit, we've been sitting here talking about you," Quershi said with a mischievous glint in his dark eyes.

"I'm glad I'm here to defend myself," Grace replied as she shook Anna's hand and they all laughed.

The evening moved along smoothly. Over a light dinner of chicken and vegetables, Quershi and Anna took turns discussing issues of the Islam faith as they saw them.

"I've lived in the country ever since coming here to college," Behram explained. "I intended to go back home, but it became evident to me this is a great country with much more opportunity. Then of course I met the lovely Miss Lorraine, and the rest is geography."

"History," Lorraine teasingly corrected, reaching across the table and placing her hand on his. Grace thought the two displayed a tone of mutual respect and sense of humor.

Behram continued, "So I became a citizen and made a reasonably successful life in America. During my career here in the restaurant business, and now as a filmmaker, I've grown not only to admire what has been created in this nation, but also to regret the decline of many of the fifty or so predominately Muslim nations, including my native land."

210

"And what do you attribute that decline to?" Gleason asked.

"Not one thing. But I've become a student of history in my search to answer that question. My studies have taken me back through successful societies of history and what made them great. Babylon, Egypt, Persia, Greece. In simple terms, all had systems of laws and individual rights, at least to some extent. And because of their adherence to fairness and order, they became catalysts for exploration of new ideas. They became economically successful. This was true of Muslims for a long time. They developed some of the most advanced creations of science, technology and the arts the world had known. While Islam led the world in many ways, Europe languished in the dark ages."

"You're implying a reversal took place somewhere along the way. Right? What happened?"

"In my humble opinion, the Muslim world went backwards in time. As Mullahs with strict dogmas took over, I think they became averse to democratic ideals. Openness to new ideas was discouraged. In many countries, women were not permitted to go to school, for example. Some Islamic societies still suppress women's rights. Saudi Arabia, for example, with all its wealth and influence, only recently has said women may drive. In a microcosm kind of way, I watched all of that regression happen in my home, Pakistan. Once a thriving, open society, much of the current Pakistan is closed to embracing Western ideals."

Grace turned to Anna Chatila, who was listening intently. "Do you agree with Behram's assessment?"

"I see the plight of Muslim people in a different light," she answered. "It's true that many Islamic nations in the Middle East and Africa have struggled, especially economically. But one

211

could argue that, as only the third largest religion in the world, technically a minority, Muslims have been held back by prejudice against them.

"We experience this bias here, in America, where Behram says the values of tolerance and individual rights are sacrosanct. A poll several years ago showed Muslims in America are the most disliked religious group—more so even than atheists. Another poll told us Americans believe the values of Islam are not commensurate with the American way of life."

Grace asked, "You represent a fairly large group of Muslims here in Atlanta. How are you attempting to deal with those perceptions?"

"First and foremost, through education," Anna said. "I married a Muslim and converted while I was still a student. So helping students gain greater understanding of our faith is important personally to me. We assist with students' research when they need it for essays, term papers, even dissertations. More than that, though, we take our message out to a great many community groups through our speakers bureau. To those who want it, we provide the Holy Book in the language of their choice. Most importantly, we have many activities designed to promote friendly relations between Muslims and non-Muslims. Our mission is to impart a message of Islam as a peaceful and loving religion, not the faith of hate and division depicted every day in the news."

"You don't deny that hate and division exists at least in some Muslim countries, do you?" Grace challenged.

"We're a faith of more than one and a half billion people. It's a thin minority of those people who cling to old ideas of 'jihad against the infidels.' But those haters put us all in a bad light. We are three and one-half million in America, and we have to endure a general atmosphere of hostility and misunderstanding, especially after nine-eleven."

Quershi surprised Grace as his voice rose for the first time. "Anna, that is partly your own fault. If more leaders of Islam would stand up and condemn the actions of those haters, as you called them—the terrorists who try to kidnap our faith—I believe more non-Muslims would be less prejudiced."

Surprising Grace, Anna fired back, "And how do you stand up, Behram? You may not be a Muslim leader, but you are influential. When an act of terrorism committed by a Muslim or an Islamic extremist group is carried out, do you speak up?"

"First of all, when my documentary comes out, you'll see Islam through the eyes of young American Muslims. They want to lead the next generation into new expressions of art and culture. Also, Anna, like you, I make speeches to many community groups," he responded. "I tell them the harsh applications of Sharia law such as stoning, the suppression of women, bombing of innocent people in a hotel or resort, is not the Islam I grew up in."

"I've heard you speak," she rejoined. "You also tell them you're embarrassed by the current state of affairs in your own native..."

"I am!" Quershi interrupted. "Nothing can justify how the radical element has torn down what so many others built."

Lorraine half rose from her chair, her brow furrowed in anguish at the outburst. "I think it's time for dessert," she said with firmness.

In other words, calm down, Grace thought as she noted Quershi's wife flashing her husband a reprimanding glare.

"I can't stay," Grace apologized. "We have an early meeting tomorrow, and Monday will come much too soon. Let me ask you both," she looked to Behram and then to Anna, "will you agree to come on our program next Tuesday?"

The two friendly rivals looked at each other and then nodded to Grace.

"Good. My producer, MaryAnne McWherter, will call you with details. Time will be short, so you'll need to keep your answers and statements succinct. But please, don't hold back. Express your views as forcefully as you have here tonight."

"I apologize for becoming agitated," Behram looked down at the table, seeming to speak to all three women.

"I apologize as well," Chatila said. "It was unseemly."

Lorraine walked Grace out to her car. "Behram is a kind man," she said, sounding apologetic, Grace thought. "He never raises his voice. It was not like him."

"It's okay," Grace assured.

"They are friends."

"I get it."

"It helps to understand where they're coming from. He arrived here from another country, a different culture, and loved it here so much he became Americanized, I guess you could say. She grew up here, had all the privileges of a happy Christian home, and because she married a Muslim from another country and converted, her life turned upside down. Many of her friends and family deserted her."

"Each seems passionate about their country and their faith in their own way," Grace said. "I meant to ask you, are you and Behram Sunni or Shia?"

Lorraine looked startled. "It's not that simple, not here at least. We don't think of it that way. We are Muslim at the heart. There are just as many kinds of Muslim groups, even in this country, as there are protestant denominations, for instance. Christians all believe in the Holy Bible. Muslims believe in the Qur'an, many neither professing to be Sunni or Shia.

"Grace, the Muslims in this country are as much a melting pot—maybe more so—as the population itself. Many people believe Muslims are Arabs, but the truth is, most are not. Behram himself is Indian, as are most Pakistanis. Over twenty percent of American Muslims are African-American. The truth is that American Muslims probably make up the most racially diverse segment of our population."

Grace took Lorraine's hand in a friendly gesture. "You're terrific. Maybe I should put you on the show."

Lorraine blushed slightly, lowering her eyes. "No, Grace, you have the right person. Behram has taught me."

As she climbed into her car, Grace felt good about the encounter. Two moderate Muslim devotees, both professing a love for the peaceful definition of their religion, yet their passion for their viewpoint came through loud and clear. It seemed no different to her than a Baptist arguing with a Methodist, or a Jew haggling over divinity with a Christian. Their presence would add important texture to the program.

She noticed the headlights as soon as she pulled from the driveway. Glancing in her rearview mirror, she watched as they stayed with her out of the subdivision and onto the main surface streets. Grace couldn't be sure, but she thought they were still behind her as she ramped onto the freeway and then off again near her own neighborhood.

Because she drove in and out of traffic, she couldn't be certain the lights behind her as she drove through Buckhead were the same ones in Quershi's neighborhood. It seemed they had never left her. But she realized the scares she had experienced were causing her to view common occurrences as potential threats.

She would continue to be vigilant. But at the same time, she realized it wouldn't take much to make her paranoid.

CHAPTER TWENTY-SIX: Counting Down

On Saturdays, the newsroom was less calamitous than normal. There was still a certain amount of computer noise, phone conversations and other news-gathering activities going on. It was a news operation, and the news never stops, nor does the reporting of it. But Grace, Bannister, MaryAnne and David were able to find a relatively quiet area to sit and put finishing touches on their plans.

They sat around a circular table with laptops and tablets in front of them. MaryAnne had pulled a whiteboard up close so she could write out the day-to-day schedule. MaryAnne was in charge. Grace and Bannister were the on-air talent, but this was the producer's show to hammer together into a single piece of news-making fabric.

"We've all agreed on the sequence of stories, but let's go down the plan, segment by segment, to be sure there are no hitches," she said. On the board, she scribbled *Monday.*

"First night. Grace will open with a brief premise of the show. It's already written and on the teleprompter. Grace, if there are any changes, we need to have them no later than Monday morning." Gleason nodded.

McWherter continued, "Then we'll focus on Aahil Moghaddam and his mosque. Footage of his capture and arrest, and of the protests by his followers. Then portions of Grace's interview with Khalila Noorani, his friend and adviser. She has agreed to be live in the studio so the two of you can ask follow-up questions.

"Okay, next." The producer scribbled *Tuesday* on the whiteboard. "Second night. Bannister will report live on the arrests and subsequent activities involving Atlanta State students Hussein Bejan and Parveen Mustafa." She turned to Walker. "There's no interview footage of either of them, but Mustafa's cousin has agreed to appear on camera during the show, right?" The young reporter nodded yes.

She continued, "I've worked it out with a camera crew in Brooklyn to give us a live feed. David, this has to work like clockwork."

"I've got it, no problem," Williams assured.

Grace repeated for emphasis, "So on the first night we have the Aahil Moghaddam perspective through the canned interview and live appearance of his associate, Ms. Noorani. Bannister and I will question her." She turned to her young colleague. "Bannister, we'll have to be careful not to appear as if we're ganging up on her. Now as follow-up we have the two young men meeting up in Moghadd- am's mosque, and subsequently being arrested and having charges of terrorism leveled against them. And Bannister's interview with the cousin professing Parveen's innocence.

"In the studio, we'll have the documentary maker, Behram Quershi and a representative of the Islamic Programs Association. Bannister will address this panel, seeking their perspectives on radi- cal terrorism and Islam more generally."

She took a deep breath and smiled. "I'm pooped already."

"And it's only Tuesday night," Bannister Walker roared.

MaryAnne joined his laughter and looked up at her notes on the whiteboard. "That second night is a heavy load. We'll need to edit the canned interviews prudently, and move the live questioning along at a pretty good clip."

She wrote, *Wednesday.*

"Third night, hump day," McWherter went on. "Radical shift, no pun intended, to the allegations of abuse against the late Father Anthony Bianci. We have the video interview Grace did with the man making the accusations, with his face hidden and voice altered. Then Grace's interview with the state legislator who introduced the Victim Fairness Act. Finally, live in the studio, to further discuss or debate the legislation, former district attorney Morgan Staton and lobbyists of the

Atlanta Archdiocese and the Boy Scouts regional office."

"One more thing," Grace interjected. She paused a beat. Discussing this story stuck in her throat. Finally, "I have also spoken to one of Father Anthony Bianci's brothers, who agreed to be interviewed remotely from the studio of our fellow network affiliate in Pittsburgh. The brother insists the allegations against Bianci are not true."

"Okay, that'll be good," the producer said matter-of-factly, not seeming to notice Gleason's discomfort with the subject. "We'll have all points of view covered."

MaryAnne wrote *Thursday* on the board, which was beginning to fill up. "Final two nights will be devoted to controversies surrounding Reverend Dontell Freeman." She said. " So on night four, we air the portions of Grace's video interview with Reverend Freeman having to do with children's spankings in church. And we'll show part of the video of the two mothers who broke from his congregation over their children's injuries. Then we'll have representatives of both factions from his parishioners—pro spanking and con—to debate his teachings and practices."

"Sounds like some sparks will fly that night," Walker said.

"What night won't they?" the producer said. She turned and wrote *Friday.*

"So night five, the final night, we have more interview with Dontell Freeman, this time about marrying the young girls off. We'll have portions of the interview Grace did with two of the newlyweds, Eddie and Pearl. Plus, video of the Tuskegee minister interview. Then Grace will have the professor in the studio live to discuss the Stockholm Syndrome. He's a definite will-show, Grace?"

"He's on board," Gleason responded, feeling her face flush a little.

MaryAnne stood staring at the board for a moment, then nodded satisfaction. "Finally, a concluding statement by Grace to wrap things up, and that's it."

They sat in collective silence. Grace stared at the whiteboard. "It's a huge bite to chew."

"It'll fly by," the producer assured.

"Time flies when you're getting religion," Walker quipped. He glanced at Grace who sat slumped over her laptop, her brow furrowed in a sullen expression. "Grace, you seem really concerned about something."

All eyes went to the lead reporter. She sat in thought for a long moment, then, "I called it a huge bite to chew, but I didn't mean just for us. We're throwing a lot of information at our viewers in a very short period of time. We have three controversial, complex stories, all with different subplots, and we're trying to sum them up in five half-hour segments. Our reporting will include a long list of names, many nearly unpronounceable to the majority of our audience. Some of us even have trouble keeping the cast of characters straight. I'm concerned about the people who watch bachelor dating shows and sitcoms and celebrity reality programs. I'm worried we'll lose them."

Everyone sat absorbing her words, not speaking. She turned to Walker. "Don't you share my concern—that after one or two segments, they'll get so confused they'll start to turn us off? Watch something that doesn't require such rapt concentration and deep thinking?"

"No," Bannister replied. "I know this is deep stuff, but can you tell me it's not relevant to what's going on in the world today?"

"No."

"Then give our viewers a little credit. They care. If we've packaged and promoted it right—and we have—they'll stay with us all week."

Grace heaved an enormous sigh. "You can't blame me for having doubts. We've worked so hard."

"Enough of this self-doubt," MaryAnne chimed in cheerfully. "There's plenty of time to worry a week from now. As for me, I'm going home to a good night's sleep."

They began closing their laptops and stuffing notepads into their bags when Buck Lohmeyer appeared. "Everything set for the big week?" he asked, scanning the whiteboard.

"Just about," MaryAnne reported. "Still a few loose ends to tie together, but we'll be ready."

"I hope you know I went out on a limb to get you this feature," Lohmeyer blustered. *Yes, and took credit for the idea,* Grace thought, attempting to control her emotions.

The news director continued, "Mr. Silver has a lot riding on this with several advertisers. We've warned them it'll be controversial and to expect some pressure from some of their customer groups. On the other hand, if ratings are good, they'll reap the rewards." He paused. "Good luck. Grace, come visit with me for a minute, will you?"

Grace followed Lohmeyer to his office, wondering what to expect. He sank into his chair and motioned for her to sit across from him. "Grace, I've spoken with Harvey about that break-in at your house. We're very concerned about it."

"As am I, Mr. Lohmeyer. But thanks for telling me."

"That's not it. I want you to know we're taking a protective step. The station has contracted with a private investigator to watch your house at night."

"That's not necessary..." she started.

He held up his hand. "No, it is necessary. It's not the first scare you've had, and it might not be the last. I just wanted you to know, if you see a mysterious silver SUV parked on the curb just up from your house, that's our guy. If you ever get frightened about anything, he's a shout away."

"That's really generous, Mr. Lohmeyer. Thank you."

Grace left feeling a slight bit of warmth toward the man she was fighting not to resent.

Leaving the station, Grace drove to the Highlands Shooting Range. She took Ned Moore's advice that she refresh her gun-handling knowledge to heart. In Dallas, where she bought her gun after a dangerous experience, she became comfortable and confident shooting. She had visited this Atlanta range twice since that conversation with Ned, and it was all coming back to her.

Pulling into the parking lot, she chuckled inwardly at how intimidated she felt the first time she visited the Dallas range. *What am I doing here?* she thought to herself that day. *I have a daughter to protect, but do I really think I can handle a firearm? Stand up to another shooter? Shoot to kill someone?*

Finally forcing herself into the building that day, she was immediately greeted by a nice, friendly guy who obviously met plenty of first-time shooters. "I see you have your own gun," he said, glancing down at the case she carried. "Nine millimeter."

"Yes," she answered, still feeling intimidated. "A friend, a detective at the Dallas PD, helped me buy it and pointed me your direction. He was going to come with me but ran into an emergency."

"That tends to happen to detectives. Have your own ammo?"

"Not with me," she answered.

"That's fine, we would have to inspect it anyway before you could use it here. You can purchase all you need for your session."

The attendant put her at ease, showing her how to load the gun, release the magazine, load the chamber, assume the proper stance and everything else she needed to get started. Even with the ear protection they provided, the pop-pop-pop of rounds being fired all around her was unsettling. Yet when she stepped into her designated lane and squeezed off the first rounds at her paper assailant, a calm settled in on her. *I can do this,* she thought. And when she retrieved and examined her target, with several bullet holes where they should be, she felt an odd exhilaration.

Now, entering the Highlands range, she felt like a veteran. A week earlier, her first time at Highlands, she introduced herself to one of the instructors named Marvin.

"Why are you here?" Marvin asked her. "What's your objective?"

"Protect myself and my daughter if we're ever attacked," she responded immediately.

He nodded. "Perfect, outstanding," he said energetically. Glancing down at her gun case, "Since you have your own Glock, I assume you know the routines?"

"Yes," she answered. "I know how it works in here, at the range." She nodded around the room as explosions went off in the firing lanes. "But the truth is, I don't know if I could really shoot anyone, much less shoot to kill them."

"Oh, you'll do it in self defense, I guarantee it. But you need to prepare yourself, not just in here with the training, but mentally. The trick is not to hesitate. Prepare in advance how you'll respond if it's 'you or them.' The average speed of a bullet is twenty-five hundred feet per second. If you react to the sound of the gun going off and it takes two-tenths of a second to react, you'd need to be at least five hundred feet away to successfully dodge a bullet."

"Really! Nearly two football fields?" Grace exclaimed.

"Right," he said. "So if you're threatened by someone with a weapon at close range, shoot first. That's the best way to stay alive."

He walked her to a lane coming open. Grace took her turn, conducting her business like a pro.

"Not bad," Marvin came back over as the paper target returned to her. "Got one right in the heart."

Grace smiled with greater confidence as she returned the ear protectors and cased her Glock. "Thanks, Marvin," she said.

The range safety officer moved toward her, nodded and held the door as she prepared to exit. "Have a nice evening, Ms. Gleason," he said. For a brief, reflexive instant she wondered how he knew her name; she hadn't registered when she arrived. Then she realized, as was often the case, he recognized her from watching the news. As many years as she had been in the public eye, she was still occasionally caught off-guard at being a well-known figure.

Entering her car, she put the gun case into the glove compartment and locked it. She sat staring at the closed door, wondering what mayhem would have to occur for her to unlock it and put her training into practice. Could she? She would only know the answer to that question if a situation ever called for it.

CHAPTER TWENTY-SEVEN: You Did It

Grace spent Sunday sleeping late, lazing on the back porch with coffee and the paper, and finally returning to her home office to go over her notes for the show. But she couldn't concentrate there. Detectives hadn't found any usable prints to lift, and they tried to wipe up the mess they made. But she had to go back over everything to meet her high standards of cleanliness. It took several hours to replace all the drawers and organize the vandalized files. The lamp they overturned was broken, and she exchanged it with an older one in her closet. But despite her efforts to clean and straighten, memories of the break-in chilled her as she tried to work.

Finally, she took her laptop to the kitchen and sat in the small eating area to work. She could even graze with snacks during the afternoon without ever changing venues, she thought. Later, she would call Dillon McAfee as promised and see if he would meet her for supper. A nice evening away from work would be a welcome digression, and she looked forward to his company.

Sometime during the afternoon she closed her laptop and dozed there, hunched over the kitchen table. She didn't know how long she slept when a loud "bang!" awoke her. Standing to look out the back door window, she saw Horace Gunter rummaging around his back yard near the fire pit. Assuming he was preparing for his buddies to come over later, she shrugged and went into the bathroom. A luxurious, hot bath would be the ticket before calling Dillon.

He was waiting for her near the front door of the Fusion Grill. He wore khakis and a button-down shirt, with a navy blazer slung over his shoulder. It was a sure sign warmer weather was encroaching.

"I've been hoping to see you again," he told her as they entered the restaurant and he gave the hostess his name.

"You wouldn't have wanted to be around me lately," she told him as they slid into their booth. "I've been an awful grouch. This show is putting a lot of pressure on all of us."

Grinning over the top of the wine list, he said, "I would've cheered you up. There's no grouch permitted, Grace Gleason."

"Well, we're here now," she said.

While they ate, Grace told Dillon about the break-in and the anonymous caller.

He responded with alarm. "Why didn't you call me?"

Grace looked at him with surprise. "I called the authorities and slept with a neighbor. It didn't occur to me to call you, Dillon. We're still getting to know each other."

He slid his hand across the table and laid it on hers. "Grace, you can call on me to help you anytime, day or night, no matter what it is."

"Thanks," she answered. "Dillon, I've been harassed quite a bit over these stories I'm chasing. An old friend, a retired detective…"

"The guy next door?" he shot back at her.

"No, not him. A good friend, a retired cop I fought some dangerous news wars with in Dallas when I lived there. He wanted me to call you and ask you to get the locks to my doors changed and a security system installed."

"Why didn't you?" Dillon sounded dumfounded.

"I honestly don't know. I just didn't. Dillon, this same detective urged me to buy a gun back in those days, to be prepared to protect myself and my daughter, and I did. Now, with all of this new harassment, he counseled me to keep up with shooting practice."

"Grace! A gun? I don't like that idea at all."

"What? Are you anti second amendment? Don't you believe I have a right to protect myself?"

"I don't go out and protest gun violence, if that's what you mean. Sure, I believe people have a right to self-protection. But at the same time, I'm familiar with enough cases of trauma from gun-related shootings, including self-inflicted accidents, I admit I'm wary about it. If it came down to it, do you really think you could shoot someone?"

Grace felt her face redden and she realized her mouth popped open in surprise. She didn't want this nice evening to turn into a political squabble. But she felt challenged. She didn't know this man well at all, yet he was expressing doubts about a personal choice she made. "Dillon," she said, her voice a little strained, "I really don't know. If someone were about to harm my daughter, there's nothing I wouldn't do. If someone confronted me with violence, could I protect myself? I think I could. I think you could, too, if a shooter came into your classroom and started shooting at your students. Or you."

"That's too hypothetical for me. All I know is you feel threatened, and you've armed yourself. I don't like the idea. Period."

A fog of silence settled on them. Grace hated the tension straining at their conversation. Wanting to ease the friction, she changed the subject to his planned appearance on her program.

As they spoke about his role, the conversation slipped back into an easy, friendly mood. "So after I interview this couple who were paired up by this minister, you'll be sitting across from me at the moderator's table. I'll ask you essentially the things we've talked about before. Describe the Stockholm Syndrome in simple terms. Tell us how that disorder could possibly be at work between Reverend Freeman and the young people he seems to hold sway over."

He paid the check, and they began to leave the restaurant.

"Sounds good," he said. "I'll be ready." Outside, he turned to her. "Do you need any bio information to introduce me?"

Grace flashed him a slightly astonished grin. "Dr. McAfee, do you think I haven't already done my homework?" He shrugged and looked down at his feet, obviously embarrassed at asking so silly a question of this professional reporter.

"Besides," she added. "I already knew what I wanted to know about you even before we talked about your coming on the show."

"Oh?" he said, looking intrigued as he pulled her a little closer to him. "And why such interest in this old bird?"

She laughed. "You made it pretty clear right up front you had more than a professional interest," she said, leaning into him, her face close to his. "I had to do my due diligence. Didn't want to consort with a chainsaw killer."

"Consort, is it?" he teased. "Is that what we're doing?"

"Dr. McAfee," she said coyly. "I have no earthly idea what we're doing."

"Let me tell you. No, better yet, let me show you." He leaned in and kissed her, lightly, letting his mouth linger just a moment longer than a friendship kiss would last. Grace could feel herself growing flustered. It was the first time she had kissed anyone in a long, long time.

Trembling slightly, she pulled back and he let her go.

"I'd better get home," she stammered, her senses still on high alert. "I'll see you at the studio on Friday evening."

"I'll look forward to it," he called after her as she walked toward her car. "Maybe we can have some food or a glass of wine after."

"Maybe," she answered back over her shoulder. "We'll see."

The silver SUV was sitting on the street as she pulled up toward her house and into her driveway. As Buck Lohmeyer promised, it did give her a modicum of reassurance.

She could see Horace Gunter firing up his pit as she gazed out the kitchen window. Ever since the break-in and her conversation with Ned Moore, she thought a lot about her neighbor. He was quick to help her out when that brick came flying through her window. She left a key with him, not a wise move, Ned told her. Horace also showed up on her doorstep immediately after she discovered her office was vandalized. She had no way to know if the black Trans Am and the anonymous, threatening calls might have been his doing. But Moore told her not to trust the man, that he had a shadowy past and was doubtless friends with the crooked cops she helped put in jail.

All of this negativity surged through her brain as she stood staring at him. *He has something to do with this stalking,* she finally thought. *Even if he's trying to make me miserable, not harm me, I can't let it go on. If it's true that he's buddies with those rogue cops, they're probably egging him on to scare me senseless.*

Grace took a deep breath, smoldering, and pushed through the back door, across her porch and out toward her neighbor's lawn.

Horace was about to throw a log on his growing fire. He looked up, startled, as she approached.

"Jeez, Grace, you scared the bejeebers out of me," he laughed. "What's up?"

"I'll tell you what's up, Horace Gunter," she shot back. "I want to know about your Atlanta cop friends."

"What do you mean? You've seen them come over here," he retorted. "They're just a bunch of old force veterans I made friends with when I moved here."

"Not those guys," she said. "Do you have friends in the Fulton County jail, Horace? Disgraced cops?"

"Come on, Grace, what gives you such an idea?"

Growing more agitated, Grace blurted out, "I think you do. I think your drinking buddies are pals with some of the scum who robbed and murdered that strip club owner. I think you've met the guys who masterminded the crooked police robbery ring I helped bring down."

She hesitated for an instant as he turned toward her, the log still in his hand. She realized he could lay her out cold with one swing of it, if this argument got out of hand. But she was past the point of rational thinking. She was angry, and despite the risk she pressed on. "I think it might have been you who broke my window and later ripped my office apart. You and my daughter are the only ones who have a key."

"Come on, Grace, settle down. You don't know what in hell you're talking about." Gunter's voice began to rise. "You're right, I have a key. So use your head. If I wanted to mess your house and had a key, why was it a break-in?"

Now she was screaming. "Because you're a cop. You know how to make it look like forced entry. That way you covered your tracks. Your new Atlanta buddies are goading you on, to scare the daylights out of me, aren't they? You had me picked up by the cop that night coming out of the restaurant. You had me followed. You tore up my office."

Gunter turned and tossed the log onto the fire. Sparks flew up with a rage. "I'm not admitting anything, Gleason," he answered, his response seeming derisive and snide to her. "I don't have to listen to this paranoid crap any longer. But I'll tell you one thing. You shouldn't be so stupid as to give your key to someone you barely know. Now, I've got people coming over and need to get ready. Get out of my face and out of my yard. Or I will give you something to be scared about."

Enraged, Grace stared at him for a long moment. Then she spun and half-ran toward her house. Tears streamed down her face. She leapt through the kitchen door, locking it behind her, and scrambled into her bedroom, flopping on the bed. She sobbed for several minutes before gaining her composure.

I used to handle these tough situations without even blinking, Grace thought. *Am I in deeper than ever before? Or getting soft?*

Whatever the answer, she disliked not being in control, navigating unchartered waters.

She didn't really know if the suspicions she voiced to Horace were true or false. She thought her subconscious mind might have propelled her across that back yard, hoping a confrontation might draw out the truth.

The scene she just initiated had no such effect. All it did was rile her neighbor and put her in a position of looking silly if her accusations were off base.

Slowly, she dragged herself off the bed. She went into the bathroom and began removing her makeup. She wrinkled her nose as she stared at the dark areas forming under her eyes. She pulled close to the mirror and stared at the newly emerging lines in her forehead. The strain of her job and the jeopardy it brought to her doorstep seemed to be speeding the aging process.

Grace washed her face and brushed her hair, trying to shake off the events of the night.

There's no more time to waste on Horace Gunter right now, she reasoned to herself. *Tomorrow is our big day. I must get ready, not just physically. Emotionally, too.*

CHAPTER TWENTY-EIGHT: Curtain Up

Jackson Davis got off to a shaky start with Grace when she first came to Big Six News. She was put off by the anchorman's bombastic mannerisms and the misogynist attitude he did little to hide. They had several conflicts over news stories until he finally acknowledged she was not an airhead. They settled into an uneasy truce.

But the aging newsman still seemed to relish throwing smoke bombs into plans that didn't revolve around him. In morning meetings, Jackson made no secret he wasn't enamored with the idea of this commentary on religious leadership being planned for the five-thirty time slot.

"People tune in to hear the news," he argued one morning as MaryAnne McWherter, the producer, ran down the stories they had planned for the series. "If they want to hear opinionated babble they'll get it on the cable networks. This thing will create a distraction. We should stick to what made us the number one station."

"What made us number one, Jackson," MaryAnne retorted, "was going out on the edge to find out who the bad actors are. That's all we're doing here. Maybe you're concerned the program will distract from your newscast to follow?"

Grace grinned inwardly at McWherter's chutzpah. The evening anchor's face reddened a little, and he sat back in his chair with a sullen expression. He voiced no more objections, but it was obvious he wasn't enthusiastic.

That lack of keenness came through loud and clear as he prepared to introduce the first night of "Unholy Mind Games." The five-day, half-hour series would air immediately before his six o'clock news, and as the news anchor, it was his job to introduce each evening.

First came a new music theme the promotions department commissioned with an ad agency, a striking religious mood piece. A Bach-type organ riff segued into a Muslim adhan, or call to prayer. Next came a brief stanza of Jewish hazzanut cantorial music, followed by the upbeat sound of a gospel choir.

Then the music faded as Jackson launched into his intro. "Tonight we begin a series of reports on religious leadership in Atlanta. Religion reporter Grace Gleason and investigative reporter Bannister Walker will introduce you to troubling questions about how a small minority of leaders of faith might take advantage of their positions of influence. Here's Grace."

Grace and Bannister sat at the moderator table. Grace watched the red light go on camera one and began the opening monologue she wrote days earlier and added onto it during the next day's rewrite.

Reading from the teleprompter, Grace ran through major positive religious stories she had covered, then went on, "…but there is another side to religion, a dark side that manipulates the positive messages of faith and forces us to ask: Do some misguided religious leaders take advantage of their positions to the detriment of others, especially the young, the impressionable, the defenseless?

"For the next week, 'Unholy Mind Games' will explore that question and attempt to answer it. Make no mistake, some of what you will see in these half-hour evening segments will be disturbing and controversial. We will show you how leaders of several different faiths in our city have created controversy and concern. Although our reports may be offensive to some of you, it is our fervent hope that at the very least we will make you think. And, when appropriate, act.

"Tonight is segment one of our five-part series." As Grace spoke, the distinctive, melodious sound of a call to prayer, the adhan, began to play in the background, and video of the tiny Masjid Al-Emaan of Atlanta came onto the huge screen behind her. "We take you to a Muslim house of worship in an Atlanta neighborhood. It is the mosque led by Imam Aahil Moghaddam, who is in prison awaiting trial on charges that he murdered a Fulton County deputy and wounded another."

Footage of Aahil Moghaddam's arrest in Tennessee filled the screen, followed by Atlanta footage of protests in the street, covered by Scott Matthews. As it ended, Grace turned to her co-reporter. "Bannister

Walker, you recently interviewed Imam Moghaddam after his arrest."

"That's right, Grace," Bannister began. "Once known as Slay T. Jefferson, a fiery, militant leader of the California Lives Matter movement, he converted to Islam while in prison on an armed robbery conviction. He has been in and out of trouble with the law over the years but says that's because of his race and religion. Now Imam Aahil Moghaddam leads a quieter life as leader of the small Atlanta mosque. That is, until he was arrested for killing Fulton deputy Thomas Putnam and wounding Putnam's deputy partner, Jeremiah Smith, as they attempted to serve him with a warrant."

"Bannister," Grace turned to her colleague, "you recently spoke off-the-record to Moghaddam in prison. Is there anything from that conversation you can share?"

"Yes, Grace, I spent about half an hour with him. We weren't allowed to take cameras in, but his lawyers have approved my relating one statement he made during that discussion. I recorded it, and here it is verbatim: 'Preaching is not doing. If I need to rally people around putting pressure on the authorities who are oppressing them, that's not proof of criminal action, is it? They put me in jail not because of crimes committed but because of the color of my skin. Because I pushed people not to accept discrimination where it exists. And now, ever since my conversion, they have pursued me like a dog for my race and my beliefs.'"

Grace said into the camera, "Bannister, a recent development unrelated to the deputy shooting has authorities taking a new look at the Imam, right?"

"Correct. Two Atlanta State students are in jail faced with charges of abetting terrorism. Authorities say they first met at the mosque led by Imam Moghaddam. I asked the Imam if any of his activities or sermons at the mosque might have encouraged the young men to take actions the prosecutors say were intended to support jihad.

"Here's more of the statement his attorneys agreed I could quote: 'I tell my followers that struggle is necessary to be free. I promote the search for justice, for freedom from the kind of persecution I've endured for many, many years. Whoever hears my message as the truth eventually understands his obligations to Allah and his duty to society.'"

"With us tonight in the studio," Grace said, "is a staunch supporter of Imam Moghaddam. Khalila Noorani is a lawyer and community organizer who has known the Imam since his California Lives Matter days as Slay Jefferson." Grace turned to the elegant woman, dressed in a colorful aqua abaya and matching hijab. "Welcome, Ms. Noorani." Grace motioned for Khalila to sit across from her and Walker. "You converted to Islam after moving to the United States. Subsequently you met Slay T. Jefferson in California and ultimately followed him here to Atlanta. Why?"

"First thank you for letting me come on your program," Noorani said in a quiet, respectful tone. "I did know Slay Jefferson in California when he was active politically there. And after his conversion, I knew immediately as I interacted with him and other young religious leaders that he would become a special force for Islam. To serve him was to serve Allah. That is why I moved to Atlanta to be part of his spiritual leadership here."

"You organized protests after he was arrested?" Bannister asked.

"Many of us talked among ourselves about the injustice of the charges. The inconsistencies of statements made by the wounded arresting officer spoke volumes. I am a lawyer and understand I cannot go into detail, to prejudice his legal case, but I can tell you every one of those protesters believes Imam is innocent of the charges against him."

Grace asked, "So is it your belief that each time he was arrested and criminally charged over the years it was on false charges? After all, there are many Imams in the United States. Why would he alone be singled out and targeted?"

Khalili smiled gently. "Because Allah has chosen him to be an example of our struggle in this world."

Bannister broke in. "Ms. Noorani, as you know two Atlanta State students are awaiting trial on charges of terrorism. We learned they attended your mosque, or masjid. What do you say to the suspicion that they might have become radicalized there?"

"You spoke with Aahil. You heard his words. Talking about righting wrongs radicalizes no one. It merely serves to stimulate one's thinking about the state of the world, and the discrimination one finds all around us."

"You steadfastly believe Aahil Moghaddam is innocent of the accusations against him, and that the accusations of the two young students are not his doing as well?"

"With all my head and heart," the lawyer answered.

"He preached violent protest in California," Bannister interjected. "He's on record as calling for aggressive resistance to authority. In his Atlanta mosque, some of his followers wear combat boots and fatigues. Several years ago, according to Federal authorities, two of his members were guilty of shipping arms to groups linked to terrorism. One of his members reportedly went to Syria and died fighting for ISIS. How can you justify that kind of activity emanating from his masjid?"

"Many Muslims will tell you they are under attack in this country. There is a movement to destroy Islamic leaders such as Imam. Each person of Islamic faith must decide for himself or herself what is justified and what is not. I can tell you, Moghaddam will be justly acquitted of the charges against him."

"Thank you, Khalila Noorani, for sharing your views with us," Grace said. Then, turning to the camera in a close-up, "That is all the time we have for tonight on 'Unholy Mind Games.' Imam Aahil Moghaddam's guilt or innocence will be decided in a court of law. So will that of Hussein Bejan and Parveen Mustafa, the Atlanta State College students who have been arrested.

"Tomorrow night we will explore their cases and probe the reasons they are charged with terrorist activity. Until then, I'm Grace Gleason for Bannister Walker, and you are watching the weeklong series of commentary, 'Unholy Mind Games.'"

The cameras went off. From the control booth, MaryAnne McWherter appeared to hold her breath for a moment, then rose and applauded, and gave the Grace and Bannister two thumbs up.

Grace stood and shook Noorani's hand. "Thank you for coming tonight," she said.

"It was my pleasure," the gentle woman answered. "My ride is waiting in the parking lot, so I'll be going." She turned and walked toward the newsroom exit, and Grace's emotions spiked. She was tempted to follow the woman and sneak a peek at the car waiting for her. Could it be a black Trans Am with gold striping? *Don't be stupid, it can't be her,* something inside said to Grace and calmed her nerves.

She thanked Bannister, shook the hand of each camera operator and walked to the booth to thank David Williams and McWherter. Feeling elated at having the first segment over without a hitch, she walked from the production studio to the newsroom and her workstation. Immediately upon returning, her cell phone rang.

For the second time within minutes, she felt her neck pulse pounding much faster than normal. Most of the anonymous threats she received from disgruntled viewers came to her desk phone. But she knew this current harasser also had her cell number.

"Hello, this is Gleason," she managed with trepidation.

"Outstanding." Immediately she recognized the voice of Rick Dent, her radio friend.

"Rick, you gave me a scare. I need to get you a distinctive ring tone."

"Sorry, Grace. I just called to congratulate you. Great start. I bet the switchboard's melting over there."

"You thought it was that good?"

"Do I ever lie to you?"

"No, Rick, you don't. Tomorrow night should be even better." She exhaled an enormous sigh of relief. "One down, four to go."

Grace shuddered, ecstatic the call came from Rick. She only hoped the troublemaker had given up and gone away.

CHAPTER TWENTY-NINE: Peace and Terror

The second night went as planned. Bannister Walker opened with direct news style reporting of the events surrounding the arrest of the two students.

"Hussein Bejan, an engineering student at Atlanta State, was arrested on charges of contributing to terrorism," he began. "Subsequently, Parveen Mustafa, a reported acquaintance of his—arresting FBI agents called him a co-conspirator—was extradited from Lebanon on similar charges."

Video footage played behind him showing Bejan's initial court appearance and then the student being accompanied by authorities and lawyers to a waiting vehicle outside the courthouse.

A camera took a mid-range shot of Bannister. "Hussein Bejan's lawyer steadfastly denies the charges against him." He turned as the brief encounter outside the penitentiary played. "As for Bejan's alleged co-conspirator, I spoke with Parveen Mustafa at his place of incarceration, the Metropolitan Detention Center in Brooklyn, New York. That conversation was granted on condition that it remain off-the-record. But while I was there, I met a cousin of the accused who has agreed to come on this program tonight by way of live feed from New York. He asked that I not give his name."

He turned toward the screen. "Good evening."

"Good evening, Mr. Walker," the cousin said as his close-up loomed behind Bannister on the screen.

"You have been in constant touch with Mr. Mustafa ever since he was returned to the United States to face charges of terrorism?"

The cousin squinted his shadowy eyes from the glare of lights. "That is right. I saw him only yesterday."

"And like him, you profess his innocence?"

"My cousin is not a terrorist, Mr. Walker," he answered with a thick Syrian accent. "He has been accused of going to Syria, his native country, to wage jihad. But I tell you now, he returned to his homeland to see relatives and to marry his fiancée. There is nothing improper or untoward about that trip, as agents have so wrongly accused."

"He attended Atlanta State as a fellow student of Hussein Bejan? They are accused co-conspirators?"

The cousin smiled for the first time and appeared to relax. "They are friends. They took vacations together and communicated on the internet with acquaintances they had in common. Those are not crimes."

"What about accusations they sent video of potential targets to known terrorists and sought out hiding places in Canada?"

"All false, Mr. Walker. They share videos of their travels with their friends, as many people often do. And they have friends in Canada they have visited more than once before."

"Mr. Mustafa attended the same Atlanta mosque to which Bejan also went to worship, is that right?"

"That is my understanding. There is nothing wrong with two young students wanting to deepen their commitment to Islam, attending masjid together, is there?"

"The masjid they attended is led by a man currently in jail on several felony charges, including murder. Is it possible his messages of violent protest and jihad had a radical effect on the belief systems of your cousin and his friend?"

"The Imam has only been accused, not convicted. I believe he is a man of peace and will put up a vigorous defense claiming he did not commit those crimes. As for my cousin, your question as to whether he became a radical has no merit. I repeat, Mr. Walker, Parveen is not a terrorist."

"Is there a final message you would like to convey to our

viewing audience on behalf of your cousin?"

"Only that he and his friend Hussein will be found innocent in a court of law, as they are in the eyes of Allah."

"Thank you for being with us tonight." The video of the cousin faded to black.

Bannister turned to Grace. "The fate of Hussein Bejan and Parveen Mustafa will be decided by juries, Grace. If they are found guilty of aiding terrorism, questions about who influenced them will loom large."

"Will both be tried in Atlanta?" she asked.

"Bejan for sure," he reported. "Authorities in Brooklyn indicated Mustafa will also probably be brought back to be tried here."

Grace turned toward the camera. "So far we've looked at an extreme ideology associated with terrorist organizations. We have justifiably turned our questions to how those views can gain momentum and radicalize young people in America, including Atlanta. Yet there's a viewpoint that Islam gets an unfair rap. Joining us are two individuals who will give you their views on the reputation of Islam in the world and right here in our community."

Behram Quershi and Anna Chatila walked on the set and sat across from Grace and Bannister. Grace's questioning was almost identical to that in Quershi's dining room over dinner. Their responses were also the same, and at one point they entered into the same disagreement. To Grace, it was as if the conversation in Behram's house was a dress rehearsal.

The two Muslims remained on the set as Grace addressed the camera, signing off. "Tomorrow night," she concluded, "a chilling subject you won't want to miss. I'm Grace Gleason for Bannister Walker, and you've been watching 'Unholy Mind Games.'"

She thanked Anna who exited gracefully as Behram hung back. "Grace, I hope we can keep in touch," he said.

"I'm sure we will," Grace answered. "How about an invitation to the premier of your documentary?"

"You've got it," he smiled widely.

Through the rest of the night, at home relaxing, and the next day at the office, preparing for the program, Grace felt an odd sense of foreboding. She didn't understand why her spirits were sagging so, or why a feeling of dread hung with her throughout the day.

Then, as time neared to open the third segment, she realized her anxiety stemmed from the looming subject matter of this evening's show. The story of the molesting priest haunted her from the moment she first met Max Morrison, the victim who sought her out. Her lifelong admiration for the church she grew up in prevented her from accepting that certain rogue priests took advantage of their positions. Knowing it was true intellectually and accepting it emotionally were two different things. Even her lack of regular attendance at mass after becoming an adult failed to diminish her admiration for all things Catholic. She recalled many times when stressful or dangerous news stories haunted her, she dropped into a church and prayed silently. On several occasions when the spirit moved her, she went to confession.

Now she was about to put a harsh spotlight on the church her parents brought her into. She could feel her legs wobble as she walked onto the set and nodded at Bannister and MaryAnne.

"You okay?" the producer asked. "You don't seem to feel well."

"I'll be fine," was all Grace could muster. But she wasn't. As Jackson Davis introduced the segment, her stomach wanted to upheave. She couldn't remember, even on the most sensational stories she had covered, when she felt such trepidation when the cameras came on.

"Good evening," she tried desperately to suppress her unease and keep her voice from shaking, "and welcome to our third evening of examination of religion, and how some rogue leaders of their particular faiths might cross over the line." She felt her throat constrict, her speech start to falter. She stared at the teleprompter in panic. The only thing she knew to do was throw it to her co-reporter. "Banister?" she stammered.

Walker glanced at her, appearing confused, but he turned back to the teleprompter and read her lines. "Recently, a man came forward alleging an Atlanta priest molested him as a boy. We have hidden his face and changed his voice to protect his privacy. But the words are his words, the charges made against the now-deceased former priest his accusations."

The video began, and Grace couldn't watch. During the actual recent interview in a quiet corner of the studio, she had immunized herself from the emotionally wrenching subject matter by focusing on the mechanics—what questions to ask, how to ask them. Now, as it played back on-air, only a few snippets came through as she sat in a semi-daze.

"...began when I was about ten..."
"...thought it can't be wrong, he was like God himself..."
"...two other boys I knew..."
"...ashamed and scared to tell my parents..."
"...statute of limitations already passed..."

As the interview faded to black, Bannister glanced at Grace, as if to say, "Do you want me to keep going?" But Grace took a deep breath, regained her composure and jumped right into the next message on the prompter. "I also talked to an expert of sorts on many other alleged incidents. Morgan Staton is a retired district attorney from Cherokee County. Mr. Staton handled dozens of child abuse cases during his tenure as DA. Here's an interview I conducted with him several days ago."

The interview played in its entirety. It began with retired DA Staton's comments about his meeting with the accused former priest, expressing surprise that Anthony Bianci showed no emotion when responding to his questions. It ended with Staton's explanation that the legislature opened a two-year window for civil suits to be filed against alleged predators.

"There could be no criminal findings, but accused child molesters would have to face their alleged victims, and their families, in a court of law. One case had been filed and was pending when Bianci died."

Cutting back in live, Grace said, "More recently, another bill in the state legislature would have permitted even more opportunity for alleged victims to face their accused molesters in court, but that measure did not pass. Here's our report on a press conference held this week by one of the bill's sponsors." Video came on showing the disorderly event Grace, Scott Matthews and Steve Jankowski attended. It ended with Steve's shaky recording of Grace's inadvertent jolt to the head.

McWherter refused to edit out the video of Grace's fall from the blow. It became a source of tension between Grace and the producer on the day of the planning meeting. Now, as Grace sat on the set and watched the scene with chagrin, she remembered how vehemently she objected to it. "It makes me look silly," Grace told Mary-Anne..

"No, it makes you look human," MaryAnne argued. "Grace, this caps off a melee and punctuates our point that people get emotional when their religious institutions are challenged. I'm going to leave it in. That's final."

At the time Grace acquiesced, but now, watching it on the huge screen in the context of the series in progress, she wondered why she did. *I should have stuck to my guns,* she thought. *It's a distraction from the real story.*

Following the showing, with only five minutes remaining, Grace introduced the lobbyists for the Atlanta Archdiocese and the Regional Boy Scouts of America office. "Organizations that opposed at least portions of State Representative Wynn's bill deserve to explain their concerns. The objectors to various aspects of the bill, a pretty long list, were extremely busy behind the scenes as they attempted to build protections into the language. These two registered lobbyists have been the most visible and vocal, so they are in our studio to give us their viewpoints."

The questioning of the lobbyists went smoothly as they aired their side of the controversy. Grace was happy this part of the story came at the end, when she could require them to give succinct answers and quickly close out the segment.

After the closing theme music played and Jackson Davis took over to report the six o-clock news, Grace put a grateful hand on Bannister's arm. "Thank you," she said, locking her eyes on his.

"No problem," he said.

"I mean it, Bannister. From the bottom. Thank you."

"Want to tell me what happened?"

"No," she replied. He nodded, rose and walked back to his workstation in the newsroom. Grace grabbed her computer bag and headed right out the door. She was exhausted. And a little embarrassed.

"Hi Mom," Megan's voice grounded Grace once again. She was about to climb into bed when her daughter's call came.

"Hi Megan."

"Mom, are you okay?"

"Why? What do you mean?"

"I watched your program. You looked...well, I don't know... spooked or something. And really pale. Did you forget your makeup?"

"It's okay, Megan. I got a little upset at a couple of the stories we had to report, that's all. I'll be fine."

"Mom, I want you to promise me something."

"Okay."

"I know you went on a vacation to Savannah after those

stressful stories you had to do earlier in the year. When you've wrapped up this week's stories, why not take a longer vacation? Clear your mind and throw off all that stress. Help me plan a wedding."

Grace loved this young woman. "Maybe I'll do just that, Megan."

"I have to get back. I'm working non-stop on my final project. It's make or break time for this would-be architect."

"Hey, young lady. Promise me something."

"If I can."

"When that project is done, and grades come out, you'll go on a little vacation with me. You can bring Joe if you like. We'll all plan the wedding together."

"I think I'd like that, Mom. I miss you."

The stars once again aligned for Grace, at least for one night.

CHAPTER THIRTY: Final Nights

The final two shows were a blur. The painstaking care with which she nurtured her news career mattered little on this Thursday and Friday night adventure. Her standing as an objective and professional newswoman, while not unimportant, took a back seat simply to getting through to Friday at six o'clock. Slogging through to the bitter end was how she thought of it, as exhaustion gripped her mind and body. To the extent she could, Grace put herself on autopilot and let the planning they had done take over.

On Thursday evening, Grace introduced the portion of the video interview she did with the Reverend Dontell Freeman in which he attempted to justify the church service spankings.

"...teach children the consequences of their actions..."

"... disrespect their parents, they're going to get spanked..."

"...parents are as misguided as their delinquent children..."

"...spare the rod, spoil the child is what we teach here..."

"...curse or get into trouble, we teach them a lesson..."

As the interview closed out, Grace said, "We have members of Reverend Freeman's congregation here with us. We've asked them to discuss the two sides of the issue—the opinions of parents who believe their minister's Sunday punishments are improper, and the viewpoint of parishioners who support Reverend Freeman's actions, even participate in them."

Shaniqua Forrester and Miranda Young walked onto the set and sat opposite Grace and Bannister. After Grace introduced them, she said, "Shaniqua, you've been very outspoken about this punishment activity. In fact, you've filed a lawsuit against Reverend Freeman and the church."

"That's right, Grace, I want it stopped," Shaniqua huffed angrily.

Grace responded, "Let's watch some of my earlier interview with you in your lawyer's office."

"My little girl Rosalee got a whupping two Sundays ago. Man pull her dress up and whacked her five times with a stick while others held her. I rushed up and got her before he could do more, but she wasn't the only one he whupped that morning."

After the screen went black, Walker interjected, "Grace, you also interviewed Miranda Young about her son's spanking?"

"That's right, Bannister. Here's some video we shot in Ms. Young's home." The footage of Miranda's son's injuries played on the screen, with his mother's anguished comments playing off-camera.

"Ms. Young," Grace asked, "you originally declined to be identified in that interview, didn't you?"

"That's right, Miss Gleason. But Shaniqua here showed such courage I couldn't let her be a lone voice. What these people did to our children is unconscionable."

Bannister said, "We have two of the people with us who helped carry out the spankings. Let's invite them in and see what they say about it."

Grace was unprepared for what happened next. Two of the men present at her interview of Reverend Freeman in his church stormed onto the set, loudly protesting the women's statements and pointing fingers at them.

"...You weak-kneed mamas want to coddle your young-uns so they grow up to be delinquents..." one spewed.

"...The reverend knows what's good for his flock," the other chirped. "We're gonna continue to support him despite your evil threats..."

Shaniqua shot back at them, rising from her chair, her face contorted in derision. "You men who help hold our kids while the man whups them got no spine. Y'all oughtta be whupped."

246

Astonishing Grace, Miranda Young, the woman she had only observed as reserved, polite and polished, also rose and screamed out, "Did you see that video? Are you proud of the damage you monster devils did to my son?"

The argument went on, with the two men and two women standing toe-to-toe, arms waving as they argued. Grace and Bannister let it go on for minutes without interfering. But finally to Grace's relief, as it appeared it could become physical, Bannister stepped around the table and between the four raging members of Dontell Freeman's congregation. He ushered the men off the set, and Shaniqua and Miranda returned to their seats, their chests heaving in anger.

"You can see the passion and hostility produced by this controversy," Grace said into the camera. "Shaniqua Forrester's lawsuit will be decided in a court of law. But whether or not the Reverend Dontell Freeman will have to curtail his spanking ways might well be decided in the court of public opinion. Thank you ladies," she said to the two who nodded and hastily left the set.

Grace continued, "Tomorrow night we'll explore another of Reverend Freeman's activities—marrying off young girls from his congregation to paroled convicts. Until then, I'm Grace Gleason, and you've been watching 'Unholy Mind Games.'"

The theme music boomed out and Grace felt the springs unwind. She quietly applauded the crew and eagerly lugged her computer bag to the newsroom exit.

One more night...

**

Grace arrived at the station late in the afternoon. Among several messages waiting for her at her workstation was one from Dillon McAfee. Since he was to be part of the evening segment, she returned his call hoping he wasn't cancelling.

"No," he laughed as she asked the question. "I'll be there, Grace. I merely wanted to see if we could have some dinner afterward. I know you'll be relieved that it's over."

"Dillon, I don't think so. Not that I don't want to see you, but I'm a bit frazzled. I'll want to close out our business and get home to bed. I might sleep all weekend."

"Well, then I hope you'll take a rain check," he said, sounding disappointed to her.

"Of course, Dillon," she encouraged. "I'll look forward to it,"

Entering the production studio, she should have been in a mood of elation. Buck Lohmeyer said calls lit up the station switchboard all week, more than seventy percent favorable. Harvey Silver reported messages from advertisers were mostly positive. The series was by any measure a hit.

All Grace could feel, however, was fatigue, mixed with a deep sense of gratitude that it was all coming to an end. As she entered the set, Bannister was already there, getting a last-minute makeup exam from one of the staff.

Grace turned to her partner. "This is it, my friend."

Bannister smiled. "We're friends now, are we?"

"Of course," she responded. "We were from the beginning. You've been my rock. I couldn't have done it without you."

Bannister reached out and squeezed her hand in a gesture of thanks.

MaryAnne counted down, and the cameras came on as the theme music ramped up in the background. Grace felt a sense of overwhelming wellbeing as she kicked off the final episode. "All week we've explored several angles of religious fervor that may have crossed a line of propriety," she opened, "begging the question of how damaging those actions can be to our youth—or not, depending on how you see it. Last night we examined the Church of Faith and its pastor, the Reverend Dontell Freeman. In that segment we discussed his admitted spankings of children in his congregation, meting out punishment he claims is justified.

"Tonight we look at another aspect of Reverend Freeman's unconventional leadership. For several years, he has arranged marriages of young girls in his congregation to parolees from the Atlanta penitentiary. It's an activity that begs the question, are these young ladies pressured into matrimony? Watch this video of an interview I had just last week with Reverend Freeman."

The big screen came to life.

"...*girls have no home life, no supervision, no role models...*"

"...*engaging in sex and running wild on the streets, getting into all sorts of mischief...*"

"...*being married sets up a stable future for them...*"

"...*These men, many of them undeserving of their jail time... deserve a good wife who can help them get their life back...*"

"...*nobody gets forced into nothing...these girls want to get married...*"

Grace cut in, "We talked to one of the couples in question. We'll only identify them as Eddie and Pearl. Here's what they had to say."

The video switched to the newlywed couple who willingly granted their interview with Grace.

"*I love Eddie,*" Pearl's young face filled the screen. "*Reverend Freeman, he doing the right thing by helping us get our husbands, giving us a good home life. And helping them out when they get paroled, you know? I ain't got no complaint about the reverend.*"

Bannister said, "So Grace, the question looms large—have these girls, many extremely young and impressionable, been conditioned somehow to accept matrimony having little or no say in the matter?"

"Bannister, I asked the minister in Tuskegee, Alabama, who performed many if not all of the weddings, what he thought."

Her internet interview with Reverend Mercedes Humphries came on. Grace cringed at the contrast in video quality from the others, but wasn't sorry it was part of the report.

"...Dontell helping those girls and those wayward young men get their lives back on track..."

"...think Mary and Joseph found each other on an online dating service?..."

"...no problem helping Reverend Freeman save souls..."

"...Some of those men were pretty rough and tough...these girls were very young and impressionable..."

"...A few of the girls he sent over didn't look over twelve or thirteen..."

As the interview ended, Bannister turned to Grace. "So are the girls coerced into marriage? If they aren't marrying of their free will, why do they stick up for their pastor? And harking back to last night's program, why are so many of Reverend Freeman's followers steadfastly loyal in the face of evidence that at least some of the children beaten in the services are physically harmed—and perhaps emotionally as well?"

"All good questions, Bannister. To close out tonight's segment we've invited an eminent professor of psychology to speak to those questions. Dr. Dillon McAfee..." She paused only slightly, marveling at the positive sensation running through her at pronouncing his name, "...is going to join us. We have wondered ever since delving into the stories about Reverend Freeman if something called the Stockholm Syndrome might be at work, promoting loyalty of his followers whether or not it's deserved. Let's ask Dr. McAfee."

Dillon strode onto the set and sat across from them, flashing a brief, warm and friendly smile at Grace. She carried out the interview with him in a bubble of numbness. She didn't know if this settling calm fell over her because Dillon was finally there, representing safety and stability to her, or if the reality that this was the final element of the entire series found its mark. Either way, Grace went through her questions about the syndrome and heard his responses in a vault of mental vacancy. Even when Bannister broke in for a question or two, Grace nodded as he asked without really registering what was appearing on camera or how the answers were coming out of the professor's mouth.

She smiled at Dillon as he left the set, an otherworldly emotion shrouding her.

"Thanks, professor, for your presence here tonight," Bannister offered. He glanced nervously over at Grace as if to say, *Come on, snap out of it.*

And then, as if up from nowhere, it was time to be over. Without consciously thinking about the words coming out, Grace read from the teleprompter. "At the outset of this five-part series on religion gone astray, beginning Monday night, we promised you 'Unholy Mind Games' would probe how untrustworthy faith leaders can take advantage of the young people under their influence. As disturbing and controversial as some of our subject matter has been, we presented it as fairly and impartially as possible, so you can decide for yourselves—are young people harmed by their youthful acceptance of what they are told by higher authorities in their faiths? We hope you will think about all you have seen, and if you believe corrective actions are justified, that you'll participate in the solutions.

"I'm Grace Gleason, and for myself and my colleague, Bannister Walker, I wish you peace."

She remained stock-still for several moments, even after the theme quit playing and Jackson Davis across the studio droned his usual "...time for the six o-clock news." Bannister was already up, removing his lapel microphone and shuffling papers into a wastebasket. Grace looked around and saw everyone clapping—the staff in the booth, camera operators, even some others in the news staff who gathered at the edge of the studio to watch the final segment. Buck Lohmeyer was there, leading the cheering. He walked to her and Bannister. "You two knocked it out of the park," he said in hushed tones as the news went on in the other set. "Sorry I gave you such a hard time, but you proved how tough you are."

Bannister and Lohmeyer shook hands. "Thank you," was all Grace could get out.

As he turned to go, Buck turned back for a final, whispered word to Grace. "Harvey knows it was your idea." He grinned broadly, turned and left.

Grace stood staring at everyone else, feeling a little embarrassed at her obvious exhausted state. She gathered herself enough to make the rounds and shake hands, embracing MaryAnne McWherter and tech David Williams, and saving one last big bear hug for Bannister Walker.

She made her way to the newsroom delighted this mountain of work ended well, but also wondering when she had ever felt so spent.

CHAPTER THIRTY-ONE: Havoc

Award-winning reporter Grace Gleason had been neck-deep in news calamities for years. Her entire career was filled with fires, murders, hurricanes, blizzards, highway pile-ups, drug busts, gang fights and all other sorts of mayhem and madness. Living on the edge of danger and finding herself face-to-face with bad actors was not foreign territory to this risk-taking newswoman.

She grew over time to recognize the rumblings of the beginning of chaos. Her instincts alerted her clearly to the peripheral sight of imminent disorder. She could sense menace, smell the stench of hazardous circumstance.

Yet she never had grown inured to such chaos. Like a prize-fighter who endured ten thousand blows, when a devastating left hook came close to landing, she still experienced that adrenaline of dread. This punch is going to hurt. This blow could be fatal.

Grace blankly scurried through papers on her desk, packed her laptop into its case, rifled through a stack of message notes, all the while eager to get out of there, to drive home and hibernate as long as she needed to. Yet there was also an undeniable apprehension that something terribly wrong was afoot. It seemed to come from some activity stirring just outside the entrance door to the newsroom. Perhaps a flash of some lights there, or the quickening plod of footsteps. Whatever was happening that didn't fit the usual newsroom pattern now had her on high alert.

Then the door burst open. Grace froze, staring straight ahead as the figure wearing a hoodie catapulted inside. With events unfolding in dizzying speed, she mentally slowed down the action and watched the intruder brandish a pistol, his covered head turning this way and that, his hideous tattooed face glowering as he shouted,

"Where's Gleason? Where is she?"

Sounds of people screaming, scrambling, diving for cover, penetrated the air. Grace stood transfixed, watching the desperate man charge through the room, pointing his weapon at this man diving behind a desk, that woman scrambling frantically toward the exit.

What she did next fell into the category of the inexplicable. It wasn't the first time. Once she challenged drug kingpins as she did a story across a bridge in the dangerous city of Nueva Laredo, Mexico. Another time she fought scratch and claw with a suspected murderer hell-bent on hurting her child. Those instances in her career when she acted without fear or concern, she could never rationalize.

This was such a time. While Floyd MacCauley, the parolee married to Jamica by Reverend Dontell Freeman, barged through the newsroom screaming for her, she calmly but hastily bolted for the exit. Grace sprinted past the black Trans Am parked at the curb. She saw it, registered its presence, but paid it no heed. Twenty yards across the lot, she deftly unlocked her door, then her glove compartment and pulled her Glock from its case. Leaving the car door swinging open, she pivoted and dashed the same twenty yards across the lot, unlocking the pistol's safety as she ran.

Racing past the Trans Am and back into the studio, she heard shots. Inside, MacCauley stood amid the rows of desk and computers, wheeling around this way and that. Somewhere in her deepest mindset, she remembered the words of the instructor at the gun range: *"…you need to prepare yourself, not just in here with the training, but mentally. The trick is not to hesitate. Prepare in advance how you'll respond if it's 'you or them'…"*

The moment she lowered her gun barrel toward Floyd Mac-Cauley, in the two-hand grip she learned in training, she saw his eyes meet hers. His creepy face curled up into a frightening grin and his pistol started in her direction.

Grace tried to pull the trigger. But when she needed most

to answer the question whether she could shoot someone, it was answered. She heard the two shots ring out in rapid-fire. Her heart jumped a beat. She watched MacCauley lower his shoulder, his arm dangling at his side, his hand useless. His pistol clattered to the floor. The ex-con's eyes rolled up and he crumpled with a thud.

In that breathless instant, Grace's gaze swept across the room to Jimmy, the security guard, standing with his unholstered .38 caliber special aimed at Floyd. Jimmy dashed toward the assailant, kicked his gun away and dropped a knee on his chest to hold him stationary. "Someone call nine-one-one," the guard yelled out.

Steve Jankowski, only several paces away, made the frantic call.

Staffers scrambled from their hiding places, crowding toward Jimmy and his captive, hugging each other, sobbing hysterically, gaping at the man who caused such bedlam only minutes before.

Grace stumbled toward MacCauley and looked down at him. His eyes were open, and he was fighting for breath. "Why?" she pleaded. "It was you who followed me and called me with threats and trashed my house. Why, Floyd?"

"Reverend Freeman," he mumbled. "Did it for him. You ruined him. He needed me to."

"No he didn't, Floyd. Reverend Freeman doesn't want people killed. He might be misguided, but he's a man of God, not a murderer."

Floyd didn't respond. His eyelids flickered and lowered, and his labored breathing began to gurgle.

"Are you all right?" Jankowski asked, wrapping his arms around Grace's shoulders.

"I think so," her voice trembled a bit.

"Festina Lente," Steve remembered.

Grace looked up at him with a startled look. "Yes, but..." She wheeled around toward the entrance door, suddenly remembering the Trans Am. Did Floyd drive it there, or did he have an accomplice?

And if someone was in it, why didn't he confront her as she ran for her gun? She dashed toward the door. Jankowski tore across the room and followed her. As Grace poked her head out, the car peeled away. It swerved through the parking lot and dashed off at high speed.

"Steve," she shouted. "Call nine-one-one back and give them the car description." The cameraman grabbed his cell phone and made the call.

Sirens wailed as several patrol cars and an ambulance lit up the parking lot. EMTs with two gurneys hustled into the building. Grace returned to the newsroom, curious about the extra gurney. She watched the medics lift MacCauley onto the stretcher as another crew pulled the second gurney to a different part of the newsroom. A small group of the staff was clustered together there.

"Was someone else hurt?" Grace screeched, then louder, more desperate, "Who was it?"

The paramedics hovered over the prone figure. Grace ran closer to see. MaryAnne McWherter, the producer, lay on her back in a pool of blood.

"My God! No!" Grace gasped. She watched as the crew lifted her friend. MaryAnne was moving, raising Grace's spirits. She reached out and offered her hand as MaryAnne's new bed rolled past. A slight squeeze came back.

**

Harvey Silver, Buck Lohmeyer and Bannister Walker were already sitting in the waiting room when she arrived. Doctors, nurses, EMTs and patients streamed in and out of the emergency room.

Lohmeyer stood as she approached and draped his big arm around her shoulder. "She's in surgery right now," the news director said. "We won't know anything for a quite a while. Grace, you look beat. No need for you to stay here. We'll keep you informed."

"I don't want to leave," Gleason fought back tears.

Harvey walked over and joined them. "Go home, Grace. The

doctor said there's a bullet lodged in her midsection, and her condition is serious and there's a lot of bleeding. But he was optimistic. We'll keep an overnight vigil. Get some sleep. We'll call in the morning when we know something about her condition."

She nodded reluctantly. Walking back out to the parking lot, her legs felt as if they weighed five hundred pounds. A half-hour later, Grace pulled into her garage. Entering her kitchen, she shrieked a sound of incredible joy. Standing there, smiling brightly, arms outstretched, stood her daughter.

"What are you doing here?" she wrapped her arms around Megan.

"Mom, it was all over the news. I couldn't let you come home alone from that madhouse. Joe dropped me off. He's still not finished with his final project. But mine's in the can—I learned that term from you. I'm spending the night with you."

A knock at the back door interrupted them. Grace peered out and to her chagrin saw Horace Gunter standing there, whistling to himself. She so wanted to ignore him, but he had to see her drive in.

"Horace," she greeted him.

"Just stopped over to see if there's anything I can do. I saw on television what happened."

"I'm fine, Horace, thanks. This is my daughter Megan." He nodded Megan's direction, and she gave him a half-wave. "Megan's going to spend the night, so I'll be in good hands."

"Good, good, Grace," he said. "I thought I should return this." He handed her the spare door key.

Grace took it, feeling sheepish. "Horace, I...I owe you an apology." He waved her off. "No, really," she insisted, "that was a stupid, foolish thing, coming over there and accusing you. I feel really bad about it."

"Not to worry, Grace. I've been accused of a lot worse, believe me. Probably done a lot worse, too."

After he left, Megan looked at her mother with curiosity. "That was a weird, kind of mean-looking guy, Mom."

"Oh, he's okay. He's an ex-cop who lives next door."

Megan nodded toward the key in Grace's hand. "What was that about?"

"Never mind, tell you later. Right now, I need to get my make-up off, take a quick shower and get into bed."

Quietly, Grace slid beneath the covers as her daughter slept beside her. Megan could have used the guest room, but Grace was glad she opted for doubling up. It was just like those old days after Jeff left them and high school age Megan would come and climb in with her mom.

Megan stirred from sleep for a moment. "Mom," she mumbled blearily, "did you shoot that man?"

"No, honey. The security guard shot him."

Silence for a moment, as the drowsy girl processed the answer. "Oh yeah. But you had a gun?"

"Yes, I did."

"Mom, a gun. Were you going to shoot him?"

Grace lay thinking about her answer, tears welling in her eyes. "Megan, I just don't know."

That was all. Megan returned to her sleeping sounds. Grace lay thinking about how triumphant this night should have been at the conclusion of some excellent journalistic work. Instead, her euphoria was shattered by havoc and tragedy. As she drifted toward slumber, the catastrophic events of the night seemed to wash away in the wake of the love and security she could feel from the gift slightly snoring beside her.

EPILOGUE

Early Saturday morning, Rick Dent was the first to call. Though their interactions were sporadic these days, the voice of her radio counterpart always brought a sense of comfort and order. She was grateful he cared enough about her to get in touch.

"Thought you might want an update," he said. "They caught the Trans Am. It was Floyd's young wife, Jamica, who drove him to the station."

Grace now was certain Floyd was the one following her all along and harassing her. She was glad at least she made peace with Horace Gunter.

"Floyd MacCauley is dead," Rick told her. "He was DOA when they got him to Southbend Hospital."

"Rick," Grace fought not to sound panicky, "What about..."

"MaryAnne McWherter?" he broke in. "I imagine you'll hear from your boss. MaryAnne is in critical condition. They took her back in for more surgery. Grace, it's touch and go for her."

"She has to pull through, Rick. I couldn't bear it if she died because of me."

"Wait, that's going too far."

"No, really, she wouldn't have even been working there anymore if I hadn't fought for her to produce the series. And Rick, the guy was looking for me when he shot MaryAnne."

"She'll make it, Grace."

There was a long, difficult pause until Rick picked it up again. "Grace, the morning paper's full of stories about the shooting and the public reaction to 'Unholy Mind Games.' Several politicians have released statements vowing to look into some of the issues raised in the program. Look, I've got to scoot. But I'll check in."

"Rick," she said. "Thanks for your friendship."

"It'll cost you that lunch."

"You've got it, buster," she laughed for the first time in twenty-four hours.

A short time later, Grace answered Dillon McAfee's call.

"Didn't want to bug you too early," he said, "but I had to see if you're all right. I called you last night several times."

"I know, Dillon, I listened to your voicemails. I'm sorry I couldn't take them. My daughter was here with me, and I needed peace and quiet. I was in no emotional state to talk to you."

"Okay, but when can I see you?"

"Maybe in a few days," she said. "My boss gave me the week off. I just need to rest, stay quiet, get the cobwebs out of my head. You understand, don't you?"

"Hey, don't you remember? I'm a psychologist." He chuckled. "Take care of yourself. Let me know when."

"Dillon, I promise."

**

It was three days later when she called him. "Let's meet for brunch at the Fushion Grill, would that be okay?" she suggested.

"Okay?" he said. "It's terrific. I don't have class till two o'clock."

"Let's sit on the patio. There's such a nice early summer smell to the air and I want to feel the sun on my face."

He was waiting at a table outside when she arrived. Grace knew he would be disappointed; she should be rested and recovered, not oozing a somber, downbeat mood. But word a day earlier of Mary-Anne's passing took its toll.

"My station manager and news director came over and told me," she said. "It was a horrible, horrible day."

"I hadn't heard," McAffee told her as she related the news. He wrapped an arm around her and stood silent, listening to her muffled sobs. "I'm really sorry, Grace."

"The service is Saturday," she finally managed, sitting down. "Dillon, I know you didn't know her, but would you go with me?"

"Of course I will, Grace," he said, and she could hear caring in his response.

They sat and ordered. She talked about Megan and Horace Gunter, and he discussed his latest classes. They seemed to touch on everything except "Unholy Mind Games" and the tragic way it ended.

The waitress brought them each a glass of Chardonnay, and Grace looked into Dillon's eyes. "I'm thinking it's a good time to leave the news business," she told him.

"Well, I don't think I'd make a rash decision, Grace. You've just come off a really tough experience, not the most ideal time to decide something that important. You're physically and emotionally drained from everything you've been through. Give it a little time. Go away and recharge. I'll bet the station would give you some time."

She shook her head no. "I already did that, when I went to Savannah after covering those horrible drug dealers and crooked cops. Now here I am again in the same old familiar place. I've decided. I'm through with reporting."

"It's all you've done since college," he protested.

She gazed out into the open sky, as if waiting for some restorative force to emerge and make everything all right again. "Dillon, several years ago in Dallas I covered a horrendous murder case that almost got me and Megan killed. After I moved here, I became embroiled in a story about drugs that nearly got me murdered on a Mexican street corner. Then I got a little too close to the business of a gang of crooked policemen, and they nearly did me in."

Grace drew a long breath. "Now this. I'm tired. I love what I do and I hate it. I'm thrilled when I get a story right, but sometimes when I do, it brings me inconsolable grief and terror." She turned her gaze back at McAfee, at his deep blue eyes. "I have some money saved up. I think I can get past the thrill of the chase. Now I'm ready to help

Megan plan her wedding, and to work in my garden, maybe travel in the Far East. Maybe write a book, and maybe…"

He smiled and interrupted, "Whoa. And maybe have some time for a guy who's falling pretty hard for you?"

Her eyes opened wide, then she beamed back. It felt incredibly good to be able to smile. "Maybe."

He pulled his chair around the table close to hers, leaned in and kissed her lips lightly. "I've been trying to figure out how to get around to this second kiss," he confessed. "You know I'm really crazy about you, right?"

Her senses heightened as she returned the kiss. He was only the second man she had kissed since her divorce from Jeff. But she was experiencing a sensation she hadn't known since long ago, early in her marriage. Maybe this man was the one. Maybe there was life after Big Six.

"We're pitiful," she said coyly, looking around to see if anyone was watching. "Right here in public."

"Get used to it," he said. "Tell me I've got a shot."

Grace didn't know for sure. It was too soon. She had a lot to recover from before anything or anyone could heal her. But she laid a hand on his, nodding. She knew she wanted to find out.

About the Authors

Donald Reichardt taught English and wrote for newspapers before launching a career as a speechwriter and public relations and advertising executive for AT&T. He was named executive director of advertising and Olympic Games programs for the BellSouth Corporation before leaving to freelance, writing more than sixty by-lined articles for magazines and business newspapers. Donald was elected to the College of Fellows of the Public Relations Society of America and is in the Georgia Public Relations Hall of Fame. He is a Distinguished Alumni of Emporia (Kansas) State University, its highest alumni honor. Emporia State houses the Donald Reichardt Center for Publication and Literary Arts. Donald is the author of a book of short stories, *Corporate Lies and Other Stories*.

Joyce Oscar began her career in radio, joined CNN as a video journalist, and was a reporter, anchor and producer at television stations in Georgia and Tennessee. A graduate of Western Illinois University, she was a reporter and fill-in anchor for top-rated WSB-TV in Atlanta for more than twenty years and received many reporting awards, including four regional Emmy nominations. Joyce was honored by the Georgia House of Representatives and interviewed by Joan Lunden on "Good Morning America" for her coverage of a winter story in 1993 that left her stranded for days in the North Georgia mountains. Joyce is an actor in two independent films for Dean Film Works LLC, *Clandestine Lives* and in *Rest Stop*, for which she was also associate line producer and assistant casting director.

30283266R00162

Made in the USA
Columbia, SC
26 October 2018